The Senior Texan
Legal Guide

Edition 5.0

Paul Premack, JD, CELA

Texas Attorney at Law
Certified Elder Law Attorney
National Elder Law Foundation as accredited by the
Texas Board of Legal Specialization and the American Bar Association
Founding Member, NAELA Council of Advanced Practitioners

Longview Publishing, San Antonio

The Senior Texan Legal Guide, Edition 5.0

Printed in the United States of America.

Distributed by
Book Marketing Plus, Fredericksburg, Texas 830-997-4776 and
Longview Publishing, San Antonio, Texas 210-826-1122

ISBN-10: 0-96387-335-0

ISBN-13: 978-0-9638733-5-4

Library of Congress Control Number: 2006907580

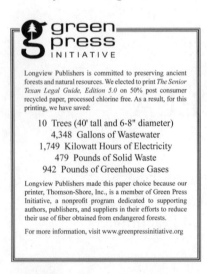

Longview Publishers is committed to preserving ancient forests and natural resources. We elected to print *The Senior Texan Legal Guide, Edition 5.0* on 50% post consumer recycled paper, processed chlorine free. As a result, for this printing, we have saved:

10 Trees (40' tall and 6-8" diameter)
4,348 Gallons of Wastewater
1,749 Kilowatt Hours of Electricity
479 Pounds of Solid Waste
942 Pounds of Greenhouse Gases

Longview Publishers made this paper choice because our printer, Thomson-Shore, Inc., is a member of Green Press Initiative, a nonprofit program dedicated to supporting authors, publishers, and suppliers in their efforts to reduce their use of fiber obtained from endangered forests.

For more information, visit www.greenpressinitiative.org

The Senior Texan Legal Guide is printed on post-consumer recycled acid-free paper using vegetable-based ink.

Table of Contents

CHAPTER 2: MANAGING HEALTH DURING DISABILITY

CHAPTER 4: PROTECTIONS DURING YOUR LIFE

CHAPTER 5: FAMILY & MARITAL ISSUES

CHAPTER 6: PLANNING YOUR ESTATE

CHAPTER 7: RESPONDING TO A DEATH

Introduction

This book provides valuable information on Texas Elder Law, but it is not intended to replace individualized legal representation. Use this book to gain general background knowledge and then seek individualized legal advice from your attorney, who should be specially trained to address your specific legal needs. Start by finding an attorney who practices Elder Law and, if possible, choose a Certified Elder Law Attorney (CELA)[1], which designates that attorney as a specialist recognized by the Texas Board of Legal Specialization via the National Elder Law Foundation.

This Guide covers new laws and it covers existing laws that have been on the books for years. It is certain that the law will continue to change after this Guide reaches you. Be sure to consult your own legal advisor before you act on any topic discussed in this book. Your purchase of this Guide does not make me your attorney.

Many of the Internet sites referred to in this Guide are maintained by government offices or by private businesses. As I do not control the content of those sites, I make no warranty regarding the accuracy of the information contained at those sites.

For your convenience, all the Internet sites referred to in the Guide have been gathered onto one web page. You can use it to reach any other site referred to in the Guide, instead of having to type all the complicated URLs on your own. Visit that page at WWW.PREMACK.COM/GUIDELINKS.HTM.

I give my loving thanks to my wife, Ruthie S. Premack, who has encouraged me and assisted me with this Guide and with the prior editions.

Paul Premack, JD, CELA

Chapter 1:   Managing Finances During Disability

You have important business to conduct: caring for your lifetime of earnings, paying monthly bills, or selling a piece of real estate. Whatever your activities, they require your personal attention.

But if you were to become disabled, all those important transactions could be brought to an untimely halt. No one has inherent authority to manage your financial affairs for you; someone must be legally authorized to take care of your business as your representative.

How do you obtain a representative? You can choose for yourself, or you can let the state decide. Here are six legal techniques:

1 - Power of Attorney. Using a Power of Attorney offers great flexibility at a reasonable cost.

2 - Guardianship. This is the default choice unless you act to avoid it. Guardianship happens in court and is expensive and slow.

3 - Community Property Administration. This judicial process allows a healthy spouse to sign for a disabled spouse without a full-blown Guardianship.

4 - Social Security Representative Payee. This allows a person to apply to Social Security to manage the monthly check received by a retiree.

5 - Account Management. You can establish a "convenience" bank account to allow someone access to your funds. However, your helper's powers are limited to dealing with that single account. Any other activities are off limits.

6 - A trust. You can set up a living trust to manage your finances. This method is very effective, but often the trust cannot handle certain details. Living trusts, testamentary trusts, charitable trusts and other forms of trust are discussed in various sections of the Guide. Consult the index for more information.

Here is a look at each of the first five options in detail.

STRATEGY 1: FINANCIAL POWER OF ATTORNEY

With a power of attorney, you select a representative to assist you. You delegate to that representative (called an "agent") whatever powers you feel will be needed.

When you sign a Power of Attorney as principal, you retain full and unrestricted rights to handle any and all business and financial matters for yourself. The agent may act on your behalf, but does not supplant you.

The agent is your fiduciary, so the first question the agent must ask before taking any action is "am I authorized by the power of attorney to do this action?" and the second questions is "does this benefit the principal?" The agent cannot legally act beyond the scope authorized, and would be acting illegally by doing anything to harm the principal.

Many powers of attorney are written to grant very broad general powers to your agent. But if you want, you can grant very narrow powers, being as specific as you want. For estate planning, the powers granted are usually extensive to allow your agent flexibility.

You must use caution when appointing an agent. If the powers are broad, your agent might dishonestly use your assets for your agent's gain. You must always take extra care to select a trustworthy agent.

If you are not sure you have anyone you trust enough, you might consider a living trust. They are more complex and more expensive up front, yet are more comprehensive solutions that could save you money in the long run. You can appoint as Trustee yourself, a family member, or a bank trust department (to be assured you will have professional asset management).

Durable Power of Attorney

Financial powers of attorney can be broken down into two types: "durable" and "regular."

A durable power of attorney stays in force even if you are disabled. It continues to work until the time of your death, regardless of the state of your health, unless you revoke it.

A regular power of attorney, on the other hand, becomes invalid if you become disabled in any way. Clearly, that is not a desirable result: just when you need it, the document's legality vanishes.

Durable powers of attorney are therefore the proper choice. They could not exist without a statute as their source. Hence, to create and use a durable power of attorney, you must follow the instructions included in state law.

Note that there is a difference between a financial durable power of attorney and a medical power of attorney. The "Durable Power of Attorney Act" (part of the Texas Probate Code[2]) authorizes a financial durable power of attorney. The "Advance Directives Act" (part of the Texas Health and Safety Code[3]) authorizes a medical power of attorney. They must be handled separately, in two distinct documents. They have different legal requirements, and cannot be blended. If you have a single power of attorney that tries to cover both medical and financial issues, your plans are out of date and should be corrected immediately.

Fundamental Requirements

If you want to create a financial durable power of attorney, the statute requires very few formalities. Fundamentally, you must write out your instructions, you must date it, sign it, and have it notarized. In it, you must say, "This Power of Attorney will not terminate upon the disability of the principal." There is no requirement that it have witnesses.

Filing a durable power of attorney with the County Clerk is not required unless your agent is using it to sign some other document that must be filed. For example, if your agent signs a deed for you, both the deed and the durable power of attorney must be filed with the clerk.

The complicated part is writing out your instructions. Perhaps you've read an old power of attorney. You would have been struck by that fact that it was, in large measure, a list of verbs. "My agent can lease, purchase, sell, exchange, acquire, bargain, contract and agree…." Several pages of that would confuse anyone.

Current legal practice in Texas is to write durable powers of attorney to include various standardized categories of powers that are spelled out in the statute itself. Each category (for instance, "the power to handle real estate transactions" or "the power to handle banking transactions") is detailed in the statute. The details do not need to be in your document. This makes it both easier to read and more likely to be useful.

The categories are all contained in the "Statutory durable power of attorney" form that can be used by consumers. Sadly, the statutory form itself falls short in some ways. For instance:

- The statutory form lacks clear language authorizing your agent to make plans for your long-term care (which may involve making transfers, that is, gifts to your family members).

- The statutory form lacks any terms allowing your agent flexibility to create a trust on your behalf. Often the agent will find that setting up a trust to manage your assets (when you become disabled) is more readily accepted for long-term management needs.

- The statutory form does not provide many options for appointing alternate, backup Agents.

Internet Resource:
The legal documents store at our website has a durable power of attorney, designed to take full advantage of the most current laws and to overcome the shortcomings of the standard statutory form. It can be found at WWW.PREMACK.COM

Capacity to Make a Power of Attorney

When a person desires to make a power of attorney, the key issues are that person's 1) ability to understand what the power of attorney is, and 2) desire to authorize an agent to provide assistance. Essentially, the person needs to have the same capacity necessary to enter into any contract. A person's location, or status as a hospital patient, does not alone eliminate the ability to create a binding power of attorney.

There is no doubt that many elderly people face the risk of not understanding complex financial transactions. Age can bring many unpleasant effects, including memory loss and dementia. But age does not universally cause mental instability, and the law does not allow us to presume that a person is incapacitated just because of age.

A case decided by the Supreme Court of Texas[4] tells us that seniors can be presumed competent until proven otherwise. In the case, a stockbroker assisted an elderly client in transferring several hundred thousand dollars of stock to her nephew. The broker had never met her before, and went to her house so she could sign the transfers. He met with her alone for several hours.

A year later, a niece decided she was unhappy with the transfers. She started a Guardianship over her elderly aunt – who was determined to be incapacitated at the time she appeared before the Judge. The niece/guardian sued the stockbroker.

The jury thought that the broker's actions were negligent and/or a breach of fiduciary duty, and that the broker had used "fraudulent, manipulative and/or deceptive" actions. However, the jury did not find that the aunt was incapacitated at the time she worked with the broker.

The broker appealed, claiming that his only duty to this client was faithfully to carry out her instructions. (Legally, a person can only be held liable for negligence if that act was a breach of a legal duty owed to the other person). On the other hand, the niece argued that the stockbroker should know, because of the client's age alone, that she would not understand the transaction.

The appeals court acknowledged that there is a real risk that an elderly person may not understand a complex financial transaction. It chose, however, to balance that risk against the need to provided services to everyone in the same manner, regardless of age. As such, the appeals court decided that there is no responsibility on the part of "service providers in general or stockbrokers in particular" to determine the competence of their clients.

The court stated that, "Stockbrokers and other service providers cannot be expected to have any expertise in assessing mental capacity… A service provider should not be put to choosing between refusing to assist an elderly person with legitimate transactions and incurring liability for providing such assistance when the provider lacks any qualification for determining competence."

Being old is not legal grounds for denial of services. It remains illegal to defraud another person, whether young or old. But a service provider is not legally expected to assess mental competence before providing a service.

Ability to Sign

As a general rule, a person must be able to sign various documents to perform financial or legal transactions. But it is not universally true that a person must be able physically to sign a document to give it effect.

First, a person's signature does not have to be "beautiful" or "presentable." Too often, an elderly person's signature is shaky, wavy or unreadable. That does not make a difference. Some people don't have a very legible signature even when in good health (is your doctor's signature legible?). Even a "mark" is often enough to act as a signature.

Texas law allows a Notary Public to sign on behalf of a person who, despite having adequate mental capacity, is prevented from making a signature or mark due to a physical impairment. The Notary's signature must be witnessed and must bear a special acknowledgement. Using this law, even a person who cannot physically sign can create a durable power of attorney. But if the person is mentally impaired, this law does not help.

Springing Power of Attorney

You are legally allowed to create a durable power of attorney that is held in reserve until you become disabled. You can specify that even though you sign a power of attorney now, your agent has no authority to act until you become disabled. This concept, often called a "springing" power of attorney, has been used for years without statutory authority. The Texas Durable Power of Attorney statute now gives a seal of approval to the concept.

What about an older springing power of attorney – say, one that you signed in 1990 before the law was updated in 1993? If you become ill now, will the agent you selected be able to use it to take care of your business? Even though there was no law before 1993 that said a springing power of attorney was valid in Texas, neither was there a law that said it was invalid.

A case decided by the Court of Appeals in Texarkana in August 1999 laid the issue to rest. The case is Comerica Bank vs. Texas Commerce Bank[5], and it discusses the actions of a Mrs. Bradfield. She wrote a springing power of attorney in 1986. In 1995, she became disabled, and her agent transferred some of her assets into a trust with Comerica using the springing power of attorney.

In 1997, Mrs. Bradfield died, and Texas Commerce Bank was appointed as her Executor. The Executor wanted the assets moved back to her estate so the funds could be given to the heirs named in her Will. Comerica Bank felt that 1) the assets were legally part of its trust, 2) the assets should go to the trust's beneficiaries and 3) using the springing power of attorney had been perfectly legal.

The court decided that while there was no explicit statute allowing springing powers of attorney, they were indeed legal. Reviewing the law, the court recognized that it had been legal to make powers of attorney that commenced at some future time, for instance, "this power of attorney becomes valid when I leave for Europe" or "when I buy a new business." If a power of attorney could be written to commence at some future event, then a power of attorney could also legally commence "when I become disabled."

However, even though a pre-1993 springing power of attorney may be valid, no one wants to go to court to enforce his or her wishes. The best thing you can do is to have a current power of attorney – based on the Texas Durable Power of Attorney Act (which the legislature most recently updated in 2001). Then it will clearly be legal and will clearly be useable without a court battle.

Naming Co-Agents

Naming those who will act for you under your durable power of attorney can be set up in a variety of ways. The most common approach is to name a single person to act as your agent, so you have only one representative. Then you name alternative agents who can act if your first choice dies or becomes incapable of action.

That does not preclude you from appointing several Co-Agents at the same time. The trick with Co-Agents is to define clearly whether they must all act together at all times, or whether you will allow one of them to act unilaterally.

That was the big issue in a case decided by the Texas Court of Appeals (13th District)[6]. This is what happened: mom signed a power of attorney appointing daughter and son as Co-Agents. Daughter did some repairs to mom's house, and then (acting alone) sold mom's house to herself (using the power of attorney to sign mom's name to the deed).

About six months later, mom died and son probated her Will. As Executor he discovered the house had been deeded out of the estate. That did not sit well with him or with the other heirs, so he sued his sister for return of the property. He claimed that by acting alone, his sister had misused the power of attorney.

The courts agreed with the Executor, and ordered that the house be returned to the estate. Since the durable power of attorney had appointed both son AND daughter as agents, the court concluded that they were required to act jointly whenever the power of attorney was used. By implication, if the power of attorney had appointed son OR daughter as agents, mom would have been authorizing either of them to act alone, and transfer of the house would have been upheld.

Thus, the wording you put into your durable power of attorney is the key. You can have Co-Agents who must act unanimously, or you may have Co-Agents who can act independently. The wording must be clear, or the courts are likely to default to requiring joint action.

Even if you allow Co-Agents to act independently, you can still give them authority to keep an eye on each other. By law, your agent must keep you fully informed of all actions taken under the power of attorney. You can delegate that oversight position by stating in the power of attorney that any action taken by only one agent must be promptly reported to the other agent, and that all books and records are open to inspection by both agents.

Fiduciary Responsibilities

The Texas Penal Code[7] says that if the agent in your durable power of attorney intentionally, knowingly, or recklessly misapplies your assets – that is, the agent uses them in a way that is not beneficial to you or in a way that contradicts the power of attorney – the act can be investigated as a crime.

The offense is called "Misapplication of Fiduciary Property." If convicted, the agent's punishment is keyed to the value of the misapplied assets. For instance, if the amount is less than $20, the crime is classified as a Class-C misdemeanor, punishable by a fine no greater than $500. It reaches the level of "state jail felony" if the amount is between $1,500 and $20,000. And it is a first-degree felony – punishable by 5 years to life in prison and a $10,000 fine – if the amount misappropriated exceeds $20,000.

In 2003 the legislature enhanced this criminal statute by passing House Bill 240. It increases the punishment if this offense is committed against an elderly individual (who is, for these purposes, someone 65 or older). Hence, if an agent misapplies fiduciary funds – say, in the amount of $2000 – for a principal who is 60 years old, the offense is treated as a "state jail felony." But if the same act is done to someone who is 65 years old, the offense is a third-degree felony. The punishment for a state jail felony is 180 days to 2 years plus a fine up to $10,000. The same crime committed against an elderly person draws punishment as a third-degree felony of 2 to 10 years plus a fine up to $10,000.

Accounting Responsibilities

A quiet battle took place in the 2001 legislature over amending the Durable Power of Attorney Act itself. The Texas Silver-Haired Legislature recommended changing the Act to require your agent to post a bond before being able to act on your behalf. They also wanted the law to require a waiting period before your agent could transfer any real estate using the Power of Attorney (and in some instances to get court authority to take some actions). It recommended re-instituting the policy requiring all durable powers of attorney to be recorded with the local county clerk's office to be valid.

House Bill 1883 was introduced to implement those recommendations. It was objected to by many attorneys, who felt that the added requirements would impose heavy restrictions on everyone to avoid but a few cases of abuse. As it proceeded through the legislature, the bill was modified. The version that passed imposes strict accounting requirements for Agents but did not include the other strict rules recommended by the Silver Haired Legislature. The new accounting rules became effective on September 1, 2001.

The accounting rules impose on the agent the duty to keep the principal informed and to account for actions taken pursuant to the power of attorney. Failure to tell the principal about a particular act does not invalidate the act, but is a breach of fiduciary duty. An agent is required to keep a record of each action taken and each decision made, so part of that record keeping should be to provide a copy to the principal on a routine schedule.

At any time, the principal can ask for a full accounting. If the agent has been routinely providing information, then a demand for accounting becomes unlikely. Nonetheless, if a demand is made, the agent has to provide all these complete details:

- A list of the property belonging to the principal that has come to the agent's knowledge or into the agent's possession;

- A list of all actions taken or decisions made by the agent for the principal;

- An account of receipts, disbursements, and other actions of the agent, including their source and nature, with receipts of principal and income shown separately;

- A list of all property over which the agent has exercised control, with a full description of each asset and its current value (if known);

- A statement of the cash balance on hand and the name and location of the depository where the balance is kept;

- A list of all of the principal's liabilities that are known to the agent; and

- A list of whatever other information the agent has for a full and definite understanding of the exact condition of the principal's assets.

The agent must keep all these records until they are either: 1) delivered to the principal, 2) the principal releases the agent from the obligation, or 3) a court discharges the agent.

The principal or a court can order the agent to provide an accounting, and the agent must deliver it in 60 days (or longer if the principal or court sets a longer period). If the agent does not promptly deliver the information, the principal can sue to force an accounting, to retrieve the assets, and to cancel the power of attorney.

A Possible Problem with the Accounting Law

The duty to account is sensible, and an agent should be trustworthy enough to comply with the principal's request. But in many instances, the agent will only be taking action after the principal has become meaningfully incapacitated. Any report to the principal won't mean much if the principal cannot comprehend it.

The law allows anyone selected by the principal to ask for an accounting. Put this in the context of a nasty family argument, and you can see the potential for mischief contained in the accounting law. For example:

> Ed and his son Tom don't get along very well because Tom is manipulative and demanding, but Ed has always wished they had a better relationship. Ed knows that he needs someone to take care of his finances as he ages, so he signs a durable power of attorney naming Tom's daughter Edith as agent. Edith doesn't get along too well with Tom either, but adores her Grandpa Ed. She drives him to the doctor, grocery shops for him, and is available to him every day.
>
> A few years later, Ed is starting to get confused. He cannot balance his checkbook or pay his bills anymore. Edith talks with him and they decide it is time for her to take over his finances using the power of attorney. Ed moves into a nursing home, and Edith pays the bills from Ed's account.
>
> Tom hears that his father's health is slipping. He starts showing up at the nursing home and plays on Ed's vulnerability. Tom's real agenda is to get control of Ed's money, so he plants the seeds of distrust in Ed's confusion. "Where has all your money gone? Isn't the bank balance a whole lot smaller since Edith took over?"

One day, Tom puts a letter under Ed's nose. It says that Ed selects Tom to ask Edith for an accounting. Ed signs it, fearing his new relationship with Tom may suffer if he refuses.

Now Tom starts to harass Edith. He demands a full accounting from her. He pesters her, and threatens to take her to court. If she is like most people, she may not have a detailed record of all the bills she paid for Grandpa Ed. Instead of fighting with or being sued by her manipulative father, Edith decides to resign as agent. Ed is left with Tom as his only resource, and is ripe for financial abuse.

Clearly, the new law gives an arguing family a new tool to manipulate a frail elder's situation. The old law provided a solution for abuse of a durable power of attorney: the contesting family member could file for guardianship. The court could require an accounting, and would invalidate the power of attorney if a guardian were appointed.

It may be very wise to modify the basic "statutory durable power of attorney" form in the future. You should have a power of attorney that waives most of the provisions of HB 1883 (the law says that the principal can give additional instructions to the agent). Those additional instructions can closely follow HB 1883's provisions, but modify them to help avoid frivolous use of its powers.

Securities Requirements

Even when you give someone a broad general power of attorney, the agent may run into frustrating roadblocks. At times, dealing with securities (stocks and bonds) through a brokerage can present difficulties. The problems grow from two factors:

First, Texas law does not require anyone to accept your Power of Attorney. When the Texas legislature changed the durable power of attorney statute in 1993, they quietly revoked an important provision. The provision had required a third party—like a bank or broker—to accept a Power of Attorney so long as they were indemnified. Because this was revoked, there is no legal requirement that a Power of Attorney be accepted when you need to use it.

On the brighter side, the 1993 law change also allowed Powers of Attorney to be more standardized. One of the standard categories (section 494 of the Durable Power of Attorney Act) goes into great detail about an agent's authority to buy and sell stocks. *So if your power of attorney is up-to-date, you have a very good chance that it will be accepted.*

Second, stock brokerages are regulated by state and federal securities laws, which often impose more requirements than the regular Power of Attorney statute.

These additional laws allow brokerages to impose additional conditions on the use of your authority. For instance, the Texas Business and Commerce Code allows a brokerage to demand the document you present be "fresh"—even a court order can be rejected if the copy was certified by the court more than 60 days before you try to use it. The law also allows a Brokerage to impose their own standards, so long as the standards are "not manifestly unreasonable."

The bottom line is that dealing with securities is complex. To simplify the process, make sure your securities are in a single "street account." Your situation might also warrant establishing a living trust to manage the account, so that no Power of Attorney is involved.

"Stale" Powers of Attorney

What if you have a power of attorney that is 10, even 20 years old? Various law changes through the years have allowed documents that were legal under prior law to continue as valid. For instance, the 1989 law change required durable powers of attorney to be witnessed. But it expressly accepted pre-existing un-witnessed durable powers of attorney as valid. The 1993 law change eliminated the witnessing requirement.

Even though law changes may not invalidate an older document, there is a good reason you should keep your durable power of attorney up-to-date. Older powers of attorney become "stale" after 8 to 10 years. There is nothing technically wrong with them – but banks and brokers may simply refuse to accept them, fearing that the principal may have made other plans during the interim. They prefer to err on the side of caution.

Keeping your power of attorney current is much safer. Whenever there is a major law change, or at least every ten years, you should update your power of attorney. Then, if your agent needs to use it when you are ill, the chances of success are enhanced.

Revocation / Termination

You can revoke your durable power of attorney anytime. However, you must notify the agent and anyone who has received a copy of the durable power of attorney that you have revoked it. Any action taken by your agent before receiving this notice is a still a valid action.

Before 1993, any durable power of attorney was terminated the moment its principal died. However, current law allows action under a durable power of attorney to continue until the agent has *actual knowledge* of the principal's death. Any action taken by the agent, even after the principal's death, is valid if the agent does not know of the death. Of course, the Agent usually finds out about the principal's death within minutes or hours, so the general rule that death terminates a power of attorney is still the basic idea that you need to remember. *An agent cannot use the power of attorney after the death occurs as a means to settle the decedent's estate; that is where the Will and probate (or other estate planning tools) come in.*

Before using the durable power of attorney, your agent can be required to sign an affidavit saying the power of attorney has not been revoked and that you are, to the best of the agent's knowledge, still alive. You should expect banks and title companies to require these affidavits to be filed with the county clerk.

What if you have named your spouse as agent and then get divorced? Texas law says that the former spouse is automatically removed from authority. However, the removal does not happen until a Judge signs the divorce decree, which can be several months after the divorce starts. If you are in a divorce or planning a divorce, you should change your Durable Power of Attorney right away.

STRATEGY 2: GUARDIANSHIP

Guardianship is a court-supervised procedure for stripping authority from one person and placing into the hands of another person. It is not a voluntary procedure; rather, it can be thrust upon you if and when you become incapacitated.

In some states, the court appointed manager is called a "conservator." Texas has stayed with the word guardian. The idea is the same. The word for the person who has his/her authority removed is "ward."

Try to Avoid Guardianship

Whenever possible, you should try to avoid Guardianship. It is expensive and slow. It is also a detailed and often troublesome task for the person appointed to be guardian. Avoiding Guardianship requires pre-planning. See your attorney for durable powers of attorney, both financial and medical. If you have them, the need for Guardianship is almost eliminated.

Powers of Attorney offer privacy, flexibility and convenience. With a financial durable power of attorney, guardianship over "the estate" can be avoided, since you've already selected someone to assist with finances. With a Medical Power of

Attorney, guardianship of "the person" can be avoided, since power to make health care decisions has already been delegated.

Declaration of Guardian

Even if you sign both medical and financial powers of attorney, someone might try to force you into Guardianship. The laws that created both types of power of attorney state that if a court appoints a permanent guardian, the powers of attorney become void.

It is not likely that anyone will try to force you into Guardianship when you've made Powers of Attorney. But there is always the chance that some relative, unhappy about your decisions, will try. If you make a "Declaration of Guardian" you have a good chance of stopping that pushy relative cold.

Any competent adult may make a Declaration of Guardian. Your declaration cannot be verbal; it must be written down and signed. In it, you list your first choice for guardian and several back-ups. If your first choice is not available when needed, your alternates will be in line to replace the first choice.

A key feature of the Declaration of Guardian is that it gives you the power to disqualify an individual from ever becoming your guardian under any circumstances. This protects you from people you may want to avoid, such as former spouses and intrusive relatives. The Declaration gives you control over the identity of your future guardian if one is ever needed.

Holographic Declaration

Starting September 1, 2001 it is legal to create a "holographic" Declaration of Guardian – that is, one that is written entirely in your own handwriting and signed by you. It is valid even if un-witnessed. All you need to do is write down your choices and sign. While it would be very wise to put a date on the document, the law does not require it to be dated.

Formal Declaration

The law continues to allow you to make a more formal typed Declaration of Guardian (or at least one that is not handwritten by you). But a formal Declaration must also be signed by two other people as witnesses. The witnesses must be age 14 or older. The person you have chosen as guardian (or alternate guardian) cannot be a witness.

Signature for the Disabled

Another change to the law, effective after September 1, 2001, affects persons with physical disabilities. If you are mentally competent but physically incapable of signing your name, then someone you select can sign a Declaration of Guardian for you. However, the signing must take place in your presence and under your direction. Clearly, this type of Declaration has to be "formal" in the sense that it is signed by two witnesses.

Self-Proof of Formal Declaration

If you want extra protection, you can add a "Self Proving Affidavit" to your formal Declaration. This would be signed by you and the two witnesses, and then notarized. Why add self-proof? Self-proving the document protects you because -- if someone later tries to impose a Guardianship on you -- the Judge who hears the case must comply with Section 679A of the Probate Code. It states that the Judge can admit the declaration into evidence without the testimony of witnesses attesting to your competency and without further evidence that the execution of the declaration was proper. Your lawyer will not have to present any additional proof that the declaration's signing was done with the "formalities and solemnities and under the circumstances required to make it a valid declaration."

If you have made a holographic Declaration, then at the time of crisis – when someone is trying to prove you are incapacitated – you have the added job of proving that the Declaration is valid. It must be "proved up" just like it was a Will, which requires people who are familiar with your handwriting to testify about the document's authenticity.

There is another very strong reason to make a formal Declaration that is self-proven. The law allows the Judge to assume that the choices you make in your self-proved formal Declarations are valid. You are assumed to have been competent when you signed it, and the Judge assumes that the person you chose as guardian will act in your best interest.

Using the Declaration

You do not need to file your Declaration with the court in advance; however, the person you chose as guardian will need to file it when he or she goes to court to become your guardian (if the need for one arises). Timing is crucial: it must be filed after someone starts the Guardianship process (by filing an Application for

Guardianship) and before the Judge signs an order appointing a guardian. In reality, that gives you about a three-week opening to bring it to the court's attention.

Keep the original in a safe place, and let your intended guardian know about it. Most likely it will be your nominee for guardian who files it with the court.

You can revoke your Declaration of Guardian by tearing it up, or by making a new Declaration that supersedes the outdated one.

Internet Resource:
You can obtain a formal self-proven Declaration of Guardian – the kind that works best—on The Premack Law Office website at WWW.PREMACK.COM

Guardianship Reform

As difficult as Guardianship can be, sometimes it is the only legal solution available for your situation. If someone you love can no longer handle his/her finances nor take care of his/her physical needs, *and has not made a durable power of attorney*, then court controlled Guardianship becomes a real possibility.

The Texas Guardianship system used to be very severe – each time a guardian was appointed the ward was stripped of many civil rights. The ward lost the right to make a binding contract, the right to vote, the privilege of driving, the right to get married, and the right to buy or sell real property. The guardian made all decisions.

However, current law handles Guardianship in an entirely new way: a ward is allowed to keep all rights and powers that are not specifically assigned to the guardian by court order.

The ward makes all decisions that are not delegated to the guardian by court order. Only when the proposed guardian can prove that the proposed ward lacks the ability to do anything can the Judge give the guardian complete control. The focus of current Guardianship law is to provide assistance to the ward while preserving, as much as possible, the ward's rights and independence.

Estate and/or Person

A guardian can be appointed to care for a ward's estate and/or person. In this context, "estate" means the ward's financial dealings and "person" means the ward's physical well-being.

These two jobs are usually given to one guardian, but legally can be split between two Guardians. Sometimes, it will be appropriate to create only a Guardianship of the Estate, or of the Person, but not of both. For example

> Martha has a son named Steven who has been severely mentally disabled since birth. While Steven was a minor (under 18) Martha had automatic legal authority to control his medical care. But when he turned age 18 she lost legal control. Since Steven has no assets, Guardianship of his Estate is not necessary. She needs Guardianship of the Person so that she again has authority to take care of him.

A guardian of the person has automatic authority to make decisions regarding the physical welfare of the ward. This includes:

- The power to have physical possession of the ward and to establish the ward's legal residence;

- The power to care for, control and protect the ward;

- The power to provide food, clothing, shelter and medical care to the ward; and

- The power to consent to medical care, outpatient psychiatric care, and surgical treatment for the ward. However, mental health commitment cannot be done without approval of the Judge.

A guardian of the estate has authority to handle the ward's financial affairs, to the degree of control the court allows in its orders. The guardian can possess and manage the ward's property, also subject to orders from the court. A court order must be obtained before the Guardian can spend or sell any of the Ward's assets.

If, for instance, the guardian wants to pay the Ward's regular monthly nursing home expenses, pay for medications and pay utility bills – which are all very proper – the guardian must first seek approval from the court. The attorney must file a request, a hearing must be set and notice must be posted. At the hearing, the Judge might consent to the expenses or decline to approve them.

Mental Health Commitment

Forcing a mentally ill person to receive clinical attention was impossible for a Guardian until late 2003. It required a mental health commitment proceeding separate from the Guardianship. But House Bill 2679 was passed to allow a Guardian of the Person to admit the Ward to an inpatient mental health facility. This change keeps the Ward out of another court-based hearing.

Of course, it is still possible that a person who does not have a Guardian may be mentally disturbed. Obtaining inpatient mental health care for such a person is quite different from Guardianship. Mental health commitment is severe and short-term. Guardianship is serious and targeted toward the long-term care of an incapacitated person.

Texas Law only allows involuntary mental health commitment under limited circumstances. It is a fairly extreme measure, and can only be done with full respect to the patient's civil rights.

As such, the law requires a Judge to find that the proposed patient is mentally ill and due to that mental illness is likely to cause serious harm to himself or to someone else. In the alternative, the Judge can find that the proposed patient is suffering severe and abnormal mental, emotional, or physical distress. This must be accompanied by substantial mental or physical deterioration in his ability to function independently, and lack of ability to make a rational and informed decision as to whether or not to submit to inpatient medical treatment. Other similar standards apply for a Judge to order outpatient medical treatment.

The purpose of a mental health commitment is to obtain immediate mental health care. The care cannot last longer than 90 days. The process does not give anyone financial control over the patient.

Temporary Guardianship

If a person is at risk, but the situation does not fit the mental health commitment guidelines, temporary guardianship may be an answer.

Temporary guardianship used to be "ex parte" procedures that were initiated and approved without involvement of the proposed ward. As of late 2003 the law was changed so that when someone applies to become a temporary guardian, the proposed ward must be notified and must have an attorney. A hearing before the court will take place quickly, no more than 10 days after the application is file (unless the proposed ward asks for a delay of up to 30 days).

When the hearing date arrives, all the parties appear in court. If the proposed ward requests it, the proceedings can be held in private. The applicant must allege to the court that the proposed ward is incapacitated and must provide substantial evidence to back up that claim. If the court agrees that a temporary guardianship is appropriate, the temporary guardian receives only those powers that are granted by the court order. The proposed ward retains all other rights and powers during the term of the temporary guardianship. The order expires in 60 days unless it is extended during a contest of the order by the temporary ward.

Interaction with Power of Attorney

If a court appoints a temporary guardian of the estate of the principal, the court may suspend the powers held by an agent under a durable power of attorney. Until September 1, 2001 filing any type of guardianship automatically revoked any durable power of attorney that existed. This was a problem in temporary guardianships. Even if the court decided there were not grounds to make the guardianship permanent, prior powers of attorney were already invalidated. At the least, the principal then had to pay to create a new power of attorney. At the worst, the principal was left without any agent to help with management.

The currently law simply states that a power of attorney is suspended during the term of the temporary guardianship. If the guardianship is made permanent, the power of attorney is revoked. If the guardianship ends, the power of attorney is restored.

Permanent Guardianship

To begin a permanent Guardianship, an interested person hires an attorney to prepare an Application for Guardianship, which is then filed with the Court Clerk.

Notifications

The proposed ward is, of course, entitled to notice that the application for Guardianship has been filed. A sheriff's deputy is often sent to serve a citation on the ward. Citation can also be served by one of the many private companies that seek such business. The same notice must be served on the proposed ward's spouse (unless the spouse is the one applying to become guardian).

A notice must be mailed to the proposed ward's adult children and siblings. It must also be mailed to the nursing home administrator if the proposed ward lives in such a facility. If the applicant is aware of that a power of attorney exists, the notice must be mailed to the agent. Finally, if the applicant knows that a Declaration of Guardian was signed, the notice must also be mailed to the ward's selected guardian.

This requirement that the family and caregivers be notified is fairly new, and should help avoid the need for unnecessary guardianships. However, it was somewhat watered-down by the 2001 legislature. They changed the law so that failure to properly mail the notices to the siblings is not a bar to going forward with the guardianship hearing.

"Court Visitor Programs" exist in the probate courts of major metropolitan areas. The Judge (on his or her own incentive) can require, or anyone involved in the Guardianship can ask the Judge to require that a Court Visitor meet with the proposed ward before the court hearing. The Visitor's job is to give an independent assessment of the proposed ward's condition.

Two other people must be involved before Guardianship can be granted. They are 1) the Court Investigator and 2) the Attorney ad litem.

The Court Investigator

When anyone files a Guardianship application, the court investigator is required to look into the circumstances alleged in the application. The investigator is supposed to decide if there is any "less restrictive alternative" than guardianship – like a durable power of attorney.

The court investigator is also the chief court visitor, and oversees that program in each county with a statutory probate court. In this role, the investigator also checks out any complaints made about guardianships and reports to the judge when necessary.

Only those counties with statutory probate courts have court investigators. As of this writing, the only Texas counties with statutory probate courts are Bexar, Collin, Dallas, Denton, El Paso, Galveston, Harris, Hidalgo, Tarrant and Travis counties.

The Attorney Ad Litem

Why does another attorney have to be involved? If the proposed ward is truly incapacitated then he/she needs legal representation. The court appoints the attorney ad litem as an advocate for the proposed ward, to protect his/her legal rights.

The ad litem will interview the proposed ward face-to-face when possible. The goal is to discuss with the proposed ward the law, the facts of the case and the legal options available. It is standard practice for the ad litem to deny the need for a Guardianship (even when it is obviously necessary). This forces the person trying to become guardian to prove completely the ward's incapacity, and offers extra protection against abuse of the system.

The attorney ad litem is paid out of the ward's money. This happens even if the ward didn't want the Guardianship, and even if the court decides a Guardianship is not necessary.

Incompetent or Incapacitated?

When the court hearing finally arrives, the applicant must prove the ward is "incapacitated." Texas lawmakers have put real effort into revising the laws to eliminate the wording "of unsound mind" or "incompetent." A person is legally incapacitated if he/she:

- Is under age eighteen;

- Is eighteen or older and, because of a physical or mental condition, is substantially unable to provide food, clothing or shelter, to provide for his/her own physical health, or to manage his/her own financial affairs. These difficulties must be proven to be recurring acts (not just isolated examples of bad judgment). They must have occurred in the six month period prior to the hearing, not back farther in the past;

- Is a "missing person;" or

- Needs a guardian in order to receive some type of government benefit.

The Applicant must also prove that he or she is eligible to act as guardian and that the ward's legal rights will be protected by appointment of a guardian. If the Judge determines these facts exist, the Judge will authorize the Guardianship by signing an Order appointing the guardian, which becomes effective when the court's clerk issues Letters of Guardianship.

Before the clerk issues Letters of Guardianship, the guardian must post a bond and file an oath pledging to act properly. Then an inventory of the ward's assets must be filed, reviewed, approved, and updated annually.

Who can be Guardian?

When appointment of a guardian is the only alternative, who will become your guardian? If you have selected someone in a Declaration of Guardian, the court will appoint that person unless he/she is disqualified. If you did not make a Declaration of Guardian, the Court will favor appointing your spouse as guardian. If your spouse is unavailable or has not asked for the job, any "next of kin" can be appointed. If no next of kin volunteer, then any person not "disqualified" can become your guardian (whether or not that person is related to you). That can include the Texas Department of Aging and Disability Services under limited circumstances.

A potential guardian is disqualified if the applicant:

- Is under age 18 or has "notoriously bad" conduct;

- Is incapacitated;

- Is a party (or his/her parent is a party) to a lawsuit on which the welfare of the proposed ward may depend. This disqualification can be waived by the court if the proposed ward and guardian are on the same side of the lawsuit, or if the court appoints a guardian ad litem to be in control while the lawsuit is pending;

- Owes money to the ward, unless the debt is paid before the applicant gets appointed to be guardian;

- Cannot prudently assist the ward due to lack of experience or education; or

- Is found to be unsuitable by the court, is disqualified in a Declaration of Guardian, or is not a Texas resident and does not submit to the court's jurisdiction.

A case in the Appeals Court in Houston helps us understand these disqualifications[8]. In the case, the husband (Mr. Trimble) failed to provide care to his ailing wife. The state, through Adult Protective Services (APS), intervened and started a guardianship over the wife.

Mr. Trimble also went to court. He argued that, as spouse, he had first right to be guardian. APS pointed out that he had already botched the job: he let his wife wander and did not pay her bills. She had been repeatedly picked up and returned to their home from her wanderings by the local Sheriff.

The appeals court applied the law that a "person is ineligible to serve as a guardian if he is incapable of properly and prudently managing and controlling the ward or the ward's estate because of inexperience, lack of education, or other good reason." They went on to decide that Mr. Trimble, by failing to provide proper care for his wife, provided ample "other good reason" that he should not be her guardian. He was disqualified, and control over her welfare was placed with the state.

After the Guardian is Appointed

The Court Order that appoints the guardian should spell out the powers given to the guardian. It will define whether the guardian has financial powers (guardian of the Estate), has medical powers (guardian of the Person), or has both sets of authority.

The ward retains any powers that are not specifically given to the guardian in the court Order. Also, the powers granted do not take effect until the guardian posts bond as required by the Judge, the Judge approves the bond, and the guardian files an oath of office. Then, the guardian must prepare an initial inventory of the ward's estate for review and approval by the court.

Each year, the guardian is required to file a thorough accounting of all income and expenses. The probate courts have a special auditor to review these records. Once reviewed, they must be presented to the Judge and an Order must be signed approving the accounting.

The guardian's powers are suspended if the annual account is not approved within 120 days of the Guardianship's anniversary. Very often, guardians are lax about filing their annual accountings. The accountings must be timely and complete – if they are not, then the guardian's authority automatically expires.

Incapacitated Adult Children

In Texas, once a person turns 18 that person is legally considered to be an adult. The law presumes a person to have capacity. What if, in fact, that person does not have capacity? If that "adult" is mentally retarded or is otherwise incapable of managing him/herself since childhood, then a guardianship may be necessary for the parent or a responsible relative to continue to provide care.

When you become guardian, you have legal authority to manage the person. But as an aging parent with a middle-aged child, you may wonder what will happen when you die or if you become incapacitated.

When that happens, the court must select a replacement guardian. Any interested person can apply; family has priority, but any person could become guardian. If there is someone who you feel would be an appropriate guardian, you can designate that person (and alternates) as successor guardian. You can therefore arrange for his/her care by selecting a replacement guardian who shares your values and will care for your adult child in the way you prefer.

This is done either in your Will or in a separate legal document. The requirements for a non-Will declaration closely resemble those for a Declaration of Guardian – except that this is called a "Declaration of Appointment of Guardian for my Children in the Event of my Death or Incapacity." One major difference: you cannot "disqualify" someone from serving as guardian – you can only affirmatively select a successor. The court must appoint your selection, unless that person refuses the job or is disqualified for some other reason. Then the court can open the job to anyone interested.

Special Needs Trust

Often, an incapacitated adult child will qualify for public benefits, either under the SSI (supplemental security income) or the SSDI (social security disability income) programs. Both programs are complex and provide a different set of benefits, and SSI has qualifying standards very similar to those that relate to qualifying for Medicaid. SSDI is an earned benefit that is not lost because the disabled person may have some money in the bank, but SSI can be denied or stopped if the disabled person has too much monthly income or too many resources.

Since an SSI beneficiary cannot have too much income or too many resources, the parents should consider other options before making a Will that simply leaves their estate to that disabled person. Some parents will select another of their adult children – one who is a capable and responsible person – to inherit the estate with the non-binding understanding that the disabled person will be cared for properly.

Alternatively, the parents may desire a more formal structure for the care of their disabled adult child. They can create a Special Needs Trust (sometimes called a Supplemental Needs Trust). This trust becomes the owner of some or all their estate when they die and the Trustee is granted broad discretion over when and how much to provide in benefits to the disabled adult child.

The trust contains provisions stating that funds should only be distributed for items not paid for with public benefits. Thus, two goals are met. First, the beneficiary's needs are fulfilled (albeit from two sources: public benefits and the trust) and second, the trust funds last many years longer (because the trust is limited to paying for things public benefits don't cover).

Special Needs Trusts are allowed by a provision of federal law referred to as section 1396p of the Social Security Act[9]. It begins with the premise that a person can<u>not</u> simply take resources, place them into a trust, and then claim they are no longer accessible… unless special conditions are met. A trust may contain assets, and those assets will not be counted against the person who is trying to qualify for public benefits if:

1. The disabled person applying for benefits is under age 65 and a) the applicant is disabled as defined by Social Security; b) the trust was established for the benefit of the applicant by a parent, grandparent, legal guardian or a court; c) the trust receives assets that belong to the applicant; and d) the State will receive all amounts remaining in the trust upon the death of the applicant up to the total medical assistance paid by the State.

2. The disabled person applying for benefits is of any age and a) the applicant is disabled as defined by Social Security; b) the trust was created for the benefit of the applicant by a parent, grandparent or other individual desiring to provide for the applicant's needs; c) the trust receives assets that belong to the person who created the trust; and d) when the applicant eventually dies, the remaining funds can be paid to anyone the trust's creator selected.

3. The disabled person applying for benefits is of any age and a) the applicant is disabled as defined by Social Security; b) the trust was established by and is managed by a nonprofit association (where a separate account is maintained for each beneficiary of the trust, but, for purposes of investment and management of funds, the trust pools these accounts but the account inside the trust was established for the benefit of the applicant by the applicant him/herself, or by a parent, a grandparent, a legal guardian or a court; c) the trust receives assets that belong to the applicant; and d) when the applicant dies, the trust keeps the remaining funds. This is called a "pooled trust." In Texas, the only established pooled trust is operated by the Association of Retarded Citizens (ARC). They can be reached for information at 1-800-252-9729.

Another way to look at this is to categorize SNTs as either "self-settled" or as "third-party" trusts. When the trust's assets originally belonged to the person who is now the trust's beneficiary (or that person had the right to receive those assets before the trust was established – as in the case of a pending lawsuit settlement) then it is "self-settled". When the trust's assets belonged to someone else, like the parents or grandparents of the disabled person, then it is "third-party" settled.

Both types convert the assets put in the trust into non-countable resources for SSI and Medicaid. That means that the applicant may qualify for public benefits even though the assets still exist (if they were outside the trust, the applicant would not qualify for public benefits).

Once qualified, the applicant begins to receive a monthly income stipend and all the applicant's medical costs are covered by Medicaid. The stipend does not amount to much (in 2005 it was capped at $552, in 2006 at $585), but the medical care can be very valuable financially. If the applicant receives income from other sources, the government figures the applicant no longer needs the stipend... and when it is lost, so is the medical coverage. Thus, it is important for the applicant's monthly income to remain at a very low level.

Since distributions from a SNT might be counted as income (or might not, depending on the purpose for which the distribution is made) it is vital to know how the government categorizes distributions from a SNT. When will funds paid from a SNT be treated as income for the applicant, and when are such funds ignored by the government? The answers are exceedingly complex and could fill a fair sized book. For instance, if funds are paid from the trust to pay rent (to provide housing for the applicant) that rent is treated as income to the applicant and may jeopardize the public benefits. However, if the trust itself purchases a home and owns title to the home, allowing the applicant to live there rent-free, it is considered "in-kind support and maintenance" and the applicant's benefits will be reduced by the "Presumed Maximum Value" which is equal to $20 plus 1/3 of the maximum SSI amount.

Examples of other distributions that are allowed include cleaning services for the home, dental care, medical insurance premiums, eyeglasses, travel and entertainment, training programs, and medical procedures that the government would consider "not medically necessary". Clearly those benefits can make an applicant's life more comfortable, and they supplement the benefits provided by the public.

When the trust focuses on paying for things that the public benefits will not cover then the applicant's life is more comfortable, the public benefits are retained, and the trust fund money will not be consumed as quickly.

Volunteer Guardianship Programs

Texas is developing a variety of "guardianship programs" throughout the state using the state Guardianship Advisory Board and its implementing arm, called the Guardianship Alliance of Texas. The goal of these programs is to develop and to put into operation "a statewide plan to ensure that each incapacitated individual in the state who needs a guardianship or another less restrictive type of assistance to make decisions concerning the incapacitated individual's own welfare and financial affairs receives that assistance"[10]. The most recent survey taken by the Guardianship Alliance shows there are 18 volunteer or government-run guardianship programs in Texas.

Internet Resources:

The Guardianship Alliance of Texas has a listing of all volunteer Guardianship and Money Management programs available in Texas. It is found at WWW.HHSC.STATE.TX.US/SI/GAT/TMMP_SELECT.ASP

A good example of a Guardianship program is Family Eldercare, based in Austin. It is on the Internet at WWW.FAMILYELDERCARE.ORG

Ending Guardianship

Guardianship is technical at all its stages: beginning, middle and end. Certainly at some future date the ward will die, and the need for Guardianship will end. It can also end if a ward has full recovery of his/her capacity. How does a person go about ending a Guardianship that is no longer necessary?

If the Ward has Recovered

Anyone interested in the ward's well being (including the ward) can file a formal written application asking the court to hold a hearing about the ward's present condition. The process is detailed, and you really should hire an attorney to help.

The law allows the ward to start the process in an even easier fashion: with an informal letter to the court. The Judge must then appoint an attorney to represent the ward, whose first job is to draw up a formal written application requesting restoration of the ward's rights. Both the ward and the guardian are served with notice of the filing.

The court is required to receive medical evidence that clearly establishes the ward's current medical condition and the outlook for his/her future health. The guardian is allowed to offer evidence of the ward's continuing difficulties. Very clear evidence of the ward's recovery is needed to allow the court to end the Guardianship. This can take time, money and a great deal of effort and could end up before a jury to decide the facts.

If the Ward Dies

Guardianship must be "closed" after the death of the ward. Usually this involves filing a final accounting of the ward's estate and obtaining a release of the guardian's bond. The court will order the remaining assets to be delivered to the ward's Executor for distribution according to the ward's Will. If there is no Will, then it may be necessary to do a "dependent administration" to handle the ward's remaining assets. (See more about that in Chapter 8: Settling an Estate).

STRATEGY 3: COMMUNITY ADMINISTRATION

If a married couple has nothing but community property, and one spouse becomes incapacitated, the well spouse can avoid guardianship with a legal process called "community administration." Of course, guardianship can also be avoided if the incapacitated spouse signed a durable power of attorney or created a living trust before becoming incapacitated. That type of pre-planning is almost always superior to court action.

Once the Judge rules the other spouse is incapacitated, the well spouse is called the "community administrator."

Community administration law is actually tucked into the Guardianship portion of the Texas Probate Code[11], so it is not well known. Think of it as a "half-way Guardianship." The well spouse is still required to pay an attorney and court costs, and to appear before a Judge. The Judge's job is to decide if the other spouse has truly become incapacitated. As such, evidence like a doctor's letter must be provided.

Authority to manage, control and dispose of community property vests in the community administrator. This even gives the well spouse power to sell the homestead without the incapacitated spouse's signature.

Process Can be Simpler than Guardianship

Unlike Guardianship, this process does not require a bond. The well spouse may not be required to file an inventory of assets, may not be required to file an annual accounting of income or assets, and is not required to obtain the Judge's permission to sell or to dispose of a community property asset. These rules make this process simpler than a guardianship.

However, the law was changed in 2001 to add requirements and possible complexities to the rules:

> First, just like a guardianship, an attorney ad litem is required in each community administration. Some Judges already imposed this requirement, but it was optional. Now appointment of an ad litem is mandatory.

> Second, any interested person who has good grounds can ask the court to order the community administrator to file an "inventory and accounting" of the community property. The Judge may also legally require an accounting in his/her discretion. Some Judges may decide to do this as a matter of routine. The Judge also has discretion to call the community administrator into court anytime after 15 months have passed. Anyone else interested (say, one of the children) can ask the Judge to call in the community administrator. The

Judge can then order an updated accounting as a method of overseeing the community administrator.

Third, the ad litem can, at any time, demand an accounting from the community administrator. The law imposes no duty on the ad litem to demand the accounting, but once demanded the administrator is legally required to provide the accounting within 60 days. The ad litem does not have to file the accounting with the court – it can just be used to oversee the well spouse's activities.

Forth, the community administrator is required to report to the court any lawsuit involving the incapacitated spouse. This specifically includes any divorce proceeding that may be brought to end the marriage.

These new oversight provisions certainly make community administration less attractive than it was prior to 2001 – but it still has the potential to be much simpler than a guardianship.

Incapacitated Spouse's Separate Property

The legislature also decided the community property administration law was not specific enough in dealing with separate property, so there is now a requirement that when the incapacitated spouse has any separate property, a permanent Guardianship must be started to handle the separate property. Guardianship is required, not optional. The well spouse will be appointed guardian unless he/she declines or is found unfit (but he/she is presumed to be suitable for the job).

If the court finds the well spouse is not qualified to be community administrator and guardian, then the court must appoint someone who is qualified. Preference goes to close relatives, but anyone who asks to be guardian and is not disqualified can be appointed.

In that case, the community administration has failed. The well spouse has no authority, and can be ordered to turn over to the guardian the ward's one-half interest in community property (in addition to the separate property over which the guardian already has control).

STRATEGY 4: SOCIAL SECURITY REPRESENTATIVE PAYEE

You may become "Representative Payee" for a retiree who:

- Is incompetent;

- Is incapable of managing his/her Social Security benefits; or

- Is legally disabled.

If someone you care for fits any of those categories, you can call the local Social Security office to request form SSA-11-BK. You must file it with proof of your identity, and under most circumstances must have a personal interview before being appointed.

When you become Representative Payee, you receive the retiree's Social Security check. You control the funds. Your legal obligation is to use the money for the retiree's expenses, and according to Social Security you have the following specific duties:

- Determine the beneficiary's needs and use his or her payments to meet those needs;

- Save any money left after meeting the beneficiary's current needs in an interest bearing account or savings bonds for the beneficiary's future needs;

- Report any changes or events which could affect the beneficiary's eligibility for benefits or payment amount;

- Keep records of all payments received and how they are spent and/or saved;

- Provide benefit information to social service agencies or medical facilities that serve the beneficiary;

- Help the beneficiary get medical treatment when necessary;

- Notify SSA of any changes in your (the payee's) circumstances that would affect your performance or continuing as payee;

- Complete written reports accounting for the use of funds; and

- Return any payments to which the beneficiary is not entitled to SSA.

Social Security can (and will) monitor your activities. If you misapply any funds, you are liable. Social Security can also be held liable if they failed to appoint a suitable Representative Payee and to monitor that Payee's performance.

Before you are appointed, Social Security must notify the retiree in writing that you have applied. If the retiree does not want you to be Payee, the retiree can contest your action and has the right to appeal a decision that has already been made.

STRATEGY 5: ACCOUNT MANAGEMENT

How you set up your bank accounts is as important as what you put into them. It is an issue of keeping your funds secure: who will be allowed to access your funds and who might be able to claim to own your funds?

Banks, Savings Banks and Credit Unions are very inventive when it comes to marketing their services. They may offer savings, checking, money funds, and certificates of deposit, but they will market them with fancy names. Opening a "Super Savers account" or "Special Senior account" may save you a few dollars on your monthly bank fees, but the marketing names are mostly hype. The important thing is how your account is legally classified, who will have access, and who may claim ownership.

Types of Accounts

Legally, there are a limited number of ways to classify your accounts. The Texas Probate Code clearly identifies your options, and asks banks to use a special form when you open a new account, called a "Uniform Single Party or Multiple Party Account Form." Sadly, most banks make things more difficult for you due to their avoidance of uniformity. Instead, they strive to make it easy for themselves by using their own internal forms – consistent from branch to branch, but very different from bank to bank.

How you set up your account will determine what happens to the money in it while you are living. It may also determine what happens to the money in it when you die. How you set up your accounts is an important choice!

Access v. Ownership

The type of account you select will vary depending on two issues: access and ownership. Some accounts only give you access to your money; some give access to multiple parties. Your Will determines ownership of some accounts; ownership to others is determined by the account type. The Henderson v. Stauffer case, discussed on page 48, is a fine example of this distinction.

Several Probate Code provisions allow you to choose among the following types of accounts, if your bank chooses to offer them. These descriptions are summarized in Table 1 on page 52:

1 - Single Party Account

If you select this type of account, then while you are alive you are the only person who can access the funds in the account. You own the account. When you die, the bank will freeze the account until your Will is probated and evidence of your heir's identity is provided.

2 - Single Party Account with Pay on Death (POD)

With this type of account, as above, you are the owner and the only person with authority to access the account while you are alive. But upon your death, the person(s) you named on the account card become the owner(s) of the account. The POD arrangement supersedes anything that your Will might say about the account.

Let that point sink in for a moment. ***"The POD arrangement supersedes anything your Will might say about the account."*** Your Will is not as powerful as the way you set up your bank accounts. What you sign at the bank takes priority. If there is a conflict between your Will and your bank account arrangement, the Will loses. That is why it is vital for you to properly coordinate what your Will says with what your bank arrangements say.

3 - Multiple Party Account

A multiple party account allows each signer to access the funds in the account without permission from each other. The person who puts the funds in the account owns them (unless the funds are community property, which are then owned ½ by each spouse).

When a party to the account dies, that party's share of the account passes according to the terms of his/her Will or (if there is no Will) by the laws of intestacy. However, the account is not frozen upon the death of its owner. Any party to the account can withdraw the funds, even though they may not be the owner of the funds.

4 - Multiple Party Account with Right of Survivorship

All of the features of this account are the same as #3 above, except that when the account owner dies the other parties to the account become its owners. No probate is needed to access the account, and the right of survivorship arrangement supersedes anything your Will might say about the account. Once again, if there is a conflict between your Will and your bank account arrangement, the Will loses.

5 - Multiple Party Account with Right of Survivorship AND Pay on Death

This account has all the features of #4 above. The difference is that when the last party to the account dies, a designated beneficiary who was not allowed to have access to the account becomes owner of the account. For example: Al and Betty open a joint checking account with ROS to each other, but POD to their son Ted. Only Al and Betty can access the funds. If Al dies, Betty becomes owner by ROS and only she can access the funds. When Betty subsequently dies, Ted becomes owner of the account even though he had no right to touch it before Betty died.

6 - Trust Account

Usually, a trust account is used to handle money you want to keep separate. Your bank may refer to this type of account as a Totten trust (after a famous 1904 case in which the Totten family were the litigants). The bank's account contract has you to list a Trustee who can access the account and is owner of the account. You can list yourself as Trustee. You also list one or more beneficiaries, who do not have access to the account. However, when the Trustee dies, the beneficiaries become owners of the funds. Totten trusts are different from Living Trusts. A Living Trust is flexible, allowing you to define your goals and design the trust to meet those goals. A Totten trust is rigid, giving you no design options at all; it must be paid out to the beneficiaries upon the trustee's death.

7 - Convenience Account

A "convenience account" is different from all of the other accounts listed above. Here are its important features:

- You set up a convenience account in your name, allowing one or more cosigner access to the account. The cosigner can withdraw funds.

- The funds in the account belong to you. When you put money in the account, a cosigner does not become owner of the funds. If a cosigner puts money in the account, you are considered to be the owner of those funds.

- You can "lock out" a cosigner by informing the bank, in writing, that access should only be allowed with your permission. The bank can impose its own procedures on this option, so be sure to discuss it with them before trying to lock out your cosigner.

- A cosigner does not have a right of survivorship to the account when you die.

- When you die, a cosigner can withdraw the funds if the bank has not received written notice of your death. The bank has no legal liability if it turns the money over to a cosigner. If the bank has received written notice of your death, the account is frozen until the Will is probated.

Texas law also allows you to name more than one co-signer. Also, a husband-wife team can own a convenience account and can name one or more other persons as co-signers.

Convenience accounts have been legal in Texas for more than a decade, but not all banks have chosen to make them available. If you can find one, it is an effective tool to grant access to your funds while retaining the right to unilaterally change your mind and cancel that access. (With a more typical joint account, once you have added someone else's name to the account you cannot take that name off without that person's cooperation short of closing the account.) A convenience account allows you to keep ultimate control over the account, allows you to change your mind, and allows you to "fire" the co-signer for any reason at any time.

Two Designations We Don't Use in Texas

Two account designations are common in other states but hardly ever used in Texas. They are "Tenants in Common" and "Tenants by the Entireties."

"Tenants in common" has the same meaning as Texas' designation "joint tenants" – that is, "we both own this together, but when one of us dies, his/her share passes according to his/her Will." There is no right of survivorship inherent in the tenants in common designation.

"Tenants by the entireties" applies only between a husband and wife, and is not used in Texas. In states where it is used, it means, "we are married, we both own this equally, and when one of us dies, the surviving spouse owns it automatically." That is essentially the same as our "joint tenants with right of survivorship" – except that the Texas language applies to anyone while the "tenants by the entirety" language only applies to a married couple. Texas does have a legal concept of community property survivorship (which only applies between husband and wife) but it must be expressed in an agreement that matches Texas law. The "tenants by the entireties" language has no application here.

Internet Banking

Most banks these days offer some type of Internet banking arrangement. Other than the routine convenience that online banking provides, stay aware that it can be a useful way to help aging parents maintain their independence. Here is an example:

> Margaret lives in Odessa, and her son Steve lives in Houston. She still lives at home, but has slowed down. She has a lady come in to help with housework and to cook. Margaret cannot balance her checkbook anymore, but still writes checks to pay her bills.
>
> Steve talks to Margaret's bank, and with proper approval from Margaret the bank activates Internet access to her accounts. Steve can run software on his home computer to balance her account and verify that her bills are being paid. He can transfer money, pay her bills that may be falling behind, and generally keep an eye on her finances.

Some banks have signed-on with the two major retail banking software packages, Quicken™ and Microsoft Money™. These programs can get pretty complex. Some banks have their own systems that work directly over the Internet. If you feel this idea is valuable in your situation, ask your bank which approach works best for them then decide which approach will work best for you.

Deposit Insurance

The Federal Deposit Insurance Corporation (FDIC) and the National Credit Union Administration (NCUA) are federal agencies set up by Congress to insure bank deposits in case the financial institution becomes insolvent.

In 2005, Congress voted to increase the deposit amounts that the FDIC an NCUA can insure. This increase, the first in 25 years, takes two forms. First, the limit on *retirement accounts* jumped from $100,000 to $250,000. The accounts covered include traditional and Roth IRAs, self-directed Keogh accounts, "457 Plan" accounts for state government employees and 401(k) accounts. The increased coverage took effect on April 1, 2006.

Second, *regular accounts* (savings, checking, CDs, money markets) are still insured up to $100,000 per depositor. At the same time and in the same financial institution, retirement accounts are separately insured up to $250,000 per depositor.

Congress also approved an increase to the standard $100,000 deposit coverage, but not in a straightforward manner. Starting in 2011, FDIC must factor inflation and other considerations into how much it will cover. Every five years after that, it must re-evaluate its coverage limits. FDIC says that "limits could rise in the future, but not until 2011, if at all."

It is fairly common for a married couple to have $200,000 coverage at a single financial institution by having joint accounts. Extra coverage can grow from adding the names of your adult children to various accounts – but you must factor in the estate planning impact (will the new account arrangements interfere with the plan you expressed in your Will?).

An unmarried person with no children would have fewer options to expand deposit insurance coverage under federal rules – but adding siblings or parents (if still living) to accounts might expand insurance coverage. The rules allow siblings, for instance, to each deposit $100,000 in joint accounts with full insurance coverage. But the rules can get tricky. For instance, if Ted deposits his own funds of $125,000 and his brother Fred deposits his own funds of $75,000, Ted's coverage still tops at $100,000. But if the funds are co-owned (each sibling owns ½) then the entire account balance is insured.

People have additional coverage when a revocable grantor trust (a living trust) is created, additional coverage for business accounts (partnerships and corporations), and additional coverage for custodial accounts under the uniform transfers to minors act.

In mid-2004 the FDIC announced simplified rules for insurance coverage of accounts owned by living trusts. The rules that were used prior to these changes tended to be confusing and difficult for your bank to track. Now, the FDIC will extend $100,000 coverage for each "qualified trust beneficiary".

Most close family members are qualified trust beneficiaries – your spouse, children, grandchildren, parents and siblings. They are covered even if their interest in the trust is contingent on some future event (unlike the old rules, which refused coverage if it was possible under some circumstances for a beneficiary to be cut-out under the trust's terms). FDIC is also dropping the requirement that your bank keep track of the beneficiaries, easing their paperwork requirements. Here are some examples of how the new rules operate:

- If you are single and, as grantor, establish a living trust that names your four children as beneficiaries (they only get funds after you die), FDIC will extend $400,000 coverage in a single bank.

- If you are married and as grantor establish a living trust with your separate property that names your spouse as beneficiary (when you die), then the coverage is only $100,000. Your spouse is the only qualified beneficiary. The limit remains $100,000 so long as your spouse is alive (even if you list your four children to get the funds in case of your spouse's death). Of course, if your spouse really does die before you, those four children then become primary beneficiaries so coverage grows to $400,000.

- If you are married and both spouses as grantors create a living trust with community property, setting up the trust for both spouses' benefit and for the benefit of four children after both spouses die, then: 1) there is $800,000 coverage while both spouses are alive, and 2) after one grantor/spouse dies, FDIC coverage is cut back to $400,000. Each grantor gets $100,000 per qualified beneficiary.

Internet Resource:
Need to verify the FDIC rules so you'll know if your deposits are insured? The FDIC has a new online coach they call EDIE that will tell you whether you are protected or exposed. Visit EDIE on the web at WWW2.FDIC.GOV/EDIE.

Right of Survivorship

"Right of Survivorship" is an easy way to give someone ownership of an asset when you die. You can grant Right of Survivorship either by agreement or by gift.

Often, Right of Survivorship is created by agreement. For example, a husband and wife can agree in writing that all of their community property will pass to the survivor between them when one of them dies. This is a "Community Property Survivorship Agreement."

Sometimes, survivorship rights can be "given" by the current owner. For example, a father can place his daughter's name onto his bank account and instruct that the bank pay all sums he has on deposit to his daughter when he dies. However, the agreement must be in writing, must be signed by father and daughter, and must specify that "Right of Survivorship" is being granted.

Use with Caution

Survivorship rights must be used with caution. Why? Because survivorship rights override your Last Will and Testament and thus may block the intentions you expressed in your Will.

Some banks try to open all new accounts automatically with Right of Survivorship. This can cause many problems, because (I repeat) the survivorship rights supersede what your Will says. To help solve this problem, Texas law allows the use of the Uniform Single Party or Multiple Party Account Form, but many banks have decided not to adopt it. They continue to use their internally approved forms, so the papers you see from bank to bank will be quite different.

Here's an example of how Right of Survivorship can interfere with the plan in your Will:

> Sheryl has three adult children. She intends for her assets to pass equally to all three children when she dies, and that is what her Last Will and Testament instructs.
>
> Her oldest son has been helping Sheryl pay bills and she decides it is time to put his name on her checking account. When she changes her account at the bank, the bank's form creates "Right of Survivorship" for her son. The bank clerk does not point this out, and Sheryl does not read the fine print on the account agreement.
>
> When Sheryl dies, her checking account contains nearly all of her assets. Her son, as survivor, becomes the owner of that money regardless what she said in her Last Will and Testament. The result: her son gets the bank account and the other children are cut out. This is not the equal distribution Sheryl wanted!

What Sheryl needed to do was more carefully coordinate her survivorship assets with her Last Will and Testament. When the bank created survivorship rights without making an issue of the impact, they altered her estate plan.

Working together, upon your death, your Last Will and Testament and Survivorship rights can pass your assets with ease. But working against each other, they can create chaos and family misery.

Your accounts should always harmonize with your Last Will and Testament. Check with your bank to see how your accounts are set up. Ask to see the "signature cards" that contain your agreement with the bank – don't rely on what the printed monthly statement says.

Stauffer v. Henderson

Right of Survivorship is an extremely useful technique for avoiding probate. It is also very cost effective. But it must be understood and used properly or it will not work for you.

A primary example of the failure to properly use Right of Survivorship was decided by the Texas Supreme Court in 1990 through its decision in Stauffer v. Henderson[12].

Here's what happened: Marion Henderson and Mary Stauffer were sisters. Henderson opened a bank account. All money in the account came from Henderson, who put her sister Stauffer's name on the account as Joint Tenant. The account card read as follows:

> " . . . upon the death of either of us any balance in said account or any part thereof may be withdrawn by, or upon the order of the survivor. It is especially agreed that withdrawal of funds by the survivor shall be binding upon us and upon our heirs, next of kin..."

Marion Henderson died, and Mary Stauffer withdrew the money. J.D. Henderson, Marion's husband, sued to get the money back. He claimed that half the money was his because of Community Property laws and that the other half belonged to his wife's estate (and should pass according to her last will and testament).

The Texas Supreme Court ruled in favor of Mr. Henderson. The Court said that the account card did *not* create a Right of Survivorship even though it appeared to give the money to Mary Stauffer. Instead, the wording of the account agreement did no more than authorize withdrawal of funds by Mary Stauffer. The ability to withdraw the money (access) contrasts with the issue survivorship (ownership).

Years ago Texas law was structured to eliminate any "presumption" that Right of Survivorship exists simply because two names are listed on an account. The only thing that can create a binding Right of Survivorship is a written agreement (like an account card) signed by all parties. Then the question becomes: what wording must the account card use in order to create survivorship rights?

In the Stauffer case, the Supreme Court decided special language must be used. Just saying "joint property" was not enough. Instead, the agreement must explicitly say the account is held as Joint Tenants with Right of Survivorship. When used, that wording will create a valid survivorship agreement. The Uniform Single Party or Multiple Party Account Form was designed to prevent this confusion, but not all banks use it.

If you intend to set up a joint account with Right of Survivorship, be certain that the words "Joint Account with Right of Survivorship" are written into the account agreement. Also, be certain that both you and the intended survivor sign the account card. If done properly, Right of Survivorship can assist you in avoiding probate.

'And' v. 'Or'

When setting up your bank accounts, two little words, "AND" and "OR," are important. If two names go onto a bank account, you need to pick between "and" and "or" to join them. What happens when you choose, and why is it important?

The word "and" binds the two listed people together as a single unit. If the account lists "Herschel and Bernice," the bank must deal with both of them. The word "or" gives the bank a choice between the two people. If the account lists "Herschel or Bernice," the bank can deal with either one of them. For example

> You become ill and need someone to pay your bills. Your bank account lists two names joined with "AND." The second person cannot pay your bills because two signatures are required for access. But if your bank account lists two names joined with "OR" then the second person can pay the bills. Only one signature is then required for access.

Choose carefully when you put another person's name on your bank account. Setting up an account that allows unrestricted access by the cosigner can be dangerous. If your cosigner is unethical, you may lose your money. An "AND" account exists to act as a control over the account by requiring double signatures. Keeping your account solo can protect your funds, but the lack of accessibility by a second person might also cause troubles down the line. For example

> Suzanne and Roger are married and have a checking account listed as "Suzanne or Roger" and a CD in only Suzanne's name.

> The checking account that lists both of them is joined by the word "or." That account is a "joint tenancy." While they are living, either of them can access the funds. If either of them becomes disabled, the other will be able to get at the checking account to pay the bills.

> If either of them dies, the Texas Probate Code gives the bank the option of allowing the other account holder to access the funds (to withdraw them or write checks on the account). Many banks will allow a surviving joint account holder to keep using the account as though no death had occurred. Some banks, on the other hand, lock the account until the estate is probated. To be certain the survivor will have access, Roger and Suzanne can add the phrase "with right of survivorship" to the account. When those words are included, the bank MUST pay the funds to the survivor.

> The CD is only in Suzanne's name. Only she can access it. It may be community property if she earned the funds during the marriage. However, putting the funds into an account with only her name gives her sole management over the funds. If Suzanne becomes disabled, Roger is locked out of the CD.

They should consider either 1) changing the CD by adding Roger's name to the account with an "or" or 2) being sure that Roger (or someone Suzanne trusts) has her durable power of attorney. The durable power of attorney would legally authorize her agent to access the funds in her name.

While the CD is only in Suzanne's name, it will be frozen if she dies. The bank is likely to hold the funds until they are presented with letters testamentary showing that her Last Will and Testament has been probated. Adding right of survivorship language to the CD will avoid the need for probate to access the account.

One warning: if the value of Roger and Suzanne's combined estates has a value greater than $2 million then they need specialized planning to avoid estate taxes[13]. Rights of survivorship offer convenience, but do not allow for certain tax savings. They should consult their Certified Elder Law Attorney for detailed advice.

Table 1: Summary of Bank Account Features

Account Type	Ownership	Access	Disposition at death
Individual	100% by owner	Owner only	To owner's estate
Individual/POD	100% by owner	Owner only	To persons listed on POD designation
Individual/ Convenience	100% by owner	Owner and co-signer	To owner's estate
Joint "or"	Each account holder according to % contributed	Equal access to all account holders regardless of % contributed	% contributed by deceased owner passes to estate; other account holder(s) retain their contributed amount
Joint "or" / WROS	Each account holder according to % contributed	Equal access to all account holders regardless of % contributed	Entire balance paid to surviving account holder(s)
Joint "or" / WROS / POD	Each account holder according to % contributed	Equal access to all account holders regardless of % contributed	Entire balance paid to surviving account holder(s). When all have died, balance paid to persons listed on POD designation
Joint "or" / WROS / Convenience	Each account holder according to % contributed (but convenience signer owns nothing)	Equal access to all account holders and to convenience signer, regardless of % contributed	Entire balance paid to surviving account holder(s). Convenience signer gets nothing.
Totten Trust	100% by Trust	Trustee	To beneficiaries of Trust

Chapter 2:   Managing Health during Disability

PATIENT SELF DETERMINATION ACT

The Patient Self Determination Act (PSDA) is the only federal law dealing directly with advance directives. It applies to any patient receiving care from a facility or care provider covered by Medicare and Medicaid, including Hospitals, Hospices, Nursing Homes, and Home Health Care Agencies.

Whenever a patient is admitted to a hospital or to a nursing home, or when a patient enrolls with an HMO, a Hospice, or a Home Health Care Agency, the following must happen:

- The agency must provide the patient written information concerning the patient's rights under state law to participate in decisions concerning medical care. This includes the right to accept or to refuse medical or surgical treatment and the right to formulate advance directives.

- The agency must provide a written statement of its policy regarding implementation of these rights.

- The agency must document in its records whether the patient has executed an advance directive under state law. Health care providers are not required to provide the documents needed to make advance directives.

Those three requirements are significant, but are not what many advocates were hoping for when Congress was debating the PSDA in 1990. Advocates hoped that Congress would impose nationwide standards for the creation of advance directives, thus ensuring that residents of all 50 states would have a uniform law to follow. The PSDA stopped far short of that broad goal, so all advance directives still vary in their form and content from state-to-state.

The PSDA did, however, impose a few uniform standards. They are:

- Covered agencies cannot discriminate when providing medical care on the basis of whether a patient has or has not executed an advance directive;

- Covered agencies are required to comply with all state laws regarding advance directives. This does not mean much, because they were already obligated to follow those laws; and

- Covered agencies must provide for staff and community education on issues related to advance directives. There has been some response to this requirement, but not enough.

BILL OF RIGHTS FOR THE ELDERLY

A person does not lose his or her civil rights upon entering a nursing home or being admitted to a hospital. The only process that can remove the person's civil rights is Guardianship, after respecting the legal due process rights of the individual.

The Bill of Rights for the Elderly[14] defines "elderly" as a person 60 or older. A care provider may not deny an elderly individual a right guaranteed by the law. Each state agency that licenses, registers, or certifies service providers must require the providers to implement and enforce these rights. Violation of any right by a service provider is grounds for suspension or revocation of a provider's license, registration, or certification.

A service provider is required to provide each elderly individual with a written list of his or her rights before providing services (or as soon after providing services as possible) and must post the list in a conspicuous location. A service provider must inform an elderly individual of changes or revisions in the list.

Many of the Rights granted to the "elderly" overlap with the rights granted to "patients" in general. Hence, it is important to realize that these rights apply to the elderly whether they are ill or healthy, whether they are patients or not.

Civil Rights

An elderly individual has all the rights, benefits, responsibilities, and privileges granted by the constitution and laws of Texas and the United States, except where lawfully restricted. The elderly individual has the right to be free of interference, coercion, discrimination, and reprisal in exercising these civil rights.

An elderly individual has the right to be treated with dignity and respect for the personal integrity of the individual, without regard to race, religion, national origin, sex, age, disability, marital status, or source of payment.

Privacy

An elderly individual is entitled to privacy while attending to personal needs and to a private place for receiving visitors or associating with other individuals unless providing privacy would infringe on the rights of other individuals. This right applies to medical treatments, written communications, telephone conversations, meeting with family, and access to resident councils.

An elderly person may send and receive unopened mail, and the service provider shall ensure that his or her mail is sent and delivered promptly. If an elderly individual is married and the spouse is receiving similar services, the couple may share a room.

An elderly individual may participate in activities of social, religious or community groups unless the participation interferes with the rights of other persons.

Financial Management

An elderly individual may manage his or her personal financial affairs and may authorize in writing another person to manage his or her money.

The elderly individual may choose the manner in which his or her money is managed, including a money management program, a representative payee program, a financial durable power of attorney, a trust, or a similar method. Additionally, he or she may choose the least restrictive of those methods.

The Bill of Rights has been ahead of its time in one sense: it has imposed legal requirements on money managers. Under the Bill of Rights, when the elderly principal (or his/her representative) so requests, the money manager shall make available the related financial records and provide an accounting of the money. A similar fiduciary accounting responsibility was not written into the Durable Power of Attorney Act until late 2001.

An elderly individual's designation of another person to manage his or her money does not affect his or her ability to exercise another right described in the law.

An elderly individual may retain and use personal possessions, including clothing and furnishings, as space permits. The number of personal possessions may be limited the health and safety of other individuals.

Medical Decisions

Under Texas law, an elderly individual has the right:

- To be fully informed, in language that he or she can understand, of his or her total medical condition and to be notified whenever there is a significant change in his or her medical condition;

- To choose and retain a personal physician and to be fully informed in advance about treatment or care that may affect his or her well-being;

- To participate in an individual plan of care that describes his or her medical, nursing, and psychological needs and how the needs will be met;

- To refuse medical treatment after being advised of the possible consequences of refusing treatment and after understanding the consequences of refusing treatment; and

- To be free from physical and mental abuse, including corporal punishment or physical or chemical restraints that are administered for the purpose of discipline or convenience and not required to treat his or her medical symptoms.

Electronic surveillance

Electronic surveillance – that is, video or audio recording – are only allowed with the resident's permission. The law is very clear that a competent resident has the final say. When a guardian has been appointed, the guardian can legally authorize electronic surveillance of the resident's room. If there is no guardian but the patient does not have capacity, then a legal representative can request surveillance. Regulations may be announced later to redefine what type of representative (in addition to the guardian) *can* authorize it[15].

Although the law seems to be written in a way designed to protect the resident's privacy, it has another major impact. If surveillance is approved and installed, and abuse or neglect of the resident is detected, the person who approved its installation can be held criminally liable for failing to report any abuse or neglect of the resident. Failure to watch a videotape is not a defense; it is assumed that the responsible party watched the tape within 14 days of its creation.

This places a huge burden on anyone who thinks that taping the resident's room is a good way to catch a thief, or to catch a nurse mishandling the patient. If that tape runs 24-hours a day, the patient will have to view all those hours of tape to look for instances of abuse or neglect. If abuse happens and the tape was not viewed (so the abuse was not reported) the patient's responsible party can be criminally prosecuted.

Transfer and Discharge

"Transfer and discharge" means moving the resident to another facility. If movement is to an uncertified part of the same facility (that is, a part that does not accept Medicare or Medicaid) it is still a transfer and discharge. Movement to another bed in the same certified facility is not a transfer.

Transfer and discharge is not allowed UNLESS:

- It is necessary for the resident's welfare, and the resident's needs cannot be met at the current facility;

- It is appropriate because of improved health of the resident, who no longer needs the care provided by the facility; or the resident requests a transfer or a discharge;

- The resident's safety is endangered in the facility, or someone else's safety is endangered due to the resident's condition or actions;

- The resident fails to pay for his or her stay. However, adequate notice is required; or

- The facility stops providing the type of services needed by the resident.

30-day prior notice is required prior to discharge or to transfer unless the resident or his or her representative requests the move. Shorter notice is allowed if the health or safety of any individual is at risk or if the resident has not yet been in the facility for 30 days.

A discharge notice can be appealed within 10 days of receiving notice. If the resident is on Medicaid, payment continues until the hearing officer makes a final determination.

A move to another room can only happen if 5-day advance notice is given, if the resident requests the move, or if there is an emergency.

INFORMED CONSENT

The basic legal premise relating to medical care is that an adult person, who is competent, is the only person who may give consent to medical treatment for him or herself.

In 1914, Judge Benjamin Cardozo (who eventually sat on the U.S. Supreme Court) voiced this principle as follows:

> "Every human being of adult years and sound mind has a right to determine what shall be done with his own body."

All adults who are not incapacitated have the right to make their own medical decisions. But to be valid, consent must be "informed"—that is, given only after full disclosure to the decision maker of the risks and benefits of any proposed medical treatment.

Frequent medical malpractice claims have made health care providers wary of acting without proper consent. A patient, operated on without his consent, may charge the caregiver with negligence or even "battery" (unlawful physical contact.)

Exceptions to the Rule

Unless you have made other arrangements, two medical situations do not require your explicit prior consent:

- First, if you are unable to communicate and your life is threatened by injury or illness, Texas law allows your caregiver to presume you give consent to medical care.

- Second, medical care is allowed without consent if your doctor says the benefits of therapy would be reduced if the therapy was explained in detail.

The only ways to overcome these presumptions are: 1) by having a court appointed guardian – see page 23 for more on Guardianship, 2) by having an advance directive, or 3) by using the Texas Consent to Medical Treatment Act.

CONFIDENTIALITY: HIPAA AND STATE LAWS

The Health Insurance Portability and Accountability Act (HIPAA) has actually been on the books since 1996. However, the federal government only got around to issuing regulations in April 2003 as standards for enforcing the law.

HIPAA's goal is to "provide patients with access to their medical records and more control over how their personal health information is used and disclosed." That sounds good, but it has mostly ended up being just another collection of paperwork people wish they could avoid. By now, almost everyone has seen and has signed a HIPAA compliance statement… repeatedly, at each place you go for medical services.

Medical providers are being careful to get signed compliance statements, since the April 2003 regulations say that a medical provider can be fined $100 per violation of the rules, up to $25,000 per year. That's enough to motivate your doctor's office and hospital to comply with the law in the most obvious way: to clam up about your personal health information.

HIPAA forbids your doctor from discussing your private medical information with an unauthorized person. There are some automatic exceptions. For instance, your "personally identifiable health information" can still be disclosed if necessary to collect payment for services (like a statement to Medicare), if necessary to comply with abuse or neglect laws, if necessary for law enforcement purposes or for public health reasons, or if ordered by a court. The law also automatically allows your Agent in a Medical Power of Attorney (or anyone else closely involved in your medical decision-making) to obtain your medical information – but restricts them by denying disclosure at any time that you (the patient) are still capable of making your own decisions.

I advocate specifically authorizing disclosure to the agent of otherwise confidential medical information under HIPAA *even while the patient has full capacity to make decisions*. A standard Medical Power of Attorney, without modification, should be legally adequate to authorize disclosure of confidential medical information to the agent *after the patient is incapacitated*. My conservative advice is that your agent, a person you have chosen and you trust, should have access to medical information as soon as your agent desires that access. That way, your agent will not be relegated to the sidelines. Your agent can get into the game early, so all decisions can then be well informed and made without undue time pressure.

To give that authority to your Agent, you must either 1) modify the standard Medical Power of Attorney with a new provision that grants access to medical information even if the other powers of your Agent have not yet been invoked, or 2) create a separate HIPAA authorization that grants that authority, but is not restricted to one doctor or to one event.

Copies of Medical Records

The Texas Occupations Code[16] specifically authorizes patients to obtain copies of their medical records. You can either ask for a copy for your own use, or ask that a copy be supplied to another doctor, a lawyer, or to another person of your choosing.

State law requires the doctor to release copies of your medical records when you submit a written request. In the written request, you must tell the doctor exactly which records you want. You must give a reason for the release, and must identify the person to whom the information is to be given.

To be certain the doctor gets your written request, you can send it by certified mail or you can hand deliver it to your doctor. The doctor does not have to honor a verbal request, but must honor your written request within 15 days of receipt. The only valid reason the doctor may have for refusing to release your records is if the doctor determines that access to the information would be harmful to your physical, mental, or emotional health.

Can the doctor legally charge you for the copies? Yes. According to the Texas Board of Medical Examiners' rules[17], the doctor can charge a "reasonable cost-based fee," which the Board sets as "no more than $25 for the first twenty pages and 50¢ per page for every copy thereafter." Copies of films (x-rays) or other static diagnostic imaging studies (MRIs) can cost up to $8 per copy. The doctor can legally require that costs be paid prior to release of the information.

The information contained in your medical records must be released at your request, but the actual files belong to your doctor. Providing copies allows you to have the information, while allowing the originating doctor to keep the actual records. Additionally, most doctors want to keep records on their patients to protect themselves if a patient decides to sue the doctor at some future date.

Here are some tips to follow when you need to request copies of medical records from your physician:

- Submit your request in writing along with a check for the fee the doctor's office requests. To get an estimate of the fee, start with a phone call to the doctor's office.

- Remember to provide a complete address and zip code for the location where you wish to have the records sent.

- If you have married or otherwise changed your name, remember to provide the former name as it appeared in your medical records.

- If your name is fairly common ("Robert Rodriguez" appears in the San Antonio phonebook 64 times and "Mary Smith" appears in the Houston phone book 71 times) then give your date of birth or social security number to ensure proper identification.

TEXAS CONSENT TO MEDICAL TREATMENT ACT

The Consent to Medical Treatment Act[18] (CMTA) is a law that makes choices for you. It selects a medical decision maker for you (called your surrogate) if you have not selected one yourself. Using the CMTA does not require any action on your part. It requires that your doctor decide you cannot provide your own medical consent. Once that decision is made, your surrogate does not need to obtain your permission to make your medical decisions. But the CMTA has limits that make using it unattractive:

- The CMTA only works if you are already in a hospital or in a nursing home. If you are in any other care setting (like at your own home) it does not apply and you are left without a surrogate decision maker.

- Even when the Act does apply it restricts your surrogate from making several types of medical decisions. Specifically, the surrogate 1) cannot make a decision to withdraw or to withhold life support systems, 2) cannot make a decision to admit you to an inpatient mental health care facility, and 3) cannot authorize electro-convulsive therapy (which may be prescribed for depression or other mental illness).

The CMTA provides a list of state-selected surrogates who may act on your behalf. They are, in order of priority and availability:

- Your spouse;

- A sole child who has written permission from the other children to act alone on your behalf. If they have not selected a representative, your medical decisions will be made by majority vote among your children;

- Your parents, if still living;

- Someone you "clearly identified" before becoming ill;

- Any other living relative; and

- Finally, any member of the clergy, whether or not you know that person.

In many instances, the surrogate will simply be your spouse. Your spouse is the person you would probably select anyway – unless the two of you are estranged, if your spouse is disabled or if you are in the process of divorcing (in which case you won't like the CMTA's choice very much). That is why it is best to make your own plan using a Medical Power of Attorney to select exactly the right person to be your surrogate, instead of the person the legislature thought you might find acceptable.

If you do not preplan, and if your spouse is unavailable, the CMTA could automatically appoint one or all of your children as surrogate. Again, if you are not estranged from the children and they are all cooperative and capable, this may be a fine arrangement for you. Regrettably, children often cannot agree on everyday matters. Getting them to agree on a parent's medical care might be very difficult. If they quibble then the majority rules. You may not want your important medical decisions made by majority rule. For example:

> You, a widowed senior, are hospitalized with heart trouble. You have been sedated and are confused, and the doctor will not proceed with surgery until he has informed consent. You do not have legal paperwork like a Medical Power of Attorney.

> The doctor's aide asks all of your children to meet, even though your oldest daughter is the one who has always "been there" for you. Legally, the burden is on the doctor to decide who should be the authorized decision maker. There are only two options: a court appointed guardian or representatives under the CMTA.

> Guardianship does not already exist. It would take a few days to start even an emergency temporary guardianship. Thus, the doctor has called together all your children, who can legally nominate one from their ranks to act as decision-maker. If they pick your eldest daughter, she can go off with the doctor and decide on your medical treatment. If they don't, then the doctor must ask for a majority vote of your children regarding your vital medical decisions.

If you don't have children, the legal proxy chosen by the law is a person increasingly remote from your life. Parents are next in line after children, but regrettably, most senior citizens' parents are long deceased. After "parents" comes "someone clearly identified." Unfortunately, no clear standard is given to decide who you may have "clearly identified." Then comes the vague "next of kin" classification, and the last resort is a clergy member (i.e., staff clergy at the hospital.) You may never have been as much as introduced, and you may even be of different religious faiths.

One purpose of this law was to remove the need for Guardianship in most medical scenarios. In many cases this removes the burden from the courts. By providing a definite line-of-command, the doctors and hospitals will always have someone to turn to for a decision, even if it is their own clergy staff.

It is best for you to avoid the uncertainties of the CMTA by selecting your own surrogates with a Medical Power of Attorney. Doing so will avoid all the sticky issues surrounding arguing children and spouses. You get to choose your decision-maker instead of defaulting to whomever the law provides. Read more about Medical Powers of Attorney beginning in the next section with detailed information beginning on page 82.

DIRECTIVE TO PHYSICIANS, FAMILY OR SURROGATE

The Advance Directives Act[19] covers three types of advance directives. They are 1) Directive to Physicians, Family or Surrogate, 2) Out of Hospital Do-Not-Resuscitate orders, and 3) Medical Power of Attorney.

Before the Advance Directives Act became law in 1999, Texas had three separate statutes addressing advance directives. The statutes had been passed in three different decades, and were not well coordinated with each other. Current Texas law on advance directives is uniform and much easier to use.

The Advance Directives Act allows any competent adult to sign a Directive regarding artificial life support. The Act recognizes that your doctor is not the only person who needs to receive your instructions. It therefore calls your written instructions a "Directive to Physicians, Family or Surrogate" (which I'll refer to as a "Directive").

The Act also makes it clear that not every person must have a Directive. By law, your physician, health facility, health care provider, insurer, or health care service plan may not require you to sign a Directive. It must be your personal choice.

Did you sign a Directive to Physicians prior to September 1, 1999? Then you have the "outdated" Directive that operates under the decades-old 1977 law.

You are not legally required to throw away your old Directive. It is still valid after September 1, 1999. On the other hand, your old Directive continues to follow the old law – you will not receive the benefits of the Advance Directives Act unless you sign a new, updated Directive.

Internet Resource:

The Directive to Physicians is available from The Premack Law Office website at WWW.PREMACK.COM. The complex statutory document is available from several sources, but the legal document from our website has been modified, in compliance with state law, so it is clearer and easier to use.

Institutional Policies

The Advance Directive Act includes a requirement that any health care provider must develop and maintain written policies regarding the implementation of advance directives. The policies must include clear and precise statements of any procedures the health care provider is unwilling or unable to provide or to withhold.

The term "health care provider" is broadly defined to include any hospital, licensed nursing facilities, home and community support services agencies, personal care facilities and special care facilities. Note that this does not require your individual physician to develop a policy. Still, most physicians must accept institutional policies of the health care facilities in which they practice.

The Act requires a health care facility to provide you a written notice of its written policies either when you (1) are admitted to receive services from the facility; or (2) begin receiving care from the facility (whichever is sooner). If you are not competent at that time, the facility must give the notice to your representative, in the following order of preference:

- Your court appointed guardian;

- The person responsible for your health care decisions (like your agent under a Medical Power of Attorney);

- Your spouse;

- One of your adult children;

- Your parent; or

- The person admitting you to the facility.

The facility must do a "diligent search" to locate the preferred representative. (The statute does not define "diligent," but typically this means a search that is persistent, attentive and untiring.) If they still cannot locate a representative, the facility is not required to provide the notice. But if you recover your competence, they must then give you the notice.

Conditions Liberalized

The Advance Directives Act liberalized the situations under which the use of artificial life support can be avoided, compared to the law that existed before 1999. The old law required that several things happen all at once: the patient had to have a diagnosed terminal condition that was incurable and death had to be imminent before life support could be withdrawn. The new law creates three separate and distinct times at which life support can be withdrawn. They are:

One: Terminal Condition

Life support can be withheld or withdrawn for a patient with a terminal condition which is expected to cause death within six months. This allows that patient to avoid life support at an earlier date than the old law allowed, and gives him/her more control over the final months of life.

Two: Irreversible Condition

The Advance Directives Act also authorizes a patient to avoid artificial life support if he/she has an "irreversible condition" that is fatal without life support. There is no six month time expectation imposed by the Advance Directives Act when the condition is irreversible; rather, the requirements are that a) the condition be incurable, b) the patient be unable to make decisions or care for him/herself, and c) that life support is all that is keeping the patient alive.

This provision can be used to remove life support from a comatose patient, even if life support could have maintained the vital signs for years. Terry Schiavo is a fitting example; she is discussed in more detail on page 72.

Three: Imminent Death

The Directive also states that if a patient is expected to die within minutes to hours (no longer) even if life support were to be provided, then the patient instructs the family, surrogates and physicians that life support is not to be used.

Context is Important

It is important to put a context around those three triggers for removal of life support. Just having one of those diagnoses is not enough to trigger removal of life support. The law requires that the patient be so ill as to be unable to make a decision (unable to communicate) and that the patient's condition be so poor that life support systems are offered (or recommended) by the physician. So in reality, a patient's condition must be terminal or irreversible or death must be imminent, the patient must be unable to issue verbal instructions, and the patient must be so ill that the doctor offers life support. Then, the Directive comes into play to refuse the life support.

Even if you have signed a Directive, your verbal instructions at any given moment always supersede your written Directive. You can change your mind.

It is also important to note that the Advance Directives Act allows a Directive to impose any conditions and restrictions that may be individually desired. While there is a statutory form provided in the law, there is no requirement that the form be used. However, at a minimum a Directive must be signed by the patient, must indicate his/her city, county and state of residence, and must be witnessed as the law requires.

Definitions

The Advance Directives Act coordinated the legal definition of several important concepts. Earlier law was often contradictory or vague, so this is an improvement. The Act includes the following terms:

✋"Artificial Nutrition and Hydration" means providing nutrients or fluids by a tube inserted in a vein, under the skin, or in the stomach.

✋ "Competent" means possessing the ability, based on reasonable medical judgment, to understand and to appreciate the nature and the consequences of a treatment decision, including the significant benefits and harms of and reasonable alternatives to a proposed treatment decision. "Incompetent" means the exact reverse.

🏷 "Life Sustaining Treatment" means treatment that, based on reasonable medical judgment, sustains the life of a patient and without which the patient will die. The term includes both life sustaining medications and artificial life support, such as mechanical breathing machines, kidney dialysis treatment, and artificial nutrition and hydration. The term does not include the administration of pain management medication nor the performance of a medical procedure considered to be necessary to provide comfort care, nor any other medical care provided to alleviate a patient's pain.

Ways to Make a Directive

Formal Written Directive

The most common approach to issuing a Directive is to do so in writing. The Act provides an approved format that meets the requirements of law. It must be signed and must be properly witnessed, but does not need to be notarized and does not need to be filed with the county clerk to be legally effective.

Frankly, the approved format is confusing, hard to understand, too long and provides opportunities to make contradictory declarations. Since the law does not require use of the approved format, the Directive that I write eliminates those negatives while complying with state law.

Life Support: Yes or No?

The Act gives you the ability to declare that you 1) desire life support to be withheld or to be withdrawn if you become terminal, or 2) desire life support to be applied and sustained if you become terminal. The choice to use a Directive to instruct withdrawal of life support is far more common than the choice to use a Directive to instruct continuation of life support.

Even if a Directive is properly witnessed, it cannot require any thing forbidden by law. For instance, the law requires that a Directive be suspended if the patient is pregnant. The law cannot be overridden by saying differently in the directive. The law requires that the physician certify in writing that the patient's condition is terminal, irreversible or that death is imminent. A lower standard cannot be set by changing the wording to, for instance, "I want life support withdrawn if my condition is serious."

However, a patient always has the legal right to refuse medical care even if death may result. As such, a Medical Power of Attorney can be written to give authority to a trusted agent. It can contain an instruction to the agent to refuse any type of medical care for the patient... even if death may result. Refer to the section below on "Self-Directed or Gatekeeper?" for more on this idea.

Witness Requirements

Texas law is extremely particular when it comes to witnessing a formal written Directive. Two witnesses are mandatory, and one of them must meet a strict list of requirements. That one witness 1) cannot be a person designated to make a treatment decision for the patient, 2) cannot be related to the patient by blood or by marriage, 3) cannot be entitled to any part of the estate, 4) cannot be the attending physician or an employee of the attending physician, 5) cannot be an employee of a health care facility in which the patient is being cared for if the employee is involved in providing direct patient care to the Declarant or is an officer, director, partner, or business office employee of a health care facility or of any parent organization of the health care facility, and 6) cannot be a person who has a claim against the estate.

The second witness must simply be a competent adult. Thus, the second witness *can* be a relative, an heir, a doctor or health care provider, etc... Prior to adoption of the Advance Directives Act in late 1999, the law required that both witnesses meet the six strict requirements of independence. As a result, it is now easier to arrange for two witnesses.

Self-Directed or Gatekeeper?

If a patient makes a written Directive, it can name a proxy to decide whether life support should or should not be withheld. The state's recommended form creates confusion in this area. It states, "*If I do not have a Medical Power of Attorney, and I am unable to make my wishes known, I designate the following person(s) to make treatment decisions with my physician compatible with my personal values: _____*". The confusion comes from an ambiguity and an impulse: 1) just how does the Medical Power of Attorney have anything to do with this? And 2) if there is a blank line, most people have an impulse to write something onto it.

The real impact is this: if you leave the blank line empty, you have not named a gatekeeper, and your Directive operates as direct communication from you to your physician that refuses life support if you become terminally ill. The "direct" method (not naming a proxy) keeps the decision entirely on your own shoulders, as you decided ahead of time in the Directive. If you feel a strong commitment to remaining off life support, consider using the direct method.

But if you fill-in the blank, you are not issuing any instruction at all about life support. Rather, you are delegating the decision to a proxy – a gatekeeper who will evaluate the situation for you and tell the physician whether to pull the plug or to leave you one life support. The "gatekeeper" method places the decision onto the shoulders of someone you select, who probably loves you very much. Naming a gatekeeper may cause him/her distress, as the burden of pulling the plug is onerous indeed.

If you desire to have a gatekeeper, the better approach is to forego entirely making a Directive. Instead, rely solely on a Medical Power of Attorney that names an Agent (and backups). Give that Agent authority to decide whether you will receive life support.

Verbal Directive

A competent patient can made a Directive either in writing or verbally. To be valid when verbal, it must be spoken in the presence of the attending physician and two witnesses (just like a written Directive) and must be recorded as part of the Declarant's medical records. The Advance Directives Act no longer requires the two witnesses to sign the medical records, but their names must be placed into the records.

Oral directives are not recommended. The process is unreliable, and should be used only in the direst of circumstances.

Never Made a Directive?

The Nancy Cruzan Case

On January 11, 1983, Nancy Beth Cruzan lost control of her car and was discovered, clinically dead, by paramedics. Though she lacked heartbeat or respiration, the paramedics restored these functions.

The physicians, after thorough examination, determined that Cruzan had been deprived of oxygen for 12-14 minutes, resulting in permanent and irreversible brain damage. She remained unconscious, and when difficulty arose in feeding her, her husband consented to surgical placement of a feeding tube.

It soon became clear that Nancy was not going to recover. Her parents became her court-appointed guardians under Missouri law and asked the hospital to terminate the artificial nutrition. The hospital refused to do so without court authorization.

The guardians went to the local circuit court, which found evidence that Nancy had verbally expressed her wish not be kept alive in a persistent vegetative state. She did not, however, have any written directive that followed her state's law. Even so, the trial court approved withdrawal of artificial nutrition, basing its decision on her right to individual liberty.

The Supreme Court of Missouri reversed the lower court. It decided that verbal testimony was not reliable when seeking to determine Nancy's wishes. The court declared that Missouri law required more convincing evidence. More boldly, it also declared that the state had an absolute interest in preserving life that overrode any individual liberty interest.

The U.S. Supreme Court's Decision

The case went to the U.S. Supreme Court[20]. Nancy's family argued that an individual has the right to refuse all medical treatment, including artificial nutrition and hydration. They argued that the state had no interest in forcing medical treatment, and that Nancy's right to privacy should allow removal of medical care.

Both the State of Missouri and the federal government argued that the government has an absolute interest in protecting life, and that when there is no clear and convincing evidence of the patient's wishes then the state has the right to force medical treatment.

The U.S. Supreme Court handed down a 5-4 decision against Nancy's family on June 25, 1990. Chief Justice Rehnquist wrote for the majority. He kept his legal analysis as narrow as possible under the circumstances. He relied on the distinction between competence and incompetence foreshadowed by Judge Cardozo in 1914.

Justice Rehnquist quickly acknowledged that a competent person has the right to refuse medical treatment because the 14th amendment declares that a person's right to "life, liberty, or property" may not be denied without due process of law.

Then he addressed the flip side: how are we to make such a decision for an incompetent person? Because of the patient's inability to decide, a surrogate decision maker is required. The court majority decided that it is constitutional to impose "procedural safeguards to assure that the action of the surrogate conforms as best it may to the wishes expressed by the patient while competent."

The court decided that Missouri's requirement that there be convincing evidence is an allowable safeguard.

Therefore, according to the U.S. Supreme Court, Nancy Cruzan had to stay on life support. (Eventually the family satisfied state law, went back to court, and Cruzan was removed from life support.)

"Living Will" Forms are Invalid

Texas has a statute relating to withdrawal of life support systems (the Advance Directives Act). That law applies constitutionally permitted procedural safeguards. Under the Cruzan decision, we are assured that a Texas Directive to Physicians is a legally valid and enforceable method for refusing artificial life support. The decision also underscored the fact that the only way to refuse such life support is by adhering to the standards established by state law. As a consequence, old style "living wills" are not usable in Texas because they do not follow the requirements of the Advance Directives Act.

How do you tell the difference between a Living Will and a Directive to Physicians? A "Living Will" says "if there is no reasonable chance of my recovery, do not use heroic measures to keep me alive." It lacks the detailed witnessing required by Texas law. Avoid "living will" forms and be sure you have a legal Directive instead.

Schiavo and Surrogate Action to Remove Life Support

Under the Advance Directives Act, if a patient has not made a directive and is incompetent or otherwise mentally or physically incapable of communication, then the attending physician along with the court appointed guardian or agent under a Medical Power of Attorney may make a treatment decision to withhold or to withdraw life-sustaining procedures.***

This is a huge expansion of the powers given to an agent compared to the prior law. From 1977 at 1999, only a court appointed guardian could authorize removal of life support systems. Even if you had appointed an agent in an old "Health Care Power of Attorney," the agent could not approve removal of life support. The Advance Directives Act, by consolidating these statutes, allowed them to interact much more reliably. As such, anyone who fails to sign a Directive, but who does sign a Medical Power of Attorney, has full benefit under the Advance Directives Act.

If there is no legal guardian and no agent under a Medical Power of Attorney then the doctor and one person from the following list may decide to withhold treatment. The list, in order of priority, is: 1) the patient's spouse, 2) the patient's reasonably available adult children, 3) the patient's parents, and 4) the patient's nearest living relative.

A treatment decision made under this provision must be documented in the patient's medical record and signed by the attending physician. Further, if the patient does not have a legal guardian or agent, and a person above is not available then another physician who is not involved in the treatment of the patient or who represents the facility's ethics committee must concur with the treatment decision. This means that two doctors can withhold life support if no family or guardian is available.

The 1999 Act is a meaningful improvement over the 1977 in the area of dispute resolution. The Advance Directives Act requires any relative who desires to challenge a decision to withhold life support to file for temporary guardianship in the local probate court. This takes advantage of a long-standing and well-understood legal process instead of inventing something new.

The Terri Schiavo Matter

Mrs. Schiavo suffered a medical crisis in 1990 at age 26 in Florida[21]. She had not signed a written directive regarding life support. Her husband was appointed Guardian. At his request, a gastrointestinal feeding tube was implanted and she was given rehab and treatment for eight years. The doctors later testified that "her cerebral cortex … sustained the most severe of irreparable injuries" and that she was in a persistent vegetative state.

Her Guardian felt strongly that she had, while healthy, expressed a choice to avoid life support. He felt that after eight years in a comatose condition she was beyond recovery, and decided to request a court order to withdraw the feeding tube. Her parents felt strongly that she could still interact and should be kept on life support. In 1998 the matter was brought to court, and in 2000 a trial determined that Mrs. Schiavo would have refused to be on artificial life support. The Florida 2nd District Court of Appeals affirmed and the Florida Supreme Court denied review of the matter. Her parents raised new issues which were upheld by the appeals court, and after more legal wrangling, a new trial was held in 2002. Again, the trial court found that life support should be removed; the appeals court upheld the decision and the Florida Supreme Court denied review.

Her parents then took the matter to federal court, claiming that the Florida advance directives law was unconstitutional. In October 2003 the federal court ruled that Florida's advance directives law was constitutional. Within days the Florida legislature changed the law as it applied to this case only. Known as "Terri's Law," it permitted Governor Bush to issue an order restoring her feeding tube. Her Guardian took the state to court, and in September 2004 the Florida Supreme Court ruled that the legislature's action violated "the fundamental constitutional tenet of separation of powers" between the executive, legislative and judicial branches. In January 2005 the United States Supreme Court declined to hear an appeal, so "Terri's law" could no longer be used.

Several more hearings were then held on various claims raised by her parents, and each claim was found to be groundless. In March 2005, her parents went to federal court a second time but the Judge ruled that he had no jurisdiction over the matter. Within days, the US Congress and President Bush enacted "Terri's Law II" specifically authorizing Mrs. Schiavo's parents to sue in federal court to "determine de novo any claim of a violation of any right of Theresa Marie Schiavo." Congress dismissed all the prior efforts in the Florida and Federal courts to protect her rights, as though the Judges who had heard the matter had complete disregard for her. In fact, the Florida courts had specifically addressed her right "to make her own decision, independent of her parents and independent of her husband."

The federal district court heard the matter quickly and determined that the prior court actions were appropriate. The 11th Circuit affirmed without addressing the issue of whether the law which granted jurisdiction was constitutional, and the US Supreme Court denied review of the decision. The feeding tube was removed for the last time, and she died March 31, 2005.

What if the Schiavo matter had happened in Texas instead of in Florida?

Under section 166.02 of our Health & Safety Code, Mrs. Schiavo's condition would have been classified as "incurable." She did not make her own *written* directive about life support, so section 166.039 allows her court appointed Guardian and attending physician to withhold life support, including artificial nutrition and hydration if that is their understanding of what she would have chosen. If her parents wanted to challenge the decision, their Texas remedy would be seeking removal of the Guardian with appointment of a parent as replacement.

It is appropriate to view the Schiavo matter as a cautionary tale and a call to action. The law supports a person's right to make his/her own medical choices, whether that means withholding life support or means having life support continue indefinitely. Mrs. Schiavo had the right but did not sign a Directive to make her choice obvious and enforceable. Your task is to make your own choice and to document it legally so that you and your family can move forward.

Revocation

You can revoke your Directive at any time. Your mental state or competence is not an issue. Revocation can be accomplished by canceling, defacing, obliterating, burning, tearing, or otherwise destroying the written declaration (which may legally be done by the Declarant or by a person in the Declarant's presence under the Declarant's directions). It is a Class A misdemeanor to conceal or to damage the Directive of another person without the Declarant's consent.

It is also legally allowed to state in writing signed by the Declarant or in an oral statement from the Declarant that the Directive is revoked.

An oral or written revocation is legally effective only if the physician is notified personally or by mail. The Physician must record the time and day when the written or oral revocation was received and must write the word "void" on each page of the Directive in the medical records.

Liability

When the Advance Directives Act is followed, the physician or health care facility that causes the withholding or withdrawal of all life-sustaining procedures is not subject to civil liability unless he/she/it is negligent.

Health professionals, including nurses, who act under the directions of a physician are not subject to civil liability unless they are negligent.

The physician or other health care professional is not guilty of any criminal act or unprofessional conduct by following the law, unless he or she acted negligently.

Noncompliance

If a physician, health care facility, or health care professional has no knowledge of a Directive, there is no civil or criminal liability for failing to act in accordance with the Directive. As such, you want to provide a copy to your physician. Also, you want to have a copy handy in case you go into the hospital (where the federal Patient Self Determination Act requires the hospital to ask if a Directive exists).

You also want the family members who are likely to be nearby during time of crisis to have a copy, so they can be sure the doctor knows about your wishes.

Review and Discipline

Your physician must comply with your Directive unless "the physician believes that the Directive does not reflect the present desire of the patient". If a physician, or a health professional acting under the direction of a physician, is aware of a Directive yet refuses to comply with its terms, that professional is subject to review and disciplinary action by the appropriate licensing board unless the review process below is used.

If the professional refuses to use the review process, he/she may temporarily provide life-sustaining treatment until a reasonable opportunity has been afforded for transfer of the patient to another physician or health care facility willing to comply with the Directive. The professional may also be subject to suit for malpractice.

The physician's refusal to disconnect life support will be reviewed by an ethics or medical committee. (The physician may not be a member of that committee.) The patient continues to receive life-sustaining treatment during the review. Hospice programs are excluded from this process.

In 2003 the legislature amended the Advance Directives Act to require a physician to provide a written explanation of the law when the physician refuses to comply with the patient's Directive. The explanation must contain this statement:

Statutory Notice:

When There Is a Disagreement about Medical Treatment: The Physician Recommends Life-Sustaining Treatment That You Wish To Stop
You have been given this information because you have requested the withdrawal or withholding of life-sustaining treatment and the attending physician refuses to comply with that request. The information is being provided to help you understand state law, your rights, and the resources available to you in such circumstances. It outlines the process for resolving disagreements about treatment among patients, families, and physicians. It is based upon Section 166.046 of the Texas Advance Directives Act, codified in Chapter 166 of the Texas Health and Safety Code.

When an attending physician refuses to comply with an advance directive or other request for withdrawal or withholding of life-sustaining treatment for any reason, the case will be reviewed by an ethics or medical committee. Life-sustaining treatment will be provided through the review.

You will receive notification of this review at least 48 hours before a meeting of the committee related to your case. You are entitled to attend the meeting. With your agreement, the meeting may be held sooner than 48 hours, if possible.

You are entitled to receive a written explanation of the decision reached during the review process.

If you or the attending physician do not agree with the decision reached during the review process, and the attending physician still refuses to comply with your request to withhold or withdraw life-sustaining treatment, then the following procedure will occur:

1. The physician, with the help of the health care facility, will assist you in trying to find a physician and facility willing to withdraw or withhold the life-sustaining treatment.

2. You are being given a list of health care providers and referral groups that have volunteered their readiness to consider accepting transfer, or to assist in locating a provider willing to accept transfer, maintained by the Texas Health Care Information Council. You may wish to contact providers or referral groups on the list or others of your choice to get help in arranging a transfer.

The patient (if competent) or patient's agent must be informed of the committee review process not less than 48 hours before the meeting called to discuss the patient's Directive (unless the time period is waived by mutual agreement). There may be strong motivation to waive this 48-hour delay, in hopes of "getting on with it."

If any party—the attending physician, the patient, or patient's agent disagrees with the decision reached, the physician must make a reasonable effort to transfer the patient to a physician who is willing to comply with the directive.

If the patient is requesting life-sustaining treatment that the attending physician and the review process have decided is inappropriate treatment, the patient shall be given available life sustaining treatment for no more than 10 days pending transfer. The patient is responsible for any costs of transfer. The 10 days can be extended by order of the appropriate district or county court – but only if the court finds that there is strong evidence a suitable facility can be found during the time extension.

The legal process to obtain an extension is very murky. As of this writing, only one case in Texas has created a vague precedent. In Nikolouzos v. St. Luke's Episcopal Hospital[22], the doctor and the ethics committee determined that further life support for Mr. Nikolouzos was futile and not medically advisable. His wife was not ready to allow life support to be withdrawn, and to obtain extra time had her attorneys seek a temporary restraining order from the court. Following the statute's requirements, the court denied her request because she could not establish that there was a suitable facility that would accept her husband's care. The appeals court ruled that it had no jurisdiction. One appeals justice wrote a concurring opinion in which she acknowledged shortcomings in the current law and called for changes to the statute to clarify the process.

Allowing a person to die naturally under this Act is not the same as allowing a suicide. The law does not allow any affirmative or deliberate act to end a life. Its focus is on permitting the natural process of dying.

ASSISTED SUICIDE

Assisted suicide is controversial from both the legal perspective and the moral perspective. The legal issues have been long settled in Texas – assisted suicide is a crime – but other states have been experimenting with their assisted suicide laws over the last decade.

Michigan's struggle with assisted suicide was in the headlines in the 1990s. It had no law regarding assisted suicide, and Dr. Jack Kevorkian used that silence to assist in a number of suicides. After his efforts began, Michigan outlawed assisted suicide. He was acquitted four times when charged with violating that law, but was eventually convicted of murder when he admitted to actually administering a fatal dosage of drugs. He is serving a term of up to 25 years in jail.

The citizens of Oregon have taken a unique approach. In 1994 Oregon became the first (and still the only) state to legalize assisted suicide. The Oregon Death with Dignity Act exempts from civil or criminal liability state-licensed physicians who, in compliance with the Act's specific safeguards, dispense or prescribe a lethal dose of drugs upon the request of a terminally ill patient.

The law was immediately challenged in court. In 1997, the US Supreme Court declined to review the case, which allowed the law to go into effect. In two other 1997 cases, the Supreme Court decided that although there was no constitutional right to assisted suicide the states were free to determine their own policies on the issue. Oregon's citizens voted in late 1997 to keep the assisted suicide statute.

Several efforts in Congress (led, in part, by then Senator John Ashcroft) to overrule Oregon were defeated. However, shortly after becoming US Attorney General, Ashcroft announced that he had reinterpreted the US Controlled Substances Act (CSA) declaring that using controlled substances to assist suicide is not a legitimate medical practice and that dispensing or prescribing them for this purpose is unlawful under the CSA. That policy raised concerns on two fronts: 1) in Oregon, assisted suicide would cease, and 2) in all the states, doctors would fear criminal prosecution for aggressively treating their patients' pain.

The State of Oregon, an Oregon physician, an Oregon pharmacist and some terminally ill Oregon residents sued Ashcroft to reverse his prescription policy. In 2002, the trial Judge ruled against Ashcroft but he appealed. In 2004, the federal appeals court also ruled against Ashcroft, holding that his policy "violates the plain language of the CSA, contravenes Congress' express legislative intent, and oversteps the bounds of the Attorney General's statutory authority." Though Attorney General Ashcroft was replaced by Attorney General Gonzales, the case was pursued to the Supreme Court.

In October 2005 the Supreme Court issued a ruling against the federal policy, holding that the CSA does not allow the Attorney General to prohibit doctors from prescribing regulated drugs for use in physician-assisted suicide when a state law authorizes the practice[23].

On this issue, Texas law is well settled: it is a crime to intentionally aid or attempt to aid another person to commit or attempt to commit suicide in Texas. Depending on the circumstances, punishment ranges from misdemeanor fines to felony jail time.

The Texas Advance Directives Act "does not condone, authorize, or approve mercy killing or permit an affirmative or deliberate act or omission to end life except to permit the natural process of dying..." But our law does allow withholding or withdrawing life support under a Directive to Physicians, honoring a do-not-resuscitate order, and declining to receive medical treatments even though that choice may result in death.

The difference is passive withdrawal of support versus active intervention to hasten death. It is legal in Texas to get medical interventions out of the way so that nature takes its course. It is illegal in Texas to use medical interventions to bring death sooner than it would have naturally occurred.

DO NOT RESUSCITATE ORDERS

The idea of a DNR is "don't bring me back." The idea of a Directive to Physicians is "don't keep me here." If a DNR order is in the patient's medical file and an emergency event occurs (like cardiac arrest) the medical responder will not resuscitate.

Do Not Resuscitate (DNR) orders come in two distinct varieties: 1) inpatient, and 2) out-of-hospital. Inpatient DNRs are used in hospitals while out-of-hospital DNRs are used in nursing homes, assisted living facilities, hospices, in emergency rooms and at your private residence.

An inpatient DNR is more limited in scope than a Directive to Physicians. An inpatient DNR is typically good for 24-48 hours (but sometimes as long as a week) as a physician's order. Inpatient DNR orders are not statutory in nature – they are based solely on a treatment decision authorized by the patient and certified by the physician.

Texas Out-of-Hospital DNR Law

The out-of-hospital DNR (OOH-DNR) exists only because Texas statute created it. The Advance Directives Act allows a patient to sign a form binding the medical providers to DNR status. If the patient cannot sign the form, his or her representative (the agent under the Medical Power of Attorney, a guardian or a qualified family member) can sign.

Current law allows any competent adult to create an out-of-hospital DNR. Before 1999, Texas law only allowed a person who was already diagnosed with a terminal illness to sign an OOH-DNR.

The OOH-DNR form was written by the Texas Department of Health. You must use the official form, and cannot make up your own wording. Anything but the official form is legally invalid.

Internet Resource:
You can obtain the OOH-DNR form free directly from the Texas Department of State Health Services at
WWW.TDH.STATE.TX.US/HCQS/EMS/DNRHOME.HTM
or free from my website at WWW.PREMACK.COM (click on "legal Documents").

The attending physician must sign an OOH-DNR. It authorizes the caregiver "not to initiate or continue" the following treatments:

- Cardiopulmonary resuscitation;

- Endotracheal intubation or other means of advanced airway management;

- Artificial ventilation;

- Defibrillation;

- Transcutaneous cardiac pacing;

- The administration of cardiac resuscitation medications; and

- Other life-sustaining procedures specified by the Texas Board of Health.

The statute does not include authorization to withhold medical interventions or therapies considered necessary to provide comfort or care or to alleviate pain or to provide water or nutrition. However, the patient's representative can (under a valid Medical Power of Attorney) give instructions to withhold artificial nutrition and hydration.

If you have signed a Directive to Physicians, the law presumes that you want an OOH-DNR if you are incompetent and cannot express your own preference at that time. The doctor signs for the patient in this case.

If the patient is awake, aware and competent, then a non-written OOH-DNR can be issued. The statement must be made in the presence of the doctor and two qualified witnesses. The doctor and the witnesses must sign the OOH-DNR form for the patient.

If Emergency Medical Service (EMS) is called to the scene, they can withhold resuscitation when an OOH-DNR or an approved ID device is presented. However, EMS must:

- Verify the identity of the patient. As such, the caregiver should have some type of photo ID for the patient ready to show; and

- Verify that the paperwork is correct. It must be signed, dated, and all the blanks must be completed. If the paperwork is not correct, the EMS technician can ignore the DNR at that time.

Non-Adult

For a minor, an OOH-DNR can be authorized by the parents, the legal guardian or the managing conservator (a court appointed individual when the parents are divorced).

Revocation

The verbal wishes of the patient, if competent, always supersede the written OOH-DNR. This applies even when the patient is a minor.

Also, if the patient is unable to communicate, then the attending physician, legal guardian, qualified relative, or agent of the person having a Medical Power of Attorney can authorize resuscitation.

ID Device

The law states that an Identification Device (a bracelet or necklace) is adequate to allow withholding resuscitation, even if the OOH-DNR paperwork is not present. The Texas Department of Health has arranged for three suppliers, listed on their website at WWW.TDH.STATE.TX.US/HCQS/EMS/DNRHOME.HTM.

Liability Shield

A caregiver who complies with an OOH-DNR cannot be held civilly liable for that action. No lawsuit should result. Further, there is no criminal liability, no "unprofessional conduct" and no violation of any licensing requirements.

Further, a caregiver who refuses to comply with an OOH-DNR (or who does not know about its existence) is not liable under the civil or criminal laws. However, the patient's representative must be informed, and the caregiver must allow a different caregiver to take over and comply with the OOH-DNR. For Example

When Bill was younger, he watched his father linger after a serious stroke. Bill decided that if he had a medical crisis like a stroke, he would not want life-prolonging treatment. Like any competent adult, Bill has the legal right to accept or to reject medical treatment—even if death will result. The legal key is how that decision is communicated. It must be legally enforceable to have any meaning.

Bill visits his lawyer and signs a Directive to Physicians and a Medical Power of Attorney. He also obtains the OOH-DNR order from the Internet, and takes it to his doctor.

The doctor makes copies of Bill's advance directives. The doctor knows that someday, if Bill becomes ill, liability won't be an issue. He will be able to discuss Bill's diagnosis and his preferred course of treatment with someone Bill appointed. If Bill's situation is critical, the doctor will already know Bill's wishes – do not put me on life support, do not resuscitate me.

Without Bill's advance directives, the doctor may have presumed that Bill wanted whatever medical treatments would prolong his life (without regard to his quality of life).

The doctor makes one other request: Bill should talk to his family so that they are aware of his wishes and understand his feelings. This will make it easier on them when the time comes, and will reduce any friction they may have with the doctor.

MEDICAL POWER OF ATTORNEY

In a Medical Power of Attorney, you as "principal" appoint an "agent" to make your health care decisions if you lose capacity to understand your medical situation. Under Texas Law, the agent may be anyone except:

- Your "Health Care Provider" or his employee UNLESS that provider happens to be the your relative, or

- Your "Residential Care Provider" or his employee UNLESS that provider happens to be your relative.

You must make the document in writing, before two witnesses. Because the Advance Directives Act rewrote prior laws to coordinate their requirements the witnessing standards for a Medical Power of Attorney are identical to those for a Directive to Physicians. Under prior law, the requirements were almost alike, but had minor variations.

The written Medical Power of Attorney must be delivered to the agent before it can be used. However, there is no requirement that the original be presented to the doctor. In fact, a photocopy is often accepted for all purposes.

Disclosure and Document

A lengthy disclosure statement must be read and signed by you before you sign the Medical Power of Attorney. The Act gives an exact quote of the disclosure statement, and also provides a form for the Medical Power of Attorney.

Interestingly, neither the disclosure statement nor the form follows the law's requirement that the disclosure statement be signed. This is problematic, because the law says the form's wording must be used without substantial changes. If changing the form to include a second signature is a "substantial change," then the Medical Power of Attorney will be invalid. If not changing the form omits the required second signature, then the Medical Power of Attorney will be invalid, too. The only hope is to interpret adding the second signature as an "insubstantial change."

Refer back to the section on page 59 entitled "Confidentiality: HIPAA and State Laws." The state's Medical Power of Attorney form has not been modified to accommodate the demands of HIPAA, so using the unaltered state form can pose problems. You need a Medical Power of Attorney that has been modified in its "limitations" section to grant authority to your agent to access your confidential medical records.

By the way, Texas law says that if you are physically unable to sign a Medical Power of Attorney (though you are still mentally competent) then someone may sign for you at your direction and in your presence.

Decisions

Your agent can make any medical decision you could make, but ONLY IF your doctor certifies in writing that you are no longer capable of understanding the risks and benefits of a proposed treatment.

When making a decision, the agent must do what he thinks you would have wanted, including consideration of your religious leanings. If unknown, the agent can decide based on your best interest.

Even though you may be incapacitated when the agent takes over, the doctor must legally make a reasonable effort to inform you of any health care decision, and you can veto the decision. Your agent cannot place you into an inpatient mental health facility, cannot authorize convulsive or psycho-surgical treatment, cannot authorize abortion, and cannot withhold comfort care.

The term "comfort care" was, under former law, undefined. However, the Act makes it clear that "comfort care" is pain management medication or the performance of a medical procedure considered necessary to provide comfort care, or any other medical care provided to alleviate a patient's pain.

Further, pain management is not, by definition, a "life sustaining treatment." As such, the requirement that the agent grant comfort care is not equivalent to a requirement that the agent provide artificial life support. And since artificial life support includes artificial feeding and hydration, comfort care does not include artificial feeding and hydration.

Conflicts

If a guardian is appointed for you, the guardian takes over from your agent unless the Judge says otherwise. You can, however, tell the Judge what you want (by writing it into the Medical Power of Attorney or with a Declaration of Guardian) and your wishes will be given great weight.

In a conflict between your Directive to Physicians and your Medical Power of Attorney, the one signed later in time has priority. There can only be a conflict if both documents name agents who are not the same person. If, however, both name the same agent then no conflict will exist. (And if your Directive to Physicians does not appoint an agent at all, then it takes priority over the Medical Power of Attorney regarding withdrawal or withholding of artificial life support).

On the other hand, if you have signed only a Medical Power of Attorney and do not have a Directive to Physicians the Act allows your agent to withhold or withdraw life support systems (and to put you into a hospice program). This power did not exist under the prior law.

Your health care provider must follow the instructions given by your agent, unless the provider feels the instructions are contrary to your wishes, to the law or to the Medical Power of Attorney's limiting statement. The provider is not liable (under either criminal or civil law) for the result of a decision by your agent nor is your agent liable if all decisions where undertaken in good faith.

Agent Liability

Your agent is not responsible for paying the bill for the medical care chosen unless the agent makes the mistake of taking on liability. Remember, when acting as an agent you must let others know you are doing so, and *you must never sign your own name*. Instead, when you sign something for the principal you literally sign that person's name, and then print below that signature the phrase "by XX, agent". Look at these two examples:

I agree to pay whatever charges are incurred for medical care of Fred Smith in this institution. *Fred Smith* Fred Smith by John Jones, Agent	I agree to pay whatever charges are incurred for medical care of Fred Smith in this institution. *John Jones*
Example 1	Example 2

In Example 1, Fred Smith is bound to pay the medical bill but John Jones is not. In Example 2, John Jones is agreeing to pay the medical bill. John may know that he is the agent, and may think that he is just being responsible, but his signature on that agreement means the care provider will expect John to pay Fred's bills, even if Fred runs out of money or insurance benefits.

> Internet Resource:
> The Medical Power of Attorney document is available from The Premack Law Office website at WWW.PREMACK.COM (Click on "Legal Documents").

ANATOMICAL GIFTS

Anatomical gifts allow you to donate useful organs upon your death. You can legally make the donation in any one of three ways:

- Through your Last Will and Testament;

- Through a written instrument like a donor card or other written declaration of anatomical gift that is signed and has two witnesses; or

- Through a statement on your driver's license (if it was declared before September 1, 1997 or after September 1, 2005).

While all three of these methods are legal, the method you select must be sensitive to the speed requirements of donation. Any lengthy delay makes an organ donation impossible. Hence, you should avoid using your Last Will and Testament because it could be days before anyone sees your statement. In the interest of speed, it is much better to carry a document on your person.

State policy on using a driver's license as a donor card has been inconsistent. Before September 1, 1997 the law allowed that practice. After that date, the legislature decided the statement on the back of the Texas driver's license was inadequate to authorize organ donation. The legislature changed its collective mind, and as of September 1, 2005 it is again legal to use the back of your driver's license as an organ donor card.

If you do use your driver's license and change your mind, you must apply to the department of public safety for an amendment to the license. As such, you might opt to use a separate card (like the LifeCare card below) that can be revoked more easily.

> Internet Resources:
> LifeGift has an organ donation card online in English or Spanish. Obtain one at WWW.LIFEGIFT.ORG/DIRECTED_DONATION.HTML
> The Texas Medical Association has an organ donation brochure online at WWW.TEXMED.ORG/TEMPLATE.ASPX?ID=453

Here is what the donor card from LifeGift looks like:

I, _____, have spoken to my family about organ and
tissue donation. The following people have witnessed my commitment to
be a donor. I wish to donate the following:

○ Any needed organs and tissue.

○ Only the following organs and tissue: _____

Donor Signature _____ Date _____

Witness _____

Witness _____

Next of Kin _____

Telephone _____

LifeGift Organ Donation Center (800) 633-6562

Texas Donor Registry

Texas is implementing a Donor Education, Awareness and Registry program
("DEAR") so individuals may publicly indicate their wishes regarding organ and
tissue donation. Starting in late 2006, Texans became able to register when renew-
ing their driver's license or their personal identification card or anytime online. The
state will request a $1 voluntary contribution to fund the program when you go to
renew your driver's license or your identification card, or when you register a vehicle. More information and a registration form are available at
WWW.TEXASDEAR.ORG.

The law that authorizes the registry also says that if you change your mind about
being a donor and want to have your name deleted from the statewide Internet-
based registry of organ, tissue, and eye donors, you must provide written notice di-
recting that your name should be deleted from the registry.

The Commissioner of State Health Services is required to select an organization to
maintain the registry, and as of this writing has not done so.

Willed Body Programs

Anatomical gifts are different from "donating your body" to science. Donation of
your whole body requires that you follow a different process. Your attorney can
write a document declaring your wishes, but it is simpler to follow the rules estab-

lished by the medical school in your area. There are nine medical schools in Texas that you can contact.

Internet Resources:
A national list of medical schools with body donation programs can be viewed at WWW.LIVINGBANK.ORG/SITE/PAGESERVER?PAGENAME=WHOLE_BODY_DONATION
Here are some Texas specific websites:
The UT Health Science Center San Antonio WWW.UTHSCSA.EDU/CSB/WILLEDBODY
Baylor College of Medicine WWW.BCM.EDU/WILLEDBODY/
UT North Texas
WWW.HSC.UNT.EDU/DEPARTMENTS/PATHOLOGY_ANATOMY/WILLEDBODY/LINKS.HTM

The medical schools will send you a "Body Bequeathal Agreement" to fill out, sign, and return. The Agreement is another type of anatomical gift declaration, and is authorized by the Texas Anatomical Gift Act.

After you return the form to the medical school, they will enter you in their records. They send a copy of the form back to you. Keep it with your other important papers, and make a photocopy to put in your car. Be sure to give a copy to the person most likely to handle your affairs when you die.

The Willed Body programs also provide bodies to the Texas State Board of Morticians so that funerary students can learn their art.

The medical school usually covers the cost of transporting the body to their facility. After their scientific study is complete (usually in six months to two years) the body will be cremated. The ashes can be returned to the family if the family so desires.

Chapter 3:   Paying for Long-Term Care

One of the greatest financial risks faced by Senior Texans is the prospect of long-term care, whether in their own home with professional help, in assisted living or in a skilled nursing facility.

The cost of care in skilled nursing facilities is steadily increasing. The Center for Medicare & Medicaid Services reports that between 1985 and 1998 the total national outlay for nursing home care grew from $30.7 billion to $88 billion, and that by 2004 the nationwide outlay for nursing home care grew to $115.2 billion[24]. That is an increase of 375% in 21 years, averaging nearly 18% annual inflation.

Paying for this care takes careful planning. To plan properly, you must understand your options and their limitations. Private and government funding of long-term care imposes some limits and exposes some opportunities. A well thought out plan can save heartache and can save money.

There are three ways to pay for long-term care. First: privately—out of your own pocket or out of your family's pocket; second: through insurance, and third: through public benefit programs.

OUT OF POCKET EXPENDITURES

Paying out-of-pocket is mostly self-explanatory, but here are a few ideas for you to consider:

- Your life savings is precious, and most people desire to leave some legacy to their children. At the same time, "saving for a rainy day" would also have been a strong motive for creating those savings. If your spouse or you need essential health care, then the rainy day has arrived and there is no shame in spending your funds. Just be aware that a safety net exists in the form of public benefits, and you should never allow yourself to become completely impoverished before you seek help.

- Your family may volunteer to assist you. Just as you likely helped them after they turned 18 even though your legal obligation of support had ended, they may have a strong desire to help you in your time of need. Even so, there is no "filial responsibility" law in Texas that requires your children to contribute to your support. Further, federal regulations forbid nursing facilities from requiring a guarantee from a family member as a condition of admittance[25].

Savings might take many forms. Consider the pros- and cons- of borrowing against the equity in your home as a way to pay for needed long-term care (but read the section on Protection of your Home starting on page 137). Also consider tapping into the reserves that may exist in your life insurance program.

Drawing on Life Insurance Reserves

You may have the option to borrow against the cash value of your policy, to take a life settlement or to draw accelerated benefits. The first option is nothing more than a traditional loan. You owe the insurance company repayment of the loan with interest, and if you do not repay before you die then the amount due is offset against the policy death benefit. The other two options are called "viatical settlements".

Viatical is from the Latin viaticus, *relating to a journey.* Thus, viatical settlement is a euphemism for "money that helps you on your journey" – that is, that assists you prior to death. There are two types:

1. "Accelerated benefits" involve early payment of benefits, directly from the life insurance company, usually for people with terminal conditions and life expectancies of six months or less. Accelerated payment of insurance benefits is *not* available from all life insurance companies.

Some insurers add accelerated benefits to life insurance policies for an additional premium, usually computed as a percentage of the base premium. Others offer the benefit at no extra premium, but charge the policyholder for the option if and when it is used. In most cases, the insurance company will reduce the benefits advanced to the policyholder before death to compensate for the interest it will lose on its early payout. There also may be a service charge.

2. "Viatical settlements" involve selling your policy to a separate company. The purchase is made for an amount less than the policy's face value, but more than the

cash surrender value of the policy. The purchaser then makes all future premium payments (often there are none) and receives the death benefit. Each viatical settlement company sets its own rules for determining which life insurance policies it will buy. For example, some companies will require that:

- The seller has owned the policy for at least two years;

- The current beneficiary signs a release or a waiver;

- The seller is terminally ill. Some companies require a life expectancy of two years or less, while others may buy the policy even if seller's life expectancy is four years; and

- The seller must sign a release allowing the company to access to his/her medical records.

In 1997, Congress changed the tax code so that proceeds from accelerated benefits and viatical settlements are tax-exempt[26]. Under the law, proceeds from accelerated benefits and viatical settlements are tax-exempt as long as client's life expectancy is less than two years and that the viatical settlement company is licensed.

Internet Resource:
In Texas, visit the Department of Insurance website for a list of who is licensed to handle viatical & life settlements at
WWW.TDI.STATE.TX.US/COMPANY/VIATLISTR_INCL.HTML

Texas regulates these licensed companies. Before purchasing a policy, the company must provide a lengthy disclosure to the seller[27] which explains:

- That a viatical or life settlement may affect an individual's ability to receive supplemental social security income, public assistance and public medical services, including Medicaid;

- That the proceeds of a viatical or life settlement may not be exempt from creditors, personal representatives, trustees in bankruptcy, and receivers in state or federal court;

- That all confidential information solicited or obtained by the purchaser will not be disclosed in any form to any person without detailed prior written consent from the seller;

- That the seller has the right to rescind a viatical or life settlement contract any time during the first 15 days after receiving the funds. If the seller dies during those 15 days, the contract is deemed rescinded and the death benefits are restored;

- That the seller may wish to contact an attorney, accountant, estate planner, financial planning advisor, their insurer, insurance agent, tax advisor, or social services agency regarding potential consequences resulting from entering into a viatical agreement; and

- That the seller may file a complaint by contacting the Texas Department of Insurance, Consumer Protection Division Help Line at 1-800-252-3439, by faxing a complaint to the department at 1-512-475-1771 or by completing a complaint on-line at WWW.TDI.STATE.TX.US.

Deducting Out-of-Pocket Nursing Home Costs

Federal law allows you to deduct "qualified long term care" expenses as an itemized deduction on Schedule A of your Form 1040. However, the deduction will only save money when it exceeds 7.5% of your adjusted gross income.

Qualified long-term care expenses include diagnostic, preventive, therapeutic and rehabilitative services when they are medically necessary. They also include personal care or maintenance services needed by a chronically ill person when prescribed by a doctor. This second definition includes nursing home care.

To be considered "chronically ill" a person must need significant assistance to perform at least two activities of daily living, like eating, toileting, bathing, dressing, and moving from place-to-place. Alternatively, a person also qualifies if he/she needs constant supervision due to cognitive impairment in order to safeguard that person's health and safety. The illness must continue for at least 90 days to be considered chronic.

If you meet all these conditions, then you can take an itemized deduction for the cost of nursing home care.

Keeping Liability under Control

It is likely that if you are ill enough to move into a nursing home, you may not have legal capacity to make your own decisions. If so, someone who cares for you may handle the paperwork necessary to move you into the nursing facility. That paperwork usually involves a contractual agreement on liability for payment of the facility's monthly bill.

The person handling your paperwork should be your legally authorized Agent under your Durable Power of Attorney. That Agent must be careful to sign documents in the proper fashion to avoid personal liability. See page 84 for a discussion on how to properly sign when acting as an Agent.

If the paperwork is signed incorrectly, your caretaker may become personally liable for your monthly bill. A case decided in Eastland tells a story that illustrates the possible complexities. In Huse v. Texas[28], a mother became very ill and found herself in a nursing home. Her son (Mr. Huse) promised to take care of things for her. She had little income and few assets, so he filed an application to get Medicaid's help with her monthly nursing home bill.

It took many months before mother was approved for Medicaid, and then only because the nursing home administrator provided information the son failed to provide. Even after mom was approved for benefits, Medicaid only paid the part of her bill her social security would not cover.

The nursing home asked Mr. Huse to pay the rest of the bill, and he agreed to take care of it. That was the moment things went wrong. He bounced a check, made more promises, and never actually paid the nursing home. The administrator eventually pressed charges against him for "theft of services." He was arrested, tried and convicted to two years in the state jail. He appealed his conviction on several technical issues, but the court decided he had induced the nursing home to provide continued services by tendering his check.

The lessons of the Huse case are to keep responsibility where it belongs, and to keep responsibility with someone who is capable. Huse's mistake was to promise he would pay the bill when he did not owe the bill and did not receive the services. His promise was a contract, and his deception was found to be a criminal act.

Had Mr. Huse relied on his mother's power of attorney naming him as agent, he should have told the nursing home his mother would pay the bill *through him, acting as her agent*. The contract for services would have stayed with her, not him. Failure to pay the bill may have resulted in her eviction or in an accusation he was exploiting his mother or breaching his fiduciary duties by keeping her monthly income, but jail time was far less likely.

LONG-TERM CARE INSURANCE

Neither your Medicare benefits nor your Medigap policy provide significant long-term coverage. Long Term Care insurance (LTC) may help avoid financial collapse caused by the high cost of long-term care. LTC insurance has improved over the last decade, from being over-priced and under-paying to being affordable and beneficial.

An LTC policy is yet another type of insurance. You must acquire it separately from your other insurance, and it will cost extra. Like any medical insurance, you have to buy the policy while you are still healthy and are able to pay premiums to the insurance company.

You need to be careful of what policy terms you buy and with what insurance company you deal.

Issues When Shopping for a Policy

- Is your budget so tight that the cost of insurance would impact your ability to pay for daily expenses now?

- Do you have enough monthly income to pay for your care without buying insurance? Nursing home costs can range anywhere from $2,500 to $5,000 or more per month. If you have enough income to pay that bill, why buy insurance?

  Remember to factor in the living expenses of your spouse. If he or she will be at home while you are in the nursing home, you'll need enough money to pay for both locations. Let's say you have income of $3,000 per month and that your spouse will need $1,500 per month to stay at home. If the nursing home will cost $3,500 per month, you'll need an extra $2,000 every month to make ends meet.

  This extra money could come out of your savings and/or investments. Or you could buy an LTC policy for $2,000 (plus inflation). The sales agent may try to sell you $3,500 coverage to pay for the nursing home, but why buy extra? Again, look at your budget and buy only what you need and can afford.

- Does the policy adjust for inflation, or will the policy pay for less-and-less as inflation makes care more expensive? Buying an inflation rider costs extra, but may make the policy more realistic.

- How does the policy define long-term care? Does the policy cover all levels: skilled, intermediate, custodial and home care? If it covers only skilled care, you might never be ill enough to draw on the benefits. On the other hand, adding home care may cost extra. The Texas Insurance Commission requires that any LTC policy issued in Texas must provide benefits for more than one level of care[29]. Generally, newer LTC policies offer coverage for both nursing home and in-home care. Texas regulations require the policy to pay for lower level care (like in-home care) without first requiring you to be in a nursing home.

- How long is the elimination period? Most policies contain a waiting period before they will pay. If the first month of care has to come out of your pocket, then the insurance company saves money. If you can afford to pay for the first three months out-of-pocket then the insurance company saves even more money. If you can cover a longer up-front expense, your policy premiums will be less expensive.

- Does the policy pay for pre-existing conditions? Most policies will not pay the bills for any illness you had before you bought the policy; some have a waiting period of up to two years before they begin to pay. The shortest wait is the best. Remember to be completely honest about pre-existing conditions when you apply for your policy. If the insurance company finds out that you lied on the application, they can deny the coverage you thought you had secured.

- Older policies often required you to be in the hospital for a certain number of days before admission to the nursing home. Texas regulations now forbid this practice. Legally, your LTC policy cannot require that you be in the hospital before admission to a nursing home. Any LTC policy issued in Texas after September 1, 1992 must pay benefits without regard to pre-hospitalization if you suffer:

  - A functional impairment in performing the activities of daily living (ADLs) like eating, transferring, bathing, walking, toileting and dressing, or

  - An impairment of cognitive ability (loss of intellectual capacity requiring continual supervision as supported by clinical diagnosis). Insurance regulations require that LTC policies pay for nursing home care due to Alzheimer's disease.

If your policy was issued before September 1, 1992, then those more liberal terms may not be in your policy. You could consider updating your policy (which may require that you cancel the existing coverage and buy a whole new policy). The problems with that are that your health may not allow you to qualify for a new policy, and a new policy will probably be significantly more expensive since you are older now.

Look for a policy where the legal contract provisions include:

- Guaranteed renewability (they cannot cancel so long as you pay the premiums);

- Waiver of payment of the premium after you enter a nursing home; and

- A flat premium that does not increase as you get older.

Internet Resource:

The Texas Department of Insurance has LTC Information online at and now has a rate guide to help you can comparison shop for LTC Insurance. It is located at HTTPS://WWWAPPS.TDI.STATE.TX.US/INTER/ASPROOT/CONSUMER/LTCRGSEARCH/LTCRGINTRO.HTML

Federal employees and retirees are eligible for a benefit called the Federal Long Term Care Insurance Program. You can read more about it at WWW.OPM.GOV/INSURE/LTC/

Premium Deduction

The "Health Insurance Portability and Accountability Act" (HIPAA) passed by Congress in 1996 included a major tax change. The premiums you pay for any LTC policy are partially deductible on your income tax return. There are two limits:

Table 2: Premium Deduction

	2006 deduction	2005 deduction
Age 40 or less	$280	$270
Ages 41 to 50	$530	$510
Ages 51 to 60	$1,060	$1,020
Ages 61 to 70	$2,830	$2,720
Ages 71 and older	$3,530	$3,400

- First, these premiums are deductible just like health insurance premiums. You need to itemize, and then they are deductible only after medical expenses reach 7.5% of your adjusted gross income.

- Second, the amount deductible depends on your age. The younger you are, the less you are allowed to deduct.

Federal law currently allows deductions only for Long Term Care policies issued after 1996 or for those that were approved by the State Board of Insurance before 1996.

PUBLIC ASSISTANCE: MEDICARE PROGRAMS

Medicare has existed as a government program since 1965. It has only a modest nursing home benefit. In 2004, Medicare spent $16 billion on skilled nursing care, about 14% of the national outlay.

Medicare is managed on a national level by the Center for Medicare Services ("CMS," formerly known as "HCFA," the Health Care Finance Administration). The Whitehouse split its management services into two groups:

- The Center for Medicare Management will focus on management of the traditional fee-for-service Medicare program. This includes deciding how much medical providers will be paid, and managing fee-for-service contractors.

- The Center for Beneficiary Choices will focus on providing beneficiaries with information on Medicare, Medicare Advantage, Medigap options and Drug coverage.

Medicare now offers several different programs.

 Part A helps pay for hospitalization, short-term nursing home care, home health care and end-of-life hospice care. You do not pay a premium for Part A.

 Part B is optional and costs extra. It helps pay the cost of physician care, some outpatient and lab services and pays for some medical equipment costs. Parts A & B are "traditional" Medicare coverage.

Medicare Advantage (formerly known as Medicare+ Choice or as Part C) applies if you opt out of traditional coverage. A variety of private care providers accept regular payments of Medicare in exchange for covering your health care needs. These Health Maintenance Organizations (HMOs) and Preferred Provider Organizations (PPOs) may offer a wider range of services and lower co-payments than traditional Medicare, but you must use the plan's physicians and must deal with the plan's efforts to save money by skimping on patient care.

Part D is Medicare's prescription drug coverage, authorized by the Prescription Drug, Improvement, and Modernization Act of 2003 (MPDIMA). It is discussed more fully beginning on page 101.

> Internet Resource:
> The Center for Medicare Services has a comprehensive website with excellent information about Medicare benefits and services. You can obtain Medicare's current handbook, called "Medicare and You" from the CMS website at WWW.MEDICARE.GOV or phone 1-800-633-4227 to ask for a free copy.

Part A Skilled Nursing Facility (SNF) Coverage

Medicare will pay for 20 days of skilled care or rehabilitation, in a nursing home or in a skilled nursing facility located at a hospital – but only when you are being discharged from an acute care hospital. This benefit is granted on a limited basis.

Qualifying for Medicare's SNF coverage requires that you first spend three days in the hospital (not including the day of discharge.) It also requires that you be sent to the SNF on doctor's orders within 30 days of the day you leave the hospital. This Part A benefit will cover the SNF's fees in full for the first 20 days so long as the patient is making progress in rehabilitation.

After the first 20 days, there is coverage for another 80 days. The patient must contribute $124 per day (2007) to his/her care during those 80 days, but that amount will change each year, so check the CMS website for new figures. Rehab in Texas can cost about $300 per day, so Medicare covers a sizeable part of the bill. This co-payment only continues until you have been in the nursing home for 100 days, after which you must pay the entire bill (or find another program to assist, like Medicaid).

The days of coverage can be repeated if enough time lapses between illnesses. You must be on your own – not in the hospital or a SNF—for at least 60 consecutive days. If you do remain in a nursing home during those 60 days, then you cannot receive any skilled care during those 60 days. If that time has passed, and if you then have another 3-day hospital stay, your SNF coverage starts over.

Part A Home Health Care

Medicare covers the cost of part-time nursing care at home, or of physical, speech or occupational therapy at home when prescribed by a physician only when:

- The patient is considered a skilled care patient or needs therapy or rehabilitative services. Medicare will not pay for custodial assistance, drugs, full-time nursing care, home delivered meals or housekeeping services. The physician determines whether the patient is in need of skilled care, subject to review by the Medicare intermediary; and

- The patient must be homebound, or must be in an institution which is not a hospital or skilled nursing facility. Current rules define homebound to mean that it is a considerable and taxing effort to leave home. You need not be a prisoner in your home, but it must be a real effort to leave; and

- Finally, the patient's doctor must prescribe and monitor the services, which must be provided by a qualified home health services agency.

You are entitled to part time home health care up to 8 hours per day but under most circumstances no more than 28 hours per week. Care is provided in 60-day "episode of care" periods. If you use up one period, your doctor may authorize another.

Part A Hospice Care

When the patient is diagnosed as terminal with 6 months (or less) to live, Medicare Part A will pay for the full cost of hospice care received in the home.

They cover two initial periods of 90 days (if the doctor certifies that the patient still needs the care). After that, the doctor must recertify the patient every 60 days – but there is no limit to the number of times the doctor can recertify the patient. Even if the patient lives beyond 6 months, if the doctor certifies that it is probable that the terminal illness will cause death within the next 6 months, hospice can continue under Medicare.

When a patient opts for Hospice Care, he/she is waiving standard Medicare benefits for that period for any problem connected to the terminal illness. The patient can cancel hospice and return to standard Medicare benefits, but will lose any "unused" hospice days for that period.

Hospice pays for:

- Doctor services

- Nursing care

- Medical equipment (such as wheelchairs or walkers)

- Medical supplies (such as bandages and catheters)

- Drugs for symptom control and pain relief

- Short-term care in the hospital, including respite care

- Home health aide and homemaker services

- Physical and occupational therapy

- Speech therapy and Social worker services

- Dietary counseling

- Counseling to help you and your family with grief and loss

Despite those benefits, the patient will still have to pay $5 of the cost of each prescription for pain relief and symptom management and 5% of the cost of respite care. Under hospice, a family member is typically "on-duty" at all times. When that person needs a break, i.e., "respite," the patient can be temporarily cared for in a Medicaid approved hospital or nursing home. The stay cannot exceed 5 days.

Part B Premiums

Medicare Part B is voluntary and enrollees pay a monthly premium. The premium has grown from $58.70 monthly in 2003 to $93.50 in 2007, and will continue to be raised annually.

Deferring Enrollment

Though Medicare Part B is optional, Medicare assumes you want the coverage and will automatically enroll anyone who qualifies for Part A. If you want to decline or to defer enrollment in Part B, you must inform them.

If someone opted-out of Part B, that person has the legal right to change that decision. However, when that person decides to opt back into Part B coverage, enrollment is only open one time per year, between January 1 and March 31. When that person enrolls, Medicare will impose an increase on its Part B premium by 10 percent for each year enrollment was delayed.

One reason someone might opt-out of Part B would be that person, age 65 or older, has not yet retired and the employer provides health care insurance. If that was the reason for opting-out of Part B, then there is no penalty for late enrollment so long as enrollment is completed within eight months of retirement. If the retiree fails to enroll during that eight-month window, federal law requires the retiree to wait for the next general enrollment period (January 1st of the following year) and imposes the ten percent penalty.

Higher Income Enrollees = Higher Premiums

Under the "Medicare Prescription Drug, Improvement, and Modernization Act of 2003" (MPDIMA) the Part B premium will be increased starting in 2007 for higher-income individuals. Specifically, those with annual incomes between $80,000 - $100,000 have an "applicable percentage" of 35%, those with income between $100,000 - $150,000 have an "applicable percentage" of 50%, those whose income is $150,000 - $200,000 have an "applicable percentage" of 65%, and those with income above $200,000 have an "applicable percentage" of 80%. The people who have paid the most in taxes through the years are the ones who will pay more for this program.

The phrase "applicable percentage" sounds like it means "rate hike", but it does not actually translate directly to the premium increase. The law provides a formula to calculate actual out-of-pocket costs. First, you take the "applicable percentage" and reduce it by 25 points. Second, multiply that by twice the regular premium rate. Finally, the law phases in the premium increase over a five-year period. In 2007, a person pays only 20% of the full increase but it ramps up to 100% by 2011.

To complicate matters, the "income" figure is not taken directly from your tax return; rather, it is adjusted by deducting any income you earn while residing in a variety of American Territories (like Puerto Rico) and by deducting income eared on education savings bonds. Then income is increased by adding in any tax-free interest earned or accrued (which should include IRA, 401k and tax-free bonds).

Here's an illustration: A single individual has adjusted income of $110,000. The standard Part B premium will reaching $93.50/month in 2007. This person would pay $102.85/month that year (110% of the standard Part B monthly premium). When the full increase hits in 2011, that person would pay approximately $140.25/month (150% of the standard monthly premium, but we won't know the actual 2011 standard monthly premium until late 2010).

In fact, the complex Part B premium calculations called for in the law could have been expressed very simply. The law could have said that those with income from $80,000-$100,000 will pay 120% of the standard Part B premium, those with $100,000-$150,000 will pay 150%, those with $150,000 - $200,000 will pay 180% and those with $200,000+ will pay 210% of the standard Part B premium.

If the increases can be expressed simply, why didn't Congress do it that way? Perhaps making it too accessible would have been a political negative ("Hey, seniors! Congress increased your costs by 210%"). Though not technically "tax increases" – they are more like the "users fees" the state uses to avoid increasing taxes – the premium increases do represent new costs to be paid by many seniors. The Congressional Budget office estimates that the Part B increase will raise $13.3 billion by 2013.

Internet Resource:
Take a look at the Premium Calculator at
WWW.PREMACK.COM/MPDIMA/PARTBPREMIUM.HTM to see the rest of the figures.

Part D Prescription Drug Coverage

The majority of Medicare-covered seniors will have struggled through the Part D sign-up already, due to the government's May 15, 2006 deadline to enroll penalty-free. Those who missed the opportunity may enroll each year between November 15 and December 31, but will pay a penalty of 1% of the premium for each month they were late. Congress has considered removing the penalty, but as of this writing it has not been removed.

Part D is optional, but the government has pushed enrollment very hard. Here are Medicare's comments[30] on when enrollment is allowed:

- If you have both Medicare and full Medicaid coverage, you can join a plan at any time.

- If you're new to Medicare, you can join during the period that starts three months before the month you get Medicare, and ends three months after you get Medicare.

- If you are eligible to join or are already a member of a Medicare Advantage Plan, you were able to make one change to your coverage through June 30, 2006. You could join or switch Medicare Advantage plans, or leave your plan and get Original Medicare. However, you can't add or drop drug coverage.

- In all other cases, if you want to change plans you are generally limited to making changes between November 15 and December 31 each year.

- In special circumstances, Medicare may give you an opportunity to switch to another Medicare drug plan. A switch is allowed if you permanently move out of your drug plan's service area, or if you qualify after May 15, 2006 for extra help paying for prescription drugs, or if the plan stops offering prescription drug coverage, or if you enter, live in, or leave a nursing home.

Formulary

When you select a Part D plan, the first step is to see whether the plan actually covers the prescriptions that you have or expect to have. Each drug plan gets to decide exactly what medicines they will cover or will exclude. The Medicare website, at WWW.MEDICARE.GOV, is a very effective way to compare formularies.

Benefits

How much money might enrolling in Part D save a typical senior? The answer is mixed. According to a 2006 New York Times/CBS News poll[31], 42% of enrollees are saving money, 30% are breaking even, and 19% are actually paying more now that they've signed up for Part D. How can someone pay more after they have signed up for the "benefit"? It is structured to provide the most assistance to those with the highest drug expenses. People with more modest monthly prescription costs are left in the so-called "donut hole" of coverage.

First, enrollees may pay a monthly premium to join a plan. Premiums range from $0 to $50 or more. The premium is paid whether you buy prescriptions or not. As a new cost, the premium can determine whether Part D saves you money or costs you extra, so finding a suitable plan with the lowest possible premium is key for all participants.

After the premium, enrollees pay the first $250 of prescription costs out of pocket. Then they pay 25% of the cost of any additional prescriptions until the costs total $2,250. Next coverage shuts off and *participants pay 100% until drug costs reach $5,100* (the donut hole). Finally most participants pay 5% for any additional prescription costs.

> Internet Resource:
> Access the calculator at
> WWW.PREMACK.COM/MPDIMA/MEDICARE DRUG BENEFIT CALCULATOR.HTM to see how you might fare under Part D.

A person with annual drug expenses of $600 will now spend $420 a year in premiums (assuming a $35/month premium). Then, he/she will spend $250 out-of-pocket for the deductible. Then he/she will pay $87.50 (25% of the remaining $350 in prescription costs). Total cost: $757.50 for $600 in prescriptions (26% higher with Part D than without it).

A person with annual drug expenses of $900 spends $832.50 out-of-pocket (a savings of 7%). At the other extreme, a person with annual drug expenses of $12,000 spends $4,365 (a savings of 64%).

The raw calculations do not tell the whole story. If you need a drug that is not covered by your plan's formulary, you have to buy it on your own. Your expenses for non-covered drugs do not count toward your deductible or your co-payments, which increases your overall share of the burden.

Further, you will have to keep close track of your drug expenses. The provider of your Medicare drug plan can ask you if you have, or expect to have, any reimbursement from a third party (like another insurance plan). Failure to give a true answer will be grounds under the new law for termination of your Part D coverage.

Extra Assistance

People whose income is below the federal poverty line and who are qualified for SSI (Supplemental Security Income) were shifted onto Part D, away from Medicaid, as of January 1, 2006. SSI and others whose drugs were formerly covered by Medicaid pay no premium, pay no deductible and do not face the donut hole. However, they do pay $2 out-of-pocket for each generic prescription and $5 for all other prescriptions until drug expenses reach $3,600 after which Part D pays all additional drug expenses.

People with slightly more income may also receive extra help with drug costs. Annual income must be below $14,355 for a single person or $19,245 for a married couple and countable resources must be below $11,500 for a single person or $23,000 for a married couple. These people then pay a monthly premium expected to average $18 plus the first $50 worth of prescriptions yearly plus 15% of the cost of prescriptions until expenses reach $3,600. After that, they pay $2 out-of-pocket for each generic prescription and $5 for all other prescriptions.

PUBLIC ASSISTANCE: MEDICAID

Medicaid is not available to everyone. As a government welfare program, much of its funding is spent on providing medical care to dependent children, disabled persons, and the poor.

Qualifying for Medicaid is like shooting at a moving target. The fundamental laws and policies that govern Medicaid are created through the political process in Washington. Congress loves to change the rules every few years, and the changes have a large impact on the entire system. The more routine rules that implement and manage the minutia of Texas Medicaid come from Austin. Texas must constantly adjust to changes handed down by Washington, and Texas frequently adjusts or rewrites its own Medicaid policies. The very agency that manages Medicaid in Texas was reorganized recently, with changes to high level personnel and to local staff. The governor decided to lay-off more that half of the state's trained Medicaid field staff in an effort to save money by centralizing the application process into call centers. His effort, implemented by the Health and Human Services Commission, has created chaos, delays, public hearings, disgruntled state employees and confused citizenry.

As a consequence, predicting Medicaid is hard and planning your way into qualifying for its benefits is complex. You should always seek advice from a Certified Elder Law Attorney before taking an action to qualify for Medicaid to be sure that you are dealing with the most current law and regulations. The following discussion of Medicaid should be read keeping in mind that once these pages were printed they could no longer be changed... but Medicaid's rules probably have changed.

One of Medicaid's basic standards, the financial limits set by Medicaid, change by design at least every year.

> As they are released annually, updated Medicaid figures will be posted at
> WWW.PREMACK.COM/TXMEDICAID.HTM

To qualify for Medicaid funds for nursing home care, the patient must clear five hurdles - Age, Residency, Level of Care, Monthly Income Amount, and Asset Amount.

1 - Aged, Blind or Disabled

The nursing home resident must be 65 or older, or must be blind or disabled. This is perhaps the most simple of the five hurdles that must each be jumped prior to qualifying for Medicaid assistance.

2 - Residency and Citizenship

An applicant for Texas Medicaid benefits must be a Texas resident. He/she must have established residence in Texas and must express intent to remain in Texas. The law and regulations do not give a technical definition of "residence," so relying on common experience, it means that the person must live in Texas and not live in another state.

If a Texas resident temporarily visits another state, with intent to return to Texas, then Texas residency is considered to have never ended. The absence from Texas must have a specific purpose, and when that purpose is fulfilled, the person must move back to Texas.

The patient must also be a legal resident of the United States: a citizen, a permanent resident alien or a person permanently living in the U.S. "under color of law."

The "color of law" exception is broad. If a person can prove that he/she has resided in the U.S. continually since January 1, 1972 until now, then he/she is a resident under "color of law." Further, any alien living in the U.S. indefinitely with the knowledge and permission of the Immigration and Naturalization Service is a resident under "color of law." Finally, any person who entered the U.S. before January 1, 1972 and who may be eligible for permanent residence at the discretion of the Attorney General is a resident under "color of law".

Proof of Citizenship

Legal aliens have their own burden to prove their status, which is understandable. And as of July 1, 2006 the burden to prove status is also being imposed on full US Citizens. Congress, in the Deficit Reduction Act of 2005 (DRA 2005) imposed a requirement that all Medicaid applicants prove their citizenship and identity before they can be approved for benefits.

Proof of citizenship and identity has been classified into four categories by the Center for Medicaid Services. They are:

- A US Passport, Naturalization certificate or Certificate of Citizenship;

- A US birth certificate or other birth certificate that establishes citizenship (including an adoption decree), a US Citizen ID card, an American Indian ID card or evidence of civil service employment before 1976;

- An extract that is at least 5 years old of a US hospital birth, or a life or health insurance record that is at least 5 years old showing a US place of birth;

- A US Census record showing citizenship or a US birthplace, admission papers to a nursing home that are at least 5 years old showing a US birthplace, various other birth notations that are at least 5 years old, or an affidavit of citizenship (but an affidavit is allowed only in rare circumstances).

Even current Medicaid beneficiaries will be required to prove US Citizenship and their identity upon their recertification review. Those who can produce the documentation will be recertified. Those who cannot produce documents but who continuously "show a good faith effort" to produce it will be allowed to retain their benefits. Regulations defining "continuously" have not been issued, but it seems that an ill nursing home resident would not be able to meet the literal meaning of the word by searching for the documentation without any type of pause or break, and thus would easily fail to meet Medicaid's new proof requirement. Until federal regulations require otherwise, the Texas Health and Human Services Commission plans to accept Affidavits of Citizenship in a liberal fashion to help people maintain their eligibility[32].

3 - Level of Care

Medicaid will not pay for custodial care. Hence, by default the patient must be classified at either the "intermediate" or "skilled" care level. The determination is made near the time of application for benefits by the Director of Nurses, an "assessor" who is a Nurse, or by the Physician. Overcoming this hurdle is usually not difficult.

4 - Monthly Income Amount

Medicaid imposes a limit on monthly income for individuals and a different monthly income limit when both husband and wife will both be in a nursing facility under Medicaid at the same time.

The income limit is raised annually. When social security benefits go up the income limit also goes up. The income limit is based on the Federal Benefit Rate (FBR), which is the limit that Social Security uses to decide if someone is eligible for SSI (Supplemental Security Income). The FBR is multiplied times three to get the Texas Medicaid income limit.

Table 3: Financial Limits on Medicaid		
	2006 Amounts	**2007** Amounts
Income Cap (single)	$1,809.00	$1,869.00
Income Cap (couple)	$3,618.00	$3,738.00
Protected Resource Amount (minimum)	$19,908.00	$20.328.00
Protected Resource Amount (maximum)	$99,540.00	$101,640.00
Protected Income allowance	$2,488.50	$2,541,00
Gift Penalty	$117.08/day	$117.08/day
The divisor to calculate the disqualification period resulting from transfers of assets was changed effective November 1, 2005 to a daily rate of $117.08 instead of a monthly rate of $2,908.00.		
For annual updates on these figures, visit WWW.PREMACK.COM/LINKS.HTM		

Money received is your income only if your name is on the check. The social security check made out to you is your income. The check made out to your spouse is not your income.

For years, the income cap was very harsh. If your income was even one dollar over the limit, Medicaid would not pay a penny for your care. Then the idea of a "Qualified Income Trust" was invented.

The Qualified Income Trust (Miller Trust)

First, be aware that a Qualified Income Trust will not shelter assets. It is not a way to "hide money" nor is it a way to save resources. Rather, it is a way to get around the income cap otherwise imposed by Medicaid.

This arrangement grew out of a federal court case brought by a family in Colorado with the last name of Miller[33]. A nursing home resident (Miller) had too much income to qualify for Medicaid. His family went to court to create a Guardianship, and obtained a court order imposing a limit on the amount of retirement funds the resident could use each month. The Court created a trust, placed all of the retirement funds in that trust, and ordered the trustee to limit withdrawals to an amount that was less than the Medicaid income cap.

Colorado contested the trust, but eventually a Federal Court decided the trust idea was legal. Mr. Miller was allowed to receive Medicaid benefits even though his income would be too high without the trust.

As a result of this case, Congress passed an amendment to the Social Security Act (it contains the Medicaid laws) to formalize the idea that the Miller case started. Medicaid officially refers to this arrangement as a Qualified Income Trust (QIT) but you may hear it called a "Miller Trust" or even a "96p trust" (because it is based on section 1396p of the federal law[34]).

The federal law says that a QIT may contain only pension funds, social security funds, and other income due to the nursing home resident. It cannot own any other asset, even a car or a savings bond. Here is an example of how a QIT works:

> Charles has regular monthly income of $1910 (a social security check of $1000 and his retirement pension check of $910) and the income cap is $1,869. His wife Margaret has income of $750 from social security. They have some resources that are below the necessary limits.
>
> Charles needs nursing home care. At this point, Medicaid looks only at the checks written to Charles totaling $1910, which exceeds the income cap of $1,869. He cannot

qualify unless he uses a QIT. The trust is written by Charles' attorney and given to Medicaid along with the application for benefits. A bank account is established for the trust, and Margaret is listed as trustee.

Each month, Margaret deposits Charles' $910 pension check to the trust's bank account. Medicaid is allowed to ignore that amount when calculating Charles' income – and since he is left with $1,000, which is below the cap of $1,869 – he qualifies for Medicaid assistance.

What happens to the money in the trust? It must be spent each month according to Medicaid's rules. Depending on the amounts involved, some of it might be paid to Margaret. Federal law sets out four priorities for spending the money in a Qualified Income Trust. They are:

- Paying the "personal needs allowance" for the resident. This has bounced between $30 and $60 per month. It was settled in at $45 for several years, but was increased again to $60 as of January 1, 2006;

- Paying the spousal allowance;

- Paying for the resident's nursing home and other medical care; and

- Paying other expenses, like bank fees, taxes or legal costs. In real life, all the money in a Qualified Income Trust is consumed for the first three priorities.

Obtaining a Qualified Income Trust

The Medicaid caseworker is an employee of the state, and is not licensed or authorized to prepare any legal documents. To obtain a Qualified Income Trust, you will need an attorney who has experience in drafting trusts relating to public benefits.

Internet Resource:
If you don't already have a qualified attorney, you can order a Qualified Income Trust online at WWW.PREMACK.COM (click on "Legal Documents"). You submit information over the Internet, pay by credit card, and receive a legally recognized, attorney-written Texas QIT by Email. You then print it, have it signed, and submit it to Medicaid. You can also order by telephone or regular mail.

5 – Asset Amount

Medicaid categorizes your assets as either "countable" or "exempt." If countable assets exceed $2,000 value for a single person or $3,000 for a married couple (both of who are applying for benefits) Medicaid will not pay for nursing home care.

Deeming of Spousal Resources

Under the federal Medicaid statutes and regulations, all assets owned by either spouse are generally considered "available" to pay for medical care of either spouse. The policy set by Congress assumes that married people will take care of each other before asking the taxpayers to do so. Thus, all assets are categorized as either "countable" or "exempt" whether they are community property or separate property.

Premarital Agreements

What if you are in your second marriage and, thinking ahead about long-term care, you signed a premarital agreement with your spouse? You both agreed that the assets you owned prior to marriage remain separate property and that you'll bear no liability to pay for each other's health care. Can you rely on the premarital agreement to shelter your assets from paying for your spouse's medical needs?

No, you cannot. Here is why: A premarital agreement operates under Texas law. As such, it makes it clear that *your spouse* cannot demand that you pay his/her medical bills. Your spouse has no right to receive support from your separate property. On the other hand, Medicaid is a federal program (it is just administered by the state). As such, its rules ignore various state laws.

Federal Medicaid law and regulations require that all of the countable resources that belong to either husband or wife be reported to Medicaid, regardless of the existence of a premarital agreement. If those combined resources leave more than $2,000 countable for the nursing home spouse, then no assistance will be provided.

Your money is still your separate property. You are not required by law to pay for your spouse's nursing home bill. But under these circumstances, Medicaid is also not required by law to pay. Federal law says that a spouse must use his or her resources before taxpayer dollars are used. So you are put to the test: do you refuse to pay with your own money - meaning that your spouse does not get needed care - or do you pay with your own money? The choice is not a pretty one.

If your goal is to shelter your assets, the better pre-plan is to investigate long-term care insurance. If your spouse's health is stable enough, and if you can afford the premium, then insurance will pay for the nursing home when that day arrives.

Finally, and I don't like this suggestion but it must be examined: divorce. When a marriage ends the separate property of one ex-spouse will no longer be counted against the other ex-spouse who is seeking Medicaid. This approach is risky, since some Judges actually refuse to grant a divorce if it is based on the need for a federal benefit (they say that state law does not allow divorce for that cause).

Standard Exemptions

Certain assets are automatically treated as exempt. The fact that you own them will not disqualify you from receiving Medicaid. Exempt assets include:

- Burial allowance of $1,500 cash, in an earmarked burial fund, or in a revocable burial contract. On the other hand, if you purchase an irrevocable prepaid burial plan it may have any value, without limit;

- A burial plot, casket and vault, regardless of their value;

- Term life insurance of any amount and other life insurance with a death benefit of $1,500 or less per insured. If the death benefit of a policy is more than $1,500 then that policy's cash surrender value is counted as a resource;

- One automobile of any value, and a second auto is allowed if the household has more than one person, and the auto is being used for work-related transportation when the first vehicle is not available for work-related transportation or is handicapped-equipped and used for a household member;

- Your home furnishings and other personal belongings. If you tell Medicaid that you own items valued over $500 that are not used for everyday living, they will inquire about the value of those items and treat them as countable. Thus, the best approach is to consider your household goods to be "used and of little value". Even expensive items, like a set of sterling silver flatware or antiques, are ignored if used for everyday living;

- Livestock that is maintained as part of a trade or business or solely for home consumption is exempt; otherwise, the livestock's current market value is a countable resource;

- Your homestead. Historically, any homestead of any value was exempt. Congress decided to place a limit on homestead values, so as of February 1, 2006 a homestead will be exempt only up to $500,000. For all but the most unusual Medicaid applicant this new limit is not a concern.

Medicaid does not care if an asset is owned just by the husband or just by the wife. It does not make a distinction for community property versus separate property. Moreover, it does not care whether you have a premarital agreement.

Other Exemptions

The law allows some other exemptions, but they are more difficult to handle. They are:

- Certain annuities, under extremely tight rules;

- An allowance for a married couple so the at-home spouse has some funds to pay for living expenses. The spouse who is living at home (called the "community spouse") is allowed to retain funds so that he or she will not become impoverished;

- Business assets that produce income you need for your self-support. For example, you can keep a rental property, and it will not be counted as a disqualifying asset if you need the income it produces. For a single person, the income will all be paid to the nursing facility (thus reducing Medicaid's share of the expenses), but for a married person, the income can be used to raise the at-home spouse's income up to the $2,541 income allowance. The key to claiming this exemption is to have a federal tax return (1040) that includes a "Schedule C" – which shows that you operated the rent house as a business. Without the proper tax return, Medicaid will not exempt the property's value;

- Non-business assets that produce income you need for your survival, but only when the equity value does not exceed $6,000 and you historically get at least a 6% net annual rate of return on the asset;

- Assets that are exempted by regulation but which are unusual, including: payments for relocation assistance and crime victim compensation, payments from radiation exposure compensation, death benefits used to pay for someone else's funeral and last illness, earned income tax credits, reparations paid by Germany to holocaust survivors, certain payments to native Americans, payments made to settle a lawsuit against Bayer Corporation, and a few other special items.

Homestead Exemption

The most significant exemption is for your homestead: the full value of your home (up to $500,000) is exempt. But there is an important condition: your home is exempt only if your spouse or a dependent continues to reside there, or if you express intent to return to it if you are able to leave the nursing home. The focus is on your intentions, not on your abilities. It does not matter that you may be too incapacitated actually to return to your home so long as you would *intend* to return if you could.

In this context, "homestead" means your principal place of residence before moving to the nursing home. It is broader than the use of the word "homestead" in Texas property law, because for Medicaid purposes there is no limit on the number of acres that are exempt.

Before you go to the nursing home, you (or your spouse or dependent) must have lived in the home you claim as exempt. You cannot claim any other type of real estate as an exemption.

Rental of the Homestead

When you apply for Medicaid, your home is exempt only so long as you intend to return to it. If you have no spouse or dependent who resides in the home, does it have to sit unoccupied? No, it can be rented out temporarily – so long as you are very careful about the process.

Do not rent it out for a long period (like a one- or two-year lease) because Medicaid might claim that you cannot return to the home. If you cannot return, it loses homestead status and becomes just another countable asset. And as a countable asset, it might disqualify you from receiving Medicaid assistance.

A short-term lease is therefore safest for Medicaid purposes. The best arrangement is a month-to-month lease, so that you can move the tenant out promptly.

When you receive rent, the money is income. You do not want that income to shove you over the $1,869 limit, or you will be disqualified from receiving Medicaid assistance (or you'll have to obtain a Qualified Income Trust).

Since 1997 up to today, the Texas Department of Human Services has had regulations dealing with rental income. In almost all situations, they will count any rental income against you. One exception: if you have a corresponding expense that offsets the rental income, then the rental income may not count against you. For instance, if your tenant pays exactly the amount needed to maintain the property then you do not have any additional income.

Home Mortgage

If the home has a mortgage, any principal paid by the tenant directly to the mortgage company on behalf of the Medicaid beneficiary does count as income. It also is not available as an offsetting expense. This means that an equal amount would have to be paid to the nursing home by someone on behalf of the beneficiary.

The regulations do offer an unusual alternative: have the tenant pay only the interest portion of the monthly mortgage. Interest is an expense, and not treated as income. A family member who does not reside in the house should pay the principal. Why would a family member do so? Perhaps he or she expects to inherit the house someday. Making the payment protects and preserves the property.

House-sitter

A vacant house is exposed to many risks. It might be vandalized. It is a drain on family funds for property taxes and for maintenance. And the homeowner's insurance company may resist covering the home against fire and theft if it is vacant for a long period. These risks motivate you to let someone occupy the home.

Many families allow a younger relative to "house-sit." Perhaps a grandchild in college could live in the home rent-free. If so, the risks of vacancy are reduced and the home is still exempt for Medicaid purposes.

If there is no relative who can occupy the home, leasing it out seems logical. Remember, however, that for the home to be exempt it must be available for the homeowner to return to it. A long-term lease makes it unavailable causing it to lose its exempt status. Thus, a short-term or month-to-month lease is preferred.

Medicaid Planning Strategies

Medicaid Planning involves legally manipulating your income and your resources so the government will pay part or all of the cost of your long-term health care. Public policy has allowed manipulation within limits for several decades, but the limits have been consistently tightened. For years, the law has imposed a civil sanction for giving away assets: you will be disqualified from receiving Medicaid assistance for a period of time. The premise is "if you could have kept the money and paid for the nursing home, Medicaid won't pay even after you've given the money away."

Restrictions on Transfers

Your assets belong to you and you have the legal right to dispose of them in any way you desire. If you choose to give away assets, Medicaid has a programmed and predicable response. First, they require that you disclose transfers made within a certain time frame. Second, they calculate the resulting disqualification period.

The "Look-Back" Period

Medicaid can only ask about any transfer you made (to another individual) within the last 60 months before your Medicaid application. Consequently, you could give away an asset and then wait five years before you apply for benefits. Medicaid cannot then ask about the transfer. Theoretically you could give away all your assets, of any value, and then wait 60 months and the transfer will not disqualify you from receiving Medicaid. But there are huge risks to making bulk transfers of all your assets.

First, Congress can change the rules in mid-game. For instance, before 2005 the look-back period was 36 months. Years earlier, it was 30 months. There is nothing to stop Congress from expanding the time again, giving Medicaid power to ask about a broader time period than it could when you made the gift. You would then be required to report the gift, and a disqualification period could be imposed. Just because the gift has been given does not give you any special status as "grandfathered" into the old law; if they set new rules, you'll be subject to the new rules.

Second, there is no guarantee that the assets will remain safe in someone else's hands. When the transfer is made, those assets become the property of the recipient. If you give the assets to one or all of your children, you have given up all legal control of and access to the assets. There are risks even if your children are meticulously honest. For instance, if your son causes an auto accident and is sued, the assets in his name may be taken to cover the liability. Or if you daughter becomes ill and runs up medical bills, the assets may be consumed for her care.

Third, the IRS may want to collect a gift tax depending on the size of the transfer. You will owe gift tax on any transfer above $12,000 to any single person in a single year. The tax may be offset by the lifetime gift tax exclusion of $1 million, but a report to the IRS is necessary to comply with the law.

Disqualification Period

When you have made a transfer, Medicaid will deny benefits for a time equivalent to the number of days those funds could have paid for your care. This is called the "disqualification period." It is calculated by dividing the amount you transferred by the cost of a day in a nursing home. Since all nursing homes are slightly different, the state uses an average amount… so it may not reflect your reality. Here's an example:

You give away $10,000 to your daughter and apply for Medicaid. On the application they ask if you have made any gifts in the last 60 months and you disclose this recent transfer (lying is fraudulent). The state's determination of the average cost of care in Texas is $117.08 per day. Take 10,000 and divide by 117.08, and you get 85 (that is, 10000÷117.08=85.4, but you round down). Because you gave the money away, Medicaid imposes a disqualification period of 85 days.

The pattern calculates the disqualification for any gift amount. Give away $65,000, get disqualified for 555 days. Give away $2,000, get disqualified for 17 days, etc.

For a short time in 1996, Congress made transfers illegal and imposed a criminal penalty. Public and media perception of the criminalization provision was very negative. The popular press referred to it as the "Send Granny to Jail Law." No one was prosecuted under the law and it was repealed in 1997. Instead, Congress made it a crime for your lawyer, for a fee, to counsel or assists you "to dispose of assets... in order for the individual to become eligible" for Medicaid. Attorneys objected to this gag law on first amendment grounds. The State Bar of New York took up the issue, and filed suit in federal court. After months of litigation, the court ruled against the government, holding the restrictions unconstitutional.

Congress' next big step did not happen until early 2006, when it passed a bill that had been proposed in 2005: the Deficit Reduction Act of 2005 (DRA 2005). This law tightened restrictions on transfers in a very effective way: it created the 60-month look back period, and it moved the disqualification period so that it would have a more certain impact.

Before DRA 2005, the disqualification days started to count off beginning with the day the gift was given. If $10,000 was given away on January 1, 2004, the 85-day disqualification period expired 85 days later, on March 26, 2004.

After DRA 2005, the disqualification days start to count off beginning when the person would otherwise qualify for Medicaid. If $10,000 was given away on January 1, 2004, the 85-day disqualification period is just stored on the shelf. If the donor is healthy until January 1, 2007 and then applies for Medicaid, the days are only then taken off the shelf to be consumed. Under the old system, the disqualification would have been far in the past, over with, and would have had no impact in 2007. Under the new system, the disqualification is stored up until public benefits become an actual necessity, and then the disqualification days are used to deny benefits.

DRA 2005 effectively eliminated the usefulness of transfers as a Medicaid planning tool. Some attorneys are still searching for loopholes, and the final regulations to implement the new rules were just recently issued in Texas. Nonetheless, the legal transfer strategies that were used before DRA 2005 are no longer valid.

Transfer Exceptions

Generally, transferring title to an exempt resource (like the homestead) incurs a transfer penalty. If the nursing home patient did not want to keep the asset, Medicaid reasons, then they could have used that value to pay for nursing home care.

However, a transfer between spouses does not trigger the penalty. Medicaid does not care if title to the house is in the name of both spouses, in the name of the patient, or in the name of the community spouse. Often, it is sensible to put the house into the name of the community spouse. Why? If the patient dies first, there will be no need to probate a Will to pass title to the survivor. If the community spouse dies first, his/her Will should recite that the assets are left to the children or to a special needs trust for the patient, but not directly to the nursing home patient. This transfers the assets away from the patient – but there is no transfer penalty since it occurred because of a death. The assets are thus protected (had they been left directly to the nursing home spouse, Medicaid would have withdrawn benefits until the assets were consumed below $2,000).

Likewise, a transfer of the home to an adult child who is either blind or disabled does not trigger the penalty, nor does transfer of the house to a specially created trust for that disabled person (so long as the disabled person is under age 65). It is also legal to transfer the home to a sibling of the Medicaid patient, when that sibling has an ownership interest in the home and has lived there for at least one year before the patient moved to a nursing facility.

Finally, transfer of the home to an adult child causes no transfer penalty if 1) that child has lived in the house for at least two years before the parent moved into the nursing home, and 2) that child provided support services to the parent that allowed the parent to avoid moving to the nursing home for some time. Proof of those services must take the form of a letter from the doctor attesting to the services provided.

Transfer Resources to a Trust?

Medicaid labels a trust that is set up by an applicant with the applicant's own money which allows the applicant to get limited benefits a "Medicaid qualifying trust." The rules count all assets in a Medicaid qualifying trust as though they still belong to the applicant. Any trust you can revoke, whether you retain other benefits or not, counts against you.

Some irrevocable trusts are useful in a very restrictive fashion. Any irrevocable trust counts against you if there are any circumstances under which you could receive benefits from the trust—whether or not you actually receive the benefits. However, if an irrevocable trust follows certain rules, it can act as an asset shelter. These rules are so restrictive and unattractive that most people seeking Medicaid planning squarely reject them. The rules are:

- The creator of the trust (called the "grantor") cannot be a trustee. An independent third party, over whom the grantor has no legal control, must be trustee.

- The trust must be irrevocable. The grantor cannot change his or her mind once it owns the resources.

- The grantor is entitled to minor benefits only—no access to the principal is allowed, and access to income is restricted.

- The 60 month look- back applies, so there is a transfer penalty for putting assets into trust unless you wait up to five years before you apply for Medicaid. Congress retains the option to expand the look-back period without warning.

Personal Service Contracts

If an adult child lives with elder parents and provides care which keeps them from having to go to a nursing home, can a "personal services contract" be used to legally transfer money to that adult child for "fair value" of those services rendered, or will the money paid be a disqualifying transfer under Medicaid?

The state regulations specifically answer that question. Compensation *is not allowed* for services that would be normally provided by a family member (such as house painting or repairs, mowing lawns, grocery shopping, cleaning, laundry, preparing meals, transportation to medical care). Compensation *is allowed* for services that are health care oriented, but there must be evidence that those services were actually performed (so that the contract is not a charade). The agreement must be established on or before the date any funds are transferred, not as an afterthought, and must be intended to provide real and needed services instead of just being a way to hide money. And the family member must have lost other income.

Here is an example of a personal services contract the state would accept. Mom and daughter agree in December that if daughter will quit her job to care for mom during her illness, mom will pay daughter $10,000. In January daughter quits her job, where she was being paid $1,000 per month. In July, mom goes to a nursing home. The state will allow six months of services at $1,000/month as legitimate, so $6,000 is not a disqualifying transfer. The balance of $4,000 was not earned but was transferred, so it disqualifies mom from getting Medicaid's help for 34 days

Shifting of Resources

So far we have been dealing with transfers of resources from the applicant to another owner and the consequences of transfers. Now let's examine another strategy: shifting resources from being "countable" into one of the exempt categories. Recall that an applicant can qualify for Medicaid even though he/she owns a home, auto, burial plan, etc. Medicaid's rules do not forbid an applicant from enhancing the value of those exempt categories at the expense of non-exempt funds. For example:

> An unmarried applicant has $50,000 in savings and a house. He cannot qualify for Medicaid because the $50,000 is a countable resource. He cannot transfer the $50,000 to his daughter because it would create a disqualification period of 427 days. Instead, he shifts a much as he can into exempt categories. He pays off the $15,000 balance on his mortgage, he purchases a non-refundable funeral plan for $8,000, he pays off his credit card debt of $3,000 and he repairs the roof on his house for $6,000 (it was in pretty bad shape). Now he has $18,000 instead of $50,000 – but the funds were spent to eliminate debt, to prepay expenses that his daughter would have been stuck with, and to enhance the value of her inheritance (the home). The $18,000 will cover 4 or 5 months in the nursing home, and then he'll qualify for Medicaid.

There are other shifting opportunities available, like purchasing a new automobile or purchasing a new more expensive homestead. Those ideas may be extreme and have consequences that make them less attractive (i.e., how is the applicant going to pay property taxes on that new, expensive home?). These strategies should always be discussed with a Certified Elder Law Attorney before you implement them.

Non-Attorney Counselors

Several businesses have popped up around the state, offering to do Medicaid planning for a fee. Be very cautious of these planners! They are not licensed attorneys, which means:

- The information you provide to them is neither confidential nor privileged. They do not owe you an obligation to protect the financial data you provide. Also, if you are sued, they can be subpoenaed into court to expose your personal data.

- They may share your financial data with insurance brokers, who may try to sell you annuities or other insurance products. They may try to sell you an annuity directly, claiming that the annuity will allow you to qualify for Medicaid.

Texas law (Human Resources Code §12.001) says that a person who is not licensed to practice law cannot charge you a fee for representing you at a Medicaid hearing or for aiding you in applying for Medicaid benefits. The offense is a Class A misdemeanor. This law allows anyone to assist you with your Medicaid application – but only a lawyer can legally collect a fee for doing so. Why? Because lawyers must follow strict rules of conduct, must place your interests before theirs, must meet continuing education standards, must pass examinations that allow them to provide legal services, etc… Non-lawyers can just say, "Hey, I can help you with that," without any imposed standards, and without the rules of conduct imposed on licensed attorneys.

A few of these companies try to avoid the law by associating with a law office. That strategy does not make their efforts legal unless the lawyer directly oversees their activities while they handle your Medicaid issues. The arrangements I have seen are much looser; you may get printed materials with the lawyers name on them, but you never meet with the lawyer and the lawyer has no involvement in your case.

These planning companies routinely and notoriously overcharge. I have spoken to many former customers of these services. They report being charged anywhere from $5,000 to $10,000 for Medicaid planning services. This is a gross overcharge –attorneys experienced in Medicaid issues often perform similar services for a small fraction of that cost.

> Internet Resource:
> Many attorneys who are members of the National Academy of Elder Law Attorneys (NAELA) have experience in Medicaid Planning. You can obtain a list of NAELA members in your area through the NAELA website at WWW.NAELA.ORG. Finding a "Certified Elder Law Attorney" is best.

Spousal Protection Rules

When one spouse lives in a nursing home and the other lives at home, the community spouse fears losing everything before any type of public benefits step in to help. The spousal impoverishment provisions (which should really be called the "non-impoverishment" provisions) help protect any married couple, one of whom was in a nursing home on or after September 30, 1989 for any period longer than 29 days.

Protected Resource Amount (PRA)

When one spouse enters a nursing home with the intent of remaining for 30 days or more, the couple can request an assessment of their resources by Medicaid. The caseworker can either send you their Form H1272 (Resource Assessment) or can send you their Form 1200 (Application for Benefits) depending on whether you are ready to apply or not ready.

Either form requests information on the assets you own, with information based on the asset value as of midnight of the first day of the month in which the ill spouse entered the nursing home. From that total, the value of all exempt assets is deducted. An allowance is then calculated by cutting the countable resources into two equal shares; however, the set aside for the community spouse cannot be less than $20,328 or more than $101,640 (2007 figures).

The most advantageous way to use the spousal resource amount is to report as high a countable asset base as possible. Why? Because you want the protected amount to be as large as possible when they cut the countable resources into two equal shares. For example:

Scenario 1: Carl and Elizabeth are married. On March 1, Carl entered a nursing home. Carl has social security income of $755. They have a house (valued at $70,000), a certificate of deposit (valued at $20,000) and stocks (valued at $30,000.) The house is not included in the calculations, but the CD and stock value of $50,000 are part of the resource assessment taken on March 1. One-half of $50,000 (that is, $25,000) is set aside as Elizabeth's share. The other half is counted against Carl. As his $25,000 share is too much to allow him to get Medicaid the caseworker will deny Medicaid coverage until those funds are down to $2,000. When that happens, Carl's application for Medicaid will be approved. Elizabeth will still have her $25,000 cash and a $70,000 house to care for her own needs. Impoverishment is avoided.

Scenario 2: What if Carl and Elizabeth had countable assets of $203,000 and their house had a $50,000 mortgage? Elizabeth wants to pay off the mortgage. If she pays off the mortgage first, before the resource assessment, she hurts herself financially. Their $203,000 would have been reduced to $153,000 – so her half upon assessment would be $76,500. If, however, Elizabeth asks Medicaid to assess the resources first and pays off the mortgage afterward, she reports countable assets of $203,000. Her protected half upon assessment is then $101,500 instead of $76,500. Since Carl's half must be spent before he qualifies for Medicaid, Elizabeth can pay off the mortgage of $50,000 from Carl's share. She ends up with a clear title to the home, a protected amount $101,500, and Carl still has $51,500 to be spent before he qualifies for Medicaid.

Income Allowance

The spousal impoverishment provisions also include an income allowance. The community spouse is allowed to keep up to $2,541 per month (2007 figure) to maintain the houschold. This is called the Minimum Monthly Maintenance Needs Allowance or the MMMNA.

> Assume that Carl has monthly income of $1,650 and Elizabeth has monthly income of $1000 from Social Security. Each month, Elizabeth would keep $2,541 from this combined income, and would pay the balance ($109) to the nursing home for Carl's care (part of that being Carl's $60 per month personal needs allowance).

This income allowance often interacts closely with the establishment of a Qualified Income Trust. If, in the above example, Carl has income of $1,900 per month and Elizabeth's income is $300 per month. Carl would only qualify for Medicaid if he has a Qualified Income Trust to bring his $1,900 below the $1,869 limit. But Elizabeth is still entitled to her $2,541 per month allowance, so part of her allowance will be paid from funds that had been diverted to the Qualified Income Trust.

Expanded Protected Resource Amount

The income allowance has another major role to play. What if the income from both spouses is not enough to cover the $2,541 income allowance? For instance, if Carl's income is $800 and Elizabeth's income is $300 she is entitled to keep the entire $1,100 for her MMMNA. But $1,100 is far less than the allowance of $2,541. To fill that gap, Medicaid will allow Elizabeth's protected resource allowance to be increased beyond the typical one-half of countable resources. The extra funds can be invested to produce the income necessary to fill the gap.

How much could a married couple expand the protected resource allowance? It depends on two factors: 1) the size of the gap, and 2) current interest rates for a one-year certificate of deposit in your community. Here is a step-by-step guide to the calculation, based on Carl and Elizabeth's situation:

	Table 4: Extended Personal Resource Allowance	
Step 1:	Enter the minimum monthly maintenance needs allowance (MMMNA)	$ 2,541.00
Step 2:	Enter combined income of both spouses	$ 1,100.00
Step 3:	Subtract Step 2 from Step 1, enter the difference:	$ 1,441.00
Step 4:	If step 3 is $0 or a negative number, STOP / otherwise, proceed to step 5	

Step 5:	Multiply the amount in step 3 by 12	$ 17,292.00
Step 6:	Multiply the amount in step 5 by 100	$1,729,200.00
Step 7:	Enter the interest rate (number, not percentage) for a 1-year CD here	4.50
Step 8:	Divide the amount in Step 6 by the above number and enter result here	$ 384,266.66

Yes, you saw that correctly. In this example, the community spouse (Elizabeth) would be allowed an investment pool of up to $384,266.66. Using the facts from Scenario 1 (page 120) where the countable resources are $50,000 and the standard protected resource allowance is $25,000, the expanded resource allowance lets Elizabeth keep all $50,0000 and Carl can go on Medicaid immediately without a spend-down. The contributing factors, again, are the amount of retirement income (step 2) and the interest rate (step 7). Interest rates can be obtained from your local bank – many of them post rates on the Internet. Just choose the lowest rate that they publish for a one-year CD.

> Internet Resource:
> Want to calculate how the Expanded PRA might affect you? I've placed an interactive calculator on my website at
> HTTP://WWW.PREMACK.COM/EXPANDEDPRA.HTM. It will allow you to input your figures, and will tell you how much you might save.

Once the expanded PRA has been established, the excess funds can be invested in any way that the community spouse elects. Just because you used a low one-year CD rate to calculate the amount does not mean that you need actually to invest the funds in CDs at that rate. If the money is tied up in stocks, it can legally stay in stocks.

Medicaid Estate Recovery Program

By federal mandate, Texas was required to recoup the funds it spends on Medicaid by making claims against recipient's estates. Texas delayed implementation of the mandate for a decade until the legislature and Governor Perry passed an estate recovery law hidden in a very lengthy bill[35]. In fact, the bill was over 68,000 words long of which the Estate Recovery portion was 67 words.

Further, those 67 words did not come right out and say "Medicaid estate recovery is being authorized". Rather, they referred to a provision of the federal code by its number and instructed the Texas Commissioner of Health & Human Services to comply with it. After the bill was passed, several legislators called for its reconsideration when they and the public became aware of its impact, but the effort to reconsider the bill went nowhere.

After considering the public's input, the Commissioner finalized regulations that were then approved by Washington. The Medicaid Estate Recovery Program (MERP) took effect in Texas on March 1, 2005. Because no warning of the program's effect had been given to people already on Medicaid, the program only applied to people who applied for benefits after March 1, 2005. It is not retroactive.

MERP is restricted to Medicaid recipients who are 55 or older. MERP applies to Medicaid's nursing home benefit, its community based care benefit and its benefit for the mentally retarded.

The MERP regulations were written to provide the state a clear and well established procedure for making a claim to recover public funds that were spent to care for a Medicaid beneficiary. When a Medicaid beneficiary dies, a notice is sent to either:

- The estate representative (Executor or administrator);

- The beneficiary's court appointed guardian;

- The beneficiary's agent under a durable power of attorney;

- The beneficiary's agent under a medical power of attorney; or

- If none of the above are known, family members who have acted on behalf of the beneficiary.

The state asks for a reply to its notice so that they will know whether any exception should be considered before they file their official claim. If no exceptions apply, the state decides whether to present a Class 7 claim under section 298 of the Texas Probate Code.

MERP will *not* bring a claim if any of these exceptions apply:

- There is a surviving spouse;

- There is a surviving child under age 21;

- There is a surviving child of any age who is blind or disabled under the Social Security standards;

- There is an unmarried adult child residing continuously in the decedent's homestead for at least one year prior to the time of the beneficiary's death;

- The assets are fit into narrow categories that belong to American Indians or Alaska Natives, or represent reparation payments from a government;

- There is an undue hardship; or

- Bringing the claim will not be cost-effective.

Avoiding Estate Recovery

Frankly, the only significant asset that most Medicaid beneficiaries still own when they die is their homestead. Thus, avoiding MERP is the equivalent of protecting the homestead so it can pass to the next generation. The law provides several opportunities to protect the homestead, the most obvious being the exceptions discussed above (for instance, an unmarried adult child resides in the home for more than a year).

What approaches can be used when the standard exemptions do not apply? The house cannot simply be given away, since that would be a transfer that causes a disqualification from getting Medicaid benefits. Title can only pass at the moment of the beneficiary's death to avoid being a disqualifying transfer. But the traditional method of passing title upon death is to invoke the decedent's Last Will and Testament as recognized in Probate Court, which is exactly where MERP wants you to be so they can bring their class 7 claim. Thus, to avoid a MERP claim the estate must stay out of probate court.

There are several ways to avoid probate of a home title. Each has its pros and cons. They are:

Lady Bird Deed

This is also called an "enhanced life estate deed" or a "life estate deed with power of appointment". No one knows for sure why the "Lady Bird" moniker was applied to it, but legend ties it back to the former first lady. The idea is this: the homeowner signs a deed with wording that retains for the homeowner a life estate (the right to occupy and use the home). Upon the homeowner's death, title transfers to the persons named in the deed. However, the deed also says that the homeowner can cancel the transaction at any time or can name different people to receive title. That eliminates any value in the deed until the moment that it can no longer be cancelled (the moment of death). Without any value being transferred there is no disqualification that arises from the deed's existence like there is for a standard life estate transfer.

Right of Survivorship Deed

In this arrangement, the homeowner sells a tiny fractional interest in the home to someone (usually the adult children who would inherit the house). That fraction has so little value that it does not have an impact on the Medicaid. The deed contains language establishing a right of survivorship among those joint owners, so that when the Medicaid beneficiary dies title passes to the other owners without probate. So long as the other owners agree that they will not interfere if the Medicaid beneficiary desires to sell the home (which never really occurs) then Medicaid considers the house "available" to the beneficiary and thus its status as an exempt homestead remains intact.

Living Trust

For Medicaid, a living trust does *not* act as a place to hide assets in order to qualify for benefits. Despite that, a living trust was considered a safe way to avoid MERP until the Health and Human Services Commission announced in late 2006 that they would begin to treat a home that had been placed into trust as though it was still owned by the Medicaid beneficiary, not by the trust. Thus, even though a living trust avoids probate, MERP says it has the legal authority to bring a claim. Unless they are challenged in court and a Judge decides against them, they plan to bring MERP claims against homes held in living trusts.

Here is an interesting twist: Texas law does not allow a decision regarding Medicaid *benefits* to be challenged in court. If an application is denied, the only legal appeal happens within the Medicaid agency, not in court. But MERP is different. It is inherently a court-based process, because MERP claims must be brought in probate court after the beneficiary dies. Hence, it may be possible for an Executor to challenge a MERP claim in court, since the probate code allows court challenges to claims brought against estates. If a house was put into a living trust, it is controlled by the Trustee of that trust not by the Executor of the estate. If MERP brings a claim to the Executor asking for the house to be used to repay the debt to Medicaid, the Executor may be able to have the Judge dismiss the claim since the house is not part of the probate estate and is not under the Executor's control.

Transfer on Death of First Spouse

MERP cannot make a claim against the house if the Medicaid beneficiary does not own it. But there are only a few ways to transfer title without creating a disqualification.

One is to have the husband and wife sign a deed of partition, converting the home into the separate property of the community spouse. That spouse then makes a Will or other arrangement to pass title to other family members upon death. If the community spouse dies first, the nursing home spouse continues to qualify for benefits but does not own a home. If the nursing home spouse dies first, there is no need to probate the estate and there is no MERP claim.

Another such opportunity is to transfer ownership to an adult child who is disabled or to a sibling who resides in and owns part of the house. Another is to transfer ownership to an unmarried adult child who lived in the home and provided care to the parent for at least two years before the parent moved into the nursing home (and who has a letter from the doctor or a social worker testifying to the care that was provided).

MERP provides an automatic exemption from a claim if there is a surviving spouse, a disabled child or an unmarried child living in the house. If MERP is already avoided, why bother to do a transfer of title? Because the person who creates the exemption could predecease the nursing home resident. If your son Jon is disabled and you count on avoiding MERP because of it, and then complications from his disability cause his death while you are still alive in the nursing home, the exemption is lost. But if you transfer title to Jon while he is alive then it is a done deal. If he dies before you, you still have no interest in the house that Medicaid can claim using MERP.

★ Caution ★

Medicaid rules change. Washington or Austin may decide that the above techniques are too forgiving and disallow them. They are valid as of the time this book went to print. Be sure to consult with a Certified Elder Law Attorney before you take action on any of the techniques discussed above.

Medicaid Annuities

For many years a cluster of insurance agents have pushed annuities as the miracle cure for Medicaid woes. This cure, if it ever really worked as advertised, is now spoiled.

The concept was to take money (which was a countable resource) and buy an annuity with it. The insurance company, in exchange, agreed to make a payment to you. The payment was income. By doing this, you effectively converted a countable resource (which would have disqualified you) into income (which can be legally manipulated). As a result, you would have qualified for Medicaid promptly.

Of course, the insurance company's representative would also make a handsome commission. Some sales representatives may tell you that the above scheme still works, but it is now illegal and specifically forbidden by Medicaid.

In broad terms, annuities are an insurance product that can be used for long-term investment purposes or to create a monthly cash flow for the purchaser. A "deferred annuity" gets special tax treatment; there is no income tax on the interest accruing in the annuity until it is paid out. Pay out occurs when the term of the annuity runs out, when funds are withdrawn as may be allowed by the annuity contract, or when the annuitant dies. An "immediate annuity" provides regular payments to the annuitant, consisting in part of return of the invested funds and in part of interest earned. Payments might be for a certain number of years or for the annuitant's entire lifetime.

When considered simply for investment purposes, deferred annuities are more popular with seniors than immediate annuities. Even without Medicaid considerations, annuities have drawbacks the sales rep may not have emphasized. For instance:

- Deferred annuities have a penalty provision for early withdrawal of funds (though minimal withdrawals may be penalty free). It is common to lose up to ten percent of your invested principal if you need to take all the funds out before the annuity matures.

- Annuities have sales commissions that may be higher than other investments. The commissions are what motivated the lecturer to invite you to a free lunch and are what pay for your lunch if you decide to invest.

From the narrower perspective of qualifying for Medicaid, annuities create many problems. Since 1993 tight restrictions have applied to annuities, forcing them to be treated like any other investment. Additional restrictions were imposed by Congress in DRA 2005, effective in early 2006. They are:

- All deferred annuities are counted as resources;

- Immediate annuities are counted as resources unless the annuity is 1) irrevocable, 2) paid out in equal monthly installments, 3) paid out entirely within the applicant's life expectancy, and 4) repays the state for its Medicaid expenditures except for payments made to the applicant's spouse. The new federal law debatably eliminates the spousal exception, but there are varying and as yet unsettled interpretations of the new law; and

- When an immediate annuity meets those requirements (and is not a countable resource) the payments made from it on a monthly basis are countable income. If the Medicaid applicant's income exceeds $1,869 per month, the patient may be disqualified from Medicaid. If the annuity payments are made to the applicant's spouse, the payments when cumulated with all the other income the couple has, cannot be retained when the income exceeds $2,541 per month.

Requiring that payments under an annuity be made in equal amounts each month over the projected lifetime of the patient (which may be only a handful of years) increases the size of the payment, making it more likely that the income limits will be surpassed. Thus, an immediate annuity with all the required restrictions is only practical if the applicant has a fairly low monthly income from other sources.

Medicaid Benefits

Once a person is approved for Medicaid, the program will provide several benefits. Although Medicaid covers a wide variety of medical needs for low income and low asset elder or disabled individuals, the elderly do not often need to access Medicaid's "hospital and doctor" coverage because they have Medicare to pay those costs.

Instead, many elders rely on Medicaid to pay all or part of the daily cost of long-term nursing home care.

Nursing Home Daily Care

In most cases, Medicaid does not simply pay 100% of the nursing home bill. The patient is still required to contribute. How much the patient contributes depends on several factors: (1) is there a spouse still living in the community, and (2) are there other medical expenses to be covered?

First example:

> Robert is the nursing home patient, and his wife Dolores lives at home. He has monthly income of $1,700 and she has monthly income of $975. Following the Spousal Allowance rules, Dolores keeps $2,541 each month. The excess is spent in two ways. First, $60 is set aside for Robert's personal needs (the MMMNA). Second, they pay the nursing home the remaining $74. This fully consumes the joint monthly income. The nursing home charge, however, is $4,000 per month. Consequently, Medicaid pays the balance of the nursing home's bill: $3,926.

Second example:

> Robert is widowed, has $1,200 per month income, and lives in the nursing home. It costs $4,000 per month. First, $60 is set aside for Robert's personal needs. The rest of his income, $1,155, is paid to the nursing home. Medicaid pays the balance: $2,845.

Medical Needs & Prescriptions in the Nursing Home

The nursing facility must provide for the total medical, nursing, and psychosocial needs of each resident. This must include room and board, social services, meals (whether on a regular, special or supplemental diet), non-legend drugs (with the exception of insulin), medical accessories and equipment, medical supplies, personal needs items and rehabilitative therapies.

Before Medicare Part D took effect in 2006, Texas Medicaid paid for the resident's prescriptions. After it took effect, all prescriptions are handled under Part D.

Internet Resource:
The Texas Health & Human Services Commission has set up a special website to advise those who are "dual eligible" (those who get Medicare and Medicaid) about prescription drugs at WWW.TEXASMEDICARERX.ORG

Community Based Alternatives

Medicaid recognizes that a Nursing Home is not always the best or the least expensive care option. It created the "Community Based Alternatives" program (CBA) to provide home and community-based services to meet patient's needs outside a nursing home setting.

CBA is designed to provide for a wide variety of needs. This includes adaptive aids and medical supplies, adult foster care, assisted living, case management by DHS staff, minor modifications to the home, physical therapy, residential nursing care services, respite care and speech pathology. It also includes basic housekeeping and laundry.

The CBA program is available to anyone who would otherwise qualify for the Nursing Home program, with a few differences. Perhaps the biggest difference is the way that the spousal Protected Resource Allowance is handled. Under the full nursing home program, the PRA is calculated only once, upon the first qualification for benefits. Under the CBA program, the PRA is calculated upon first qualification as well… but if the beneficiary becomes ineligible for a short time for

some reason, on reapplication the PRA is recalculated based on the couple's resources at that later date. The effect is that the couples protected resources are cut
in half each and every time the patient re-qualifies for CBA.

CBA is a Medicaid "waiver" program, which means that it was created as an exception to the broader requirements imposed by Washington. The US Supreme
Court, in its Olmstead decision[36], mandated that states must provide the least restrictive living environment for persons needing long-term care services. The state
has provided a limited budget for CBA and can only handle a limited number of
patients at a time – about 27,000 statewide. When it deems that the program is
fully enrolled, it places new applicants on a waiting list until a space opens.

There is one way to bypass the CBA waiting list to get on CBA faster: a patient
who is being discharged from a nursing home back to the homestead goes to the
head of the line. This shortcut is not required by law, and may become unavailable
in the future.

QMB – Help with Medicare Costs

QMB is a Medicaid program that helps seniors pay for their health care in much
the same way that a Medigap policy might. QMB stands for "Qualified Medicare
Beneficiary." Under QMB, certain aged and disabled people are entitled to have
Medicaid pay their Medicare premiums, deductibles and coinsurance. It is an effort
to shift some cost burden from Medicaid onto Medicare. This has nothing to do
with paying for a nursing home stay. It is an entirely separate program designed to
benefit low income Senior Texans.

To qualify, you must meet three standards (using 2006 figures):

First, you must have income below $837 per month for an individual and $1,120
per month for a couple. This is calculated by taking 100% of the amount the government labels the "federal poverty level[37]" and adding a $20 per month buffer.

Second, your countable resources must be below $4000 for an individual and
$6000 for a couple. Some things, like your homestead, an automobile, burial plots
and personal possessions usually do not count as resources.

Third, you must be enrolled in Medicare Part A. Most seniors receive Part A because of their (or their spouse's) employment record. However, some seniors age
65 and up only get Part A if they elect to participate in Part B and to purchase Part
A as an extra. Some people under 65 can get Part A if on kidney dialysis or if on

disability benefits from either Social Security or the Railroad Retirement Board for more than 24 months.

Generally, seniors enroll in Medicare either 1) during the seven-month period surrounding their 65th birthday or 2) during the annual enrollment period from January 1 through March 31 each year. If a senior waits beyond the time surrounding the 65th birthday, then a premium is charged for Part A coverage.

If a senior has low income, then the Medicare premiums are unaffordable. This is where QMB comes in. If a person qualifies for QMB, Texas will pay:

- Medicare premiums for both Part A and Part B;

- Part A and Part B deductibles;

- The daily coinsurance charges for extended hospital and skilled nursing facility stays;

- The 20% Part B coinsurance, depending on which doctor you use.

To qualify for QMB, you MUST already be signed up for Part A, or must apply for Part A before the end of the day on March 31 each year. Contact Social Security at 1-800-SSA-1213 or visit the local Social Security office. If you are already enrolled in Part A, you are not affected by the March 31 deadline.

When an individual's monthly income is between $837 and $1000, or a married couple's monthly income is between $1120 and $1340, it may be possible to qualify for the Specified Low Income Medicare Beneficiary program (SLMB). It pays only the monthly Medicare Part B premium, but over a full year that saves over a thousand dollars. A SLMB or QMB participant may also qualify for additional benefits directly from Medicaid.

The Texas Department of Aging and Disability Services (DADS) says that only half of the people who might qualify for these Medicare Savings Plans have applied for the benefits. They recommend that people call the Health & Human Services Commission Office of Eligibility Services (OES) to ask about the programs, even if the caller is uncertain about qualifying. DADS can be reached toll free at 1-888-902-9990.

PUBLIC ASSISTANCE: VA BENEFITS

The Department of Veterans Affairs provides some long-term care. The biggest problem is the long waiting list. Several VA Hospitals have "Extended Care and

Therapy Centers." These are like nursing facilities, but their goal is to rehabilitate patients and return them to the community. Not all patients will be accepted for care. Contact your local VA office for details.

Veterans with a service-connected disability are given top priority for nursing home care. All other Veterans are taken on a space-available basis.

No income assessment is done by the VA for any "Eligible Veteran", which is defined as a (1) Veteran with service-connected disability, (2) Veteran who was exposed to herbicides (i.e., agent Orange) while serving in Vietnam, (3) Veteran exposed to radiation during atmospheric testing or in the occupation of Hiroshima and Nagasaki, (4) Veteran with a condition related to an "environmental exposure" in the Persian Gulf war, (5) Former prisoner of war, (6) Veteran on VA pension, (7) Veteran of the Mexican Border period or World War I, and (8) Veteran otherwise eligible for Medicaid[38].

Veterans needing nursing home care can be moved at VA expense to a private nursing home when discharged from a VA medical center or nursing home. Generally, VA care does not exceed six months, except when a Veteran needs nursing home care due to a service-connected disability.

Texas Veterans Nursing Homes

In coordination with the VA, the Texas Veterans Land Board operates a series of subsidized nursing facilities. To qualify for care in a State Veterans Home, the veteran must be an "eligible veteran" as defined above, and must:

- Have both a physician and the VA concur in the need for long-term nursing care;

- Be 18 or older;

- Be a Texas resident now and when he/she began military service, or have resided in Texas continuously for a full year before seeking admission to the facility; and

- Not have a dishonorable discharge from the service.

Additionally, a spouse or surviving spouse of a veteran or a gold star parent of a veteran qualifies for care in a State Veterans Home.

Facilities are available in Temple, Big Spring, Floresville, Bonham, McAllen and El Paso, and will be available in Amarillo by mid-2007. Since the government pays part of the cost of care, a resident's out of pocket is approximately $70 per day, but that varies according to several criteria.

> Internet Resource:
> More information on State Veterans Homes is available at
> WWW.GLO.STATE.TX.US/VLB/VETHOMES/INDEX.HTML or by phoning
> 1-800-252-8387.

ASSISTED LIVING FACILITIES

Perhaps you don't quite need the range of services provided by a Nursing Home. You might consider Assisted Living. These facilities are usually less expensive than nursing homes, and provide a lower level of care.

Until 1999, Texas called these facilities "Personal Care Facilities," but the 76th legislature expanded the law to require licensure for a wider variety of facilities. Licensure is overseen by the Texas Department of Aging and Disability Services.

Technically, an Assisted Living Facility is any residential setting for four or more persons that also provides specific services. State regulations categorize facilities as either:

- Type A: facilities that accept residents capable of evacuating the premises unassisted, of following directions under emergency conditions, and of handling their own routine care during the night.

- Type B: facilities that accept residents inappropriate for Type A placement because of immobility, but who are not permanently bedfast.

- Type C: facilities with four beds that meet minimum standards set for adult foster care.

- Type E: facilities very similar to Type A, but can include those in wheelchairs or electric carts who can transfer and evacuate themselves in an emergency. They provide more general care services (supervision of medications and welfare, but no substantial assistance with meals, dressing, movement, bathing or other needs).

If you reorder that list by the amount of care and supervision provided, you get Type B, Type A, Type E then Type C. In other words, Type B facilities offer the most care and supervision and Type C offer the least.

Beware Unlicensed Facilities

Be aware that another category exists: unlicensed care facilities. If a facility houses less than four residents then a license is NOT legally required and there is no regulation by the state. If a facility is operated by a tax-exempt religious organization that has operated for at least 35 years, then regardless of the number of residents it is NOT legally required to have a license to run an assisted living facility, and the state does not oversee its operation.

The state can suspend or revoke the facility's license if conditions threaten the health or safety of the residents. A licensed assisted living facility can be shut down. But if your family member is in an unlicensed facility, the state is far less likely to intervene. Also, the owner(s) of an unlicensed facility may try to impose unreasonable terms for the care they provide (no refund for unused days, extra fees for services that should be included, limited visitation hours). Also be aware that claiming a religious motivation to care for the elderly does not guarantee honesty or quality services, and may be more of a sales pitch than a reality.

> Internet Resource:
> The Texas Dept. of Aging and Disability Services has a list of all long-term care facilities they oversee, with quality ratings. The list can be viewed by county, city, zip code or area code and is found at FACILITYQUALITY.DHS.STATE.TX.US. Further, you can phone them for information at 1-800-458-9858.

MEDIGAP POLICIES

Medicare Supplement Insurance Policies, commonly called Medigap policies, are tightly regulated by the Texas Department of Insurance.

You should only need ONE Medigap policy, if any. If you qualify for Medicaid and the QMB program in addition to your Medicare then a Medigap policy should not be necessary at all. If your employer offers group health coverage then your needs may also be met. If you sign up for a Medicare Choice+ HMO, then a Medigap policy is not necessary. Keep your money if possible.

When you turn 65 and sign up for Part A and Part B of Medicare, you are entitled to purchase a Medigap policy regardless of your health condition. This window stays open for 6 months.

If you buy a policy, it can exclude coverage for pre-existing conditions. But the insurance company cannot refuse to sell you a policy during that time period, even if your health is bad.

Standardized Medigap Plans

Federal law mandates standardization of Medigap policies, with the varieties labeled type A through L. All policies must offer a "core package" of benefits that cover:

- All co-payments for hospitalization under Part A;

- 365 days of additional hospitalization after Medicare benefits run-out;

- The Part B 20% co-payment; and

- The cost of the first three pints of blood per year.

These core benefits still leave significant gaps in coverage. You still pay the deductibles. You still pay for prescriptions (or at least the gaps left by Medicare Part D), preventive care, and nursing home care. Companies may offer policies that offer more than the core benefits, but will charge more for them.

> Internet Resource:
> The Texas Department of Insurance has consumer information and a rate guide to Medigap policies offered in Texas at
> WWW.TDI.STATE.TX.US/CONSUMER/MEDSUP.HTML

Medigap Sales Reform

For years, one rip-off that seniors were exposed to was the Medigap policy oversell. It wasn't unusual for a trusting yet frightened senior to buy two, three or even four duplicative Medigap policies. Congress passed a law forbidding double coverage. An insurance agent offering Medigap policies must provide you a written warning that:

- You probably only need one Medigap policy;

- People on Medicaid generally do not need Medigap insurance; and

- Counseling services are available if you are confused about your options.

The salesperson is not allowed to sell you a policy if he/she fails to get the listing of your current policies. The salesperson is legally forbidden to sell another policy to you if you have another Medigap policy, or if you are on Medicaid. However, if you sign a statement that the new policy replaces one you are canceling, or that it does not duplicate coverage, he/she can still sell you the policy. Do not sign a release without first understanding your rights.

By law, you get a 30-day "free-look" at any Medigap policy. Even after you agree to purchase the policy and pay the first premium, the company must allow you to cancel and give you a refund during the first 30-day period. If you do return the policy, send it to the insurance company by certified mail so you'll have a record of the date.

Chapter 4: Protections During Your Life

PROTECTION OF YOUR HOME

Homestead Tax Reductions

Texas law grants an exemption to lower the amount of property taxes paid by homeowners who reach age 65. It is a "65-plus" exemption, not an "over-65" exemption as many people believe. The homeowner qualifies for the exemption in the year that he/she turns 65 – as though on January 1st of that year his/her 65th birthday had already arrived. For example:

> Sarah turns 65 in October 2008 and her husband Peter turns 65 in June 2009. Sarah is treated as though she was 65 on January 1, 2008, so she gets the exemption in 2008. Note that only one spouse need reach age 65 for the tax exemption to begin.

65-plus homeowners qualify for a $10,000 homestead exemption on the home's value against school taxes. Additionally there is a general exemption of $15,000. A taxing unit—including a school district—can offer an additional exemption of at least $3,000 for 65-plus taxpayers. The taxing unit is not required to offer this additional exemption.

65-plus homeowners who qualify for the exemption also have a school tax ceiling for that home. The school taxes are frozen at their age-65 level and do not increase unless the home is significantly improved (like adding a game room, but not doing normal repairs or maintenance). The tax ceiling changes if the house is sold and a replacement is purchased, using a formula keyed to the original tax freeze.

The school tax ceiling transfers to the surviving spouse if he/she is 55 or older and has ownership in the home. The survivor must, however, apply to the local appraisal district for the tax ceiling to transfer.

The 65-plus exemptions are not automatic. You must apply for them, which can usually be started with a phone call to your local Appraisal District. They will ask for your birth date and the property tax account number, so have last year's tax receipt handy. Once they verify the information against their records, they'll send a form to complete and return.

Internet Resource:
You can obtain the Application for Exemption free from The Premack Law Office website at WWW.PREMACK.COM (click on "legal documents").

Death of the 65-Plus Homeowner

What if a homeowner is already receiving the 65-plus exemption, the spouse is younger than 65, and the older spouse dies? Texas law allows the exemption to rollover to the younger spouse so long as he/she is 55 or older. The younger spouse must also become owner of the house after the death and must reside in the home. This is another good reason to have a valid and up-to-date Will. The school tax freeze also rolls over to the younger spouse's benefit.

Home in Living Trust

If you decide to set up a living trust and transfer ownership of your home to it, you will lose your 65-plus homestead tax exemption *unless* your trust complies with section 11.13(j) of the Texas Tax Code. To comply, your living trust must have several features. They are:

- The trust must allow the Grantor to use the homestead without paying any rent, and must require the Grantor to pay the property taxes when they become due;

- The Grantor must be allowed to use the homestead for his/her entire lifetime, for a specified number of years, or until the trust is revoked; and

- The trust must become owner of the homestead in a properly recorded deed. The deed must contain the homestead's legal description and must be signed by the Grantor of the trust.

If your living trust does not contain those provisions, they can and should be added with an amendment.

Tax Deferral

"Defer" means to delay payment. The taxes are still owed by you or your estate; payment is just delayed until you sell, move out, or die (and consequently your homestead is no longer a homestead). Texas allows residents 65-plus (or disabled) to defer payment of property taxes on their homestead. This includes taxes imposed by the school district, the county and the city. It does not include any federal tax collected by the IRS.

To obtain a deferral, you must sign form 33.06 in front of a notary and file it with the local Appraisal District office. You need to know the legal description of your home. You need to swear that you are 65 or older and that you occupy the described property as your homestead.

There is no penalty during a valid property tax deferral period. A tax lien may still be placed against the property. Interest continues to accrue. But no penalty many be imposed during a deferral period.

Just remember that a tax deferral does not eliminate the need to pay the taxes eventually. It allows them to be paid at a later date, but they must still be paid (with interest). You must note that the deferral procedure is quite different from the 65-plus tax exemption. Deferral is not a tax reduction, while the exemption does indeed reduce the amount of taxes you owe.

> Internet Resource:
> Get "Form 33.06" from your local Tax Appraisal District, or on the Internet for free from the Premack Law Office website at WWW.PREMACK.COM (click on "legal documents").

Tax Abatement

"Abate" means to stop an already existing tax collection lawsuit. This only happens if the taxing authority has already sued you, and you want to stop them in their tracks. Abatement is granted only to persons 65-plus or disabled.

To receive abatement, you must file form 33.06 with the court that has jurisdiction over the tax collection lawsuit. The tax authority can try to disprove your right to abatement, but the final decision is the Judge's. If the tax authority raises no objection, the collection lawsuit is suspended until you no longer own and occupy the homestead property.

Filing for abatement does not mean you no longer owe the taxes. The collection authority can still place a lien against your home but cannot act to enforce it at that time. In the future, the tax dispute must still be settled and the taxes must still be paid.

Capital Gain Exemption

Your house, like any other investment, is a capital asset. Typically, when you sell a capital asset, you pay federal income tax on the "capital gain"—that is, the difference between your basis and the sale proceeds. Think of your basis as the home's purchase price adjusted for any improvements you've added.

Unlike other capital assets, Congress has granted your home special tax treatment. Married couples may sell their home and exclude any capital gain on up to $500,000 profit. An unmarried person may exclude up to $250,000. However, these rules must be followed:

- You must own and live in the home for 2 of the last 5 years;

- A married couple must file a joint income tax return for the year of the sale; and

- You cannot have used the exclusion to sell another home in the last two years.

You may recall that the rules before 1997 allowed a home-seller to (a) defer paying capital gain tax if another more expensive home was purchased, and (b) avoid capital gain on up to $125,000 in profit if the seller was 55 or older. This was limited to once per lifetime.

The updated exclusion is not only worth more money, it can also be used every two years, over and over, each time a homestead is sold.

There are two situations where you can claim a prorated exclusion if you have not yet lived in the house for two years: 1) if you have to move early because your work requires you to relocate, or 2) if your poor health forces you to move to a licensed nursing home.

The proration is calculated by dividing the number of months you occupied the home during the last five years by 24 months. If you lived there for 14 months, the ratio would be 14/24 of the $500,000 available – or $291,666. So if you are selling your house for $400,000, and you paid $190,000 for it, your $210,000 gain is free of capital gain tax because it is less than your allowable exclusion.

Exemptions from Judgment

The Homestead: Urban or Rural

The Texas Constitution and Texas Property Code make your homestead legally exempt from claims of most creditors. If, for example, you get into a dispute over payment of a large bill and the creditor obtains a court judgment requiring you to pay, the creditor cannot collect against your homestead.

There are two types of homestead: urban and rural. If your home is located in a municipality (or its extraterritorial jurisdiction or in a platted subdivision) and is served by municipal police and fire protection and three types of utilities (choosing from electricity, gas, sewer, storm sewer and water) then you have an urban homestead. Rural homesteads are in all the places that are not urban.

Legally an urban homestead can include up to ten acres of land and improvements. A rural homestead is defined similarly as up to 200 acres with improvements if you are married or only up to 100 acres with improvements if you are single.

Valid Liens Against the Homestead

Protection of your homestead is not universal. The law allows your homestead to be taken in eight situations:

- Failure to repay a mortgage or home improvement loan. The lender can foreclose for failure to pay back purchase money or money you borrowed for home improvements.

- Failure to pay taxes. The federal or local government can take your home for failure to pay taxes. As to Texas property taxes, there is specific protection for people age 65-plus: your home cannot be taken for failure to pay Texas property taxes if you have filed for a deferral of tax or an abatement of collection. A federal tax lien (by the IRS) is not affected by the Texas deferral or abatement procedure.

- Placing an "owelty of partition" against the homestead. This is a debt arising through an agreement (or by court order) to recognize the different interests of persons in property upon division of the property between the persons, usually in a divorce.

- Failure to repay a loan taken to pay off a different lien against the homestead. This is sometimes done to pay-off a federal tax lien owed to the IRS. Of course, failure to pay the new loan would also end in foreclosure.

- Failure to pay a contractor for home improvements. The contractor can place a "mechanics and materialmen's lien" against your home. You and your spouse must both agree to the lien in writing before work is started or materials are furnished. You must also be given a specific written warning in the contract that failure to follow its terms may result in the loss of your home.

- Abandonment of the homestead. If you surrender your rights by walking away from your homestead, pre-existing creditors can take it. However, you do not surrender your rights simply because of prolonged absence (especially if you express intent to return to your home). Texas court decisions also state that lengthy absence from home due to illness is not considered abandonment of your homestead.

- Voluntary equity loans. You can place a home equity loan or reverse mortgage against your homestead. This is a fairly new vulnerability for the Texas homestead.

- Voluntary manufactured housing loans. The law relating to titles for "mobile homes" has been changed several times since the mid-1990's. The current iteration was passed as Senate Bill 521 by the 2003 legislature. One of the biggest changes is the option, given to the buyer, to declare that the mobile home is real property once it is installed – that is, parked and hooked to utilities. If it becomes real property, then the seller can negotiate a lien against the mobile home and the land on which it is parked. If the buyer defaults, he/she not only loses the mobile home but can now lose the land as well.

Personal Property Exemption

In addition to your homestead exemption, Texas law provides a personal property exemption. While the personal property exemption is less well known than the homestead exemption, is still very important. It shelters your personal necessities by forbidding the authorities from seizing, garnishing, attaching, or executing against a very specific list of items—even to satisfy a court judgment.

Under current law, a family is allowed to shelter assets with a market value up to $60,000. A single adult is limited to $30,000 value. Over and above the $60,000 limit, the law forbids the authorities from seizing your current wages and from seizing "professionally prescribed health aids." This means that if you have special medical equipment in your home for an ill family member, the equipment is exempt from seizure regardless of its value.

If a judgment is entered against you, you must be given the opportunity to set aside assets valued up to the value limits granted by law. You are allowed to choose any combination from the following items:

- Home furnishings and family heirlooms;

- Foodstuffs;

- Tools, equipment, books and vehicles used in your trade;

- Farm or ranch vehicles, implements, and some livestock;

- Clothing;

- Jewelry (so long as it does not exceed ¼ of your limit);

- Two guns;

- A car for each driving member of the family; and

- Athletic equipment.

Due to the homestead and personal property exemptions, you are certain that you will never be stripped of the necessities of life even though there is no limit to the possible size of a court judgment against you.

Insurance, Retirement Funds and 529 Plans

Another law — found in the Texas Insurance Code — shelters all insurance benefits from seizure to satisfy a judgment. It specifically protects money, policy proceeds, and cash values that come from insurance.

There is one exception: your insurance company may keep any part of the insurance proceeds allowed by the policy. This might be used, for instance, to pay off a loan against a whole life policy or to collect back-due premiums. Other than that, no one may legally claim any money from the insurance except you or the beneficiary.

The protection for your insurance investment is broad. It includes any insurance policy issued by a life, health, or accident insurer (including fraternal societies like Hermann Sons). It also includes an annuity or benefit issued by an employer. Hence, your retirement annuity is exempt and cannot be seized to pay a judgment lien or a bankruptcy claim.

Some people tend to view life insurance as a necessary evil; tolerated when necessary, eliminated when possible. But since this law shelters cash values, proceeds, and any other insurance benefit from seizure and bankruptcy, you may have a good reason to continue to include insurance as part of your investment portfolio.

Be sure you buy insurance from a reputable, well-rated company. If all else fails, you will have sheltered the insurance assets from seizure, guaranteeing that you and your loved ones will not be left empty-handed.

Texas law also protects—to a large degree but not absolutely—assets held in, and the money you can take as withdrawals from, any plan, contract, or account that qualifies under the Internal Revenue Code as:

- A Stock bonus, pension, profit-sharing, or similar plan, including a retirement plan for self-employed individuals;

- An Annuity or similar contract purchased with assets distributed from the above type of plan;

- A retirement annuity or account that is qualified under section 403(b) of the Internal Revenue Code; and

- Any individual retirement account or any individual retirement annuity (IRA) including a simplified employee pension plan (SEP) and a Roth IRA;

- College savings plans – both 529 plans and prepaid tuition plans (like the Texas Tomorrow Fund) – are now also protected. This was extended in Senate Bill 1588 by the 2003 Texas legislature.

Home Equity Loans

Texas was the last of the 50 states to authorize home equity lending, and it took two constitutional amendments to become legal. Pushed by many banks, the Texas legislature passed (and Governor Bush signed) a law exposing the highly protected Texas homestead to voluntary liens. This was powerful and required an amendment to the Texas Constitution. The public approved the amendment in the November 1997 election.

Homeowners can now use the equity in their home as security for a personal loan. Want a boat? Need money to pay for nursing home care? Proponents of this approach tell you to take a loan against your home.

On the bright side, interest on a home equity loan tends to be lower than other loans. And the interest is deductible on your federal income tax return. On the dark side, home equity loans tempt you to risk the biggest asset you own – your home. Banks are aggressively marketing home equity loans.

Since Texas homesteads had the highest level of protection in the nation before this law change, the legislature felt that it should design the equity lending law with some very strict consumer protection mechanisms. Among them are:

- Both spouses must agree in writing voluntarily to place the lien against the homestead.

- Only one equity loan at a time can be put on the homestead.

- The loan cannot be for more than 80% of the home's market value. Any existing loan must be factored in. If the home is worth $100,000 and has an original mortgage of $30,000, then the home equity loan cannot be for more than $50,000 (50 + 30 = 80).

- Installment payments must be handled like a mortgage. Payments cannot be made so small that the loan balance actually grows while interest is left unpaid. Additionally, the loan must be pre-payable without penalty.

- There must be at least 12 days between the loan application and loan funding. During this time, the homeowners can change their minds. When closing time arrives, papers must be signed at the bank, at a title company or at an attorney's office. They cannot come to your home for signing.

- The loan cannot include personal liability for the homeowners; that is, it can only be collected by foreclosing on the house. Other assets of the homeowner cannot be put at risk. Of course, if the homeowner has other assets he/she probably wouldn't be defaulting on the equity loan anyway.

- Closing costs cannot be more than 3% of the loan amount. If you borrow $50,000 they can't charge more than $1,500 to originate, evaluate, maintain, re-cord, insure, or service the loan. Interest, however, is at market rates.

Until the voters changed the Texas constitution yet again in 2003, the loan could not be treated like revolving credit. It was illegal to have an open line of credit, taking a little now, a little later. Now, the opposite is true.

Home Equity Lines of Credit

Proposition 16 in the 2003 constitutional election received 65% of the vote. It allows banks to offer home equity lines of credit; that is, open-ended accounts that homeowners can draw against in varying amounts at varying times.

However, Texas law imposes certain requirements. For instance, any single draw against the line of credit must be at least $4,000. Smaller amounts are not allowed.

The method of making a withdrawal must be by direct contact with the lender; credit cards, pre-authorized checks and debit cards are not allowed.

One good feature is that the bank can only charge a fee when the loan is originally established. There cannot be an additional fee each time a draw is made on the line of credit.

How much credit can be offered? By law, the total loan cannot exceed 50% of the fair market value of the home as it was determined when the loan was established.

Similar to regular home equity loans and mortgages, repayment is made during the homeowner's lifetime. The bank cannot legally require payments more often than every 14 days, nor less often than monthly. Payments can be delayed for a short initial period of two months for the first extension of credit.

These are the highlights. There is a lengthy list of other rules that must be followed. If you apply for a home equity loan, all the rules must be provided to you in words mandated by the law.

Equity Loans Expose the Home to Liability

Some people may be temped to convert a high interest unsecured loan (like a credit card debt) into a low interest secured home equity loan. An unsecured loan is based on your promise to pay, but is not linked explicitly into the things that you have purchased. A secured loan is attached by a lien to a specific asset. Failure to make the payments on a secured loan puts that asset at risk of seizure after proper legal procedures have been followed.

Many banks push home equity loans, and they can be useful in the right situation. Conversion of an unsecured loan may make sense if you will have no trouble paying the loan. But if you are at any risk of going into default (poor health, tough economic times) you must protect your home above all other obligations. If you go into default, a credit card company that gave you an unsecured loan cannot sue to take away your home, but a bank that gave you a secured home equity loan can take away your home.

Internet Resource:
Home equity lending can put you at risk of losing your shelter. Here is an informative article from the Federal Trade Commission on home equity scams that you should read: WWW.FTC.GOV/BCP/CONLINE/PUBS/ALERTS/EQTYALRT.HTM

Reverse Mortgages

The only other category of home equity loans is the reverse mortgage. The first constitutional amendment (from 1997) was faulty in the sense that it did not match federal underwriting regulations. As a result, there was no resale market for Texas reverse mortgages. So in November 1999 the voters were asked to revise the constitution again – to let it match the federal regulations. Reverse mortgages actually began to appear on the market in mid-2001.

Reverse Mortgages are often of greatest interest to seniors who have acquired extensive equity in their homes. They allow monthly payments to be made from the lender to the homeowner. The owner can spend the money for any purpose. The loan must, of course, be repaid – but not until either:

- All of the borrowers have died; or

- The homestead property securing the loan is sold or otherwise transferred; or

- All borrowers cease occupying the homestead property as a principal residence for more than 12 consecutive months without prior written approval of the lender; or

- The borrower:

  - defaults on an obligation specified in the loan documents to repair and maintain, pay taxes and assessments on, or insure the homestead property; or

  - commits actual fraud in connection with the loan; or

  - fails to maintain the priority of the lender's lien on the homestead property, after the lender gives notice to the borrower, by promptly discharging any lien that has priority or may obtain priority over the lender's lien within 10 days after the date the borrower receives the notice, unless the borrower:

    - o Agrees in writing to the payment of the obligation secured by the lien in a manner acceptable to the lender;

    - o Contests in good faith the lien by, or defends against enforcement of the lien in, legal proceedings so as to prevent the enforcement of the lien or forfeiture of any part of the homestead property; or o Secures from the holder of the lien an agreement satisfactory to the lender subordinating the lien to all amounts secured by the lender's lien on the homestead property.

Texas law and federal lending regulations restrict reverse mortgages to people age 62-plus, or whose spouse is 62-plus. In addition, these rules must be followed:

- The lien must be voluntary and both spouses must sign it. It is not possible for only one spouse, acting alone, to place a lien against the homestead unless that spouse either a) has a durable power of attorney from the other, or b) is the court-appointed guardian of the other.

- The loan must be without recourse for personal liability against each owner.

- The lender is not allowed to reduce the amount or the number of advances because of an adjustment in the interest rate if periodic advances are to be made.

- The Texas constitution requires that before signing a reverse mortgage, the owner must attest in writing that he or she received counseling on the advisability and availability of reverse mortgages. The counseling must include a discussion of other financial alternatives.

If the lender doesn't live up to its end – if it fails to make loan advances as contracted and doesn't cure its default as required in the loan contract – then the lender forfeits all principal and interest of the reverse mortgage.

The voters of Texas also approved a constitutional amendment in 2003 that allows a 62-plus homeowner to refinance a home equity loan by taking a reverse mortgage.

> Internet Resource:
> A good source for information on Texas Home Equity loans is the Texas Finance Commission. Their information is online at
> WWW.FC.STATE.TX.US/HOME%20EQUITY/HEINDEX.HTM

How about a Cooperative?

Will a member of a Homeowner Cooperative be able to place a reverse mortgage or home equity loan on his unit?

The answer appears to be "NO". Under Texas law, someone who buys into a cooperative is a "subscriber" and owns a share in the project. This ownership entitles the subscriber to reside in a unit of the project. The Cooperative Association, however, owns the real property.

It may appear to the subscriber that the unit is his/her homestead, but it is not. The Association owns the unit. The subscriber owns stock. Stock cannot be a homestead.

Why then do subscribers receive TAX BILLS that identify the property as their homestead? Because special tax breaks were written into the Texas Tax Code for Cooperatives. Although the Cooperative Association owns the units, they are appraised separately so that each owner knows his/her share of the taxes. The Tax Code then allows the subscriber the same tax breaks that would be available had the subscriber purchased a freestanding homestead.

A coop is not a homestead for other purposes. Texas law requires a homestead to be composed of real property. People who own an interest in a Cooperative Housing Association do not own any real property. They own shares in the Association. This entitles them to lease a unit for their residence, often with a "proprietary lease" for their unit. While the interest of the resident is legally binding, it is not a homestead interest.

PROTECTION AS A CONSUMER

A seller of goods or services cannot legally use any type of deceptive tactics. If you are deceived and it causes you monetary or physical damage, Texas law may allow you to make a claim against the company that caused the harm.

Deceptive Trade Practices-Consumer Protection Act

This law defines a wide variety of prohibited schemes as "deceptive." Among these are:

- Taking advantage of a customer's lack of knowledge, experience or capacity to an unfair degree;

- Telling a customer that work has been performed on or parts replaced in goods when the work was not performed nor the parts replaced;

- Making misleading statements concerning the need for parts, replacement, or repair service; and

- Telling a customer that goods are original or new if they are deteriorated, reconditioned, reclaimed, used, or second hand.

Before you can take legal action, the law requires that you give the business a written notice of your complaint and the amount of damages. The business has a chance to offer a settlement—but if they do not make an offer, or if you reject their offer, then you may sue the business 60 days after you sent the original notice.

Texas Residential Construction Commission

Anti-Consumer Law Reduces Protections

The Texas Residential Construction Liability Act poses as a consumer protection law, but offers more protection to homebuilders than it does to homebuyers.

The Act completely changed the way a builder can be held accountable for construction defects. It created a new government entity: the Texas Residential Construction Commission. The Governor appoints the nine members, and is required to select four registered builders, one licensed professional engineer, one architect or building inspector, and three at-large members. One consumer law expert has likened this to putting the foxes in charge of the henhouse, since at least six of the nine members are in the building trade.

The Act requires that the homeowner notify the builder, in writing, of each defect, and must give the builder 30 days to respond. If the builder fails to respond or responds inadequately, the homeowner must submit the dispute to the Commission at the expense of the homeowner, along with evidence of the defects. Thus, the homeowner should hire an inspector – since overlooking a hidden defect means that defect is not part of the claim.

The Commission will then assign a private inspector to look at the home. There is concern that the inspectors will be biased toward the builders. After all, each homeowner has only one case to bring – but the builders may be involved in multiple claims, and an inspector who desires repeat business will not want to come down too hard on the builder. No doubt there are honest inspectors out there, but be careful to be sure you are not hurt by a biased inspector.

If the homeowner disagrees with the recommendation of the inspector, an appeal can be brought before the Commission. However, the homeowner has no right to make a presentation at the appeal; the Commission simply reviews the documentation. Again, be aware the Commission, composed mostly of those in the building trade, may be biased toward the builder[39].

Only after appeal to the Commission is complete can a homeowner turn to the courts with a lawsuit. Before September 1, 2003, a homeowner could sue to recover damages including cost of repairs, out of pocket expenses like inspector's fees, attorney's fees plus mental anguish and punitive damages. After September 1, 2003, the homeowner is limited to recovering for "breach of warranty" (which eliminates mental anguish and punitive damages). Additionally, the Act strips the homeowner of protections that were granted under the Texas Deceptive Trade Practices Act, including the right to sue that previously existed under the Deceptive Trade Practices Act.

Consumer Protection Division

For a Broad Range of Consumer Problems

If you are not ready to take legal action yourself, you can contact the Texas Attorney General's Office. They have a "Consumer Complaints" division. From anywhere in the state you may call the Attorney General toll free by dialing 1-800-621-0508.

The Consumer Protection division can also take direct action against a company it thinks is violating the law. They can seek an injunction and monetary penalties against companies that act deceptively.

The legislature, aware that deceptive business practices are especially harsh when the victim is elderly, imposed a special penalty. If a Judge rules that a company has violated the Deceptive Trade Practices-Consumer Protection Act by preying upon the elderly, the Attorney General can seek a fine of $10,000 per occurrence, with a maximum fine of $100,000. (Here, "elderly" is anyone 65 or older).

Compared to the standard fine of only $2,000 per occurrence with a cap of $10,000, this penalty should be a significant deterrent to deceptions that focus on the elderly. Is it? Perhaps one of the most nefarious deceptive schemes practices against the elderly is the sale of living trusts by unlicensed businesses. When this issue was raised by a State Senator, the Attorney General's office acknowledged the problem but refused to take any enforcement action. A call to complaint to the Attorney General may not result in any action, but may still be worthwhile as a way to get your complaint on the record.

Internet Resource:
The Attorney General's office complaint form can be completed online and submitted for assistance online. To do so, visit the Attorney's General's office at
WWW.OAG.STATE.TX.US/CONSUMER/CONSUMER.SHTML

Home Solicitations

As a consumer, you are legally able to cancel many in-home sales within a few days after you buy. This legal right to change your mind helps you avoid the pressure wielded by a salesperson sitting in your living room. The purchase can be real property, personal property or services – but they must be sold to you for personal, family, or household purposes. The law does not cover any business-to-business transaction. (And although "in-home" is the usual setting, the law actually applies to any consumer transaction above $25 that takes place outside the merchant's place of business).

When you are an individual consumer, you can cancel an in-home sale until midnight of the third business day after you agreed to purchase the items. If, for example, on Wednesday you sign an agreement to buy aluminum siding, you may cancel anytime until midnight on Saturday.

The salesman is required by law to provide you with a pre-printed "notice of cancellation" so you can more easily exercise your rights. Failure to give you the pre-printed form is defined by law as a deceptive trade practice.

There are a few big exceptions to the home-sales law. First, any sale of insurance is exempt from the law. You don't have a three-day right of cancellation if you buy an insurance policy in your home, including annuities. Second, any transaction that you started at the seller's place of business but that is closed at your home is exempt. Third, any in-home transaction where your attorney is present is exempt. Finally, any transaction by phone, even though you are at home, is exempt.

If the law covers the sale and the merchant delivers the goods to you during the three-day cancellation period, you can still cancel. You must, however, return any goods to the merchant when he refunds the payments you have made. The merchant is not entitled to any compensation for the services he provided before the three days have passed.

You must take reasonable care of any goods that are to be returned. The law, however, does not require that you deliver the goods to the merchant. Ordinarily, the merchant must come get the goods back from you at your home.

Phone Solicitations

Texas Law also regulates computerized telephone calls. It is illegal for any business to use a machine to solicit you unless:

- The machine immediately identifies the caller by name, tells what business is being represented, tells the purpose of the call and gives a phone number where you can contact the company making the call;

- The call is made between the hours of 9 a.m. and 9 p.m., except on Sunday when they must be between noon and 9 p.m.; and

- The machine releases your phone within 30 seconds after you hang up.

If you ever get repeat calls or if the calls continue after the legal hours you should phone the business and instruct them to stop the calls. If they do not, you should complain to the Texas Attorney General's office, which can sue on your behalf. Each violation proven in court can cause a penalty of up to $10,000 against the solicitor.

Texas and federal law also allow you to reject telephone solicitations by registering with the "do not call" lists. The Texas list applies to any telephone marketer calling a Texas residential or wireless phone number. Registration is valid for 3 years, and you can get on the list by mail, by phoning 866-896-6225 or on the Internet. Internet registration is free, but phone or mail registration costs $2.25 for each phone number you list.

> Internet Resources:
> Register for the Texas do not call list at WWW.TEXASNOCALL.COM . Register for the National do not call list at WWW.DONOTCALL.GOV

Illegal Debt Collection Practices

What if you get into financial hot water, and have trouble paying your bills? It is legal for your creditor to hire a collection agency to contact you, but there are limits to what they can do.

A debt collector cannot harass you. Texas law limits the actions a debt collector can take. It is illegal to 1) threaten or use violence, 2) falsely accuse you of fraud or other crimes, 3) threaten that you will be arrested for failure to pay the debt, or 4) to harass you.

When communicating with you, it is illegal for the debt collector to "oppress, harass, or abuse" you. The collector:

- May not use profane or obscene language;

- May not phone you without providing identification; and

- May not call you on the phone repeatedly or allow your phone to ring continuously.

If the debt collector violates these laws, he/she has committed a misdemeanor. You can also sue the collector for deceptive trade practices. You can report violations to the Texas Attorney General's office.

Federal law also provides some protection. If you get repeated calls from a debt collector, you can instruct the collector in writing to communicate with you only in writing. You can also instruct the collector to stop communications with you altogether. After that, all calls and letters must stop (except that the collector can send you one letter saying "see you in court").

> Internet Resource:
> If a debt collector violates these rules, you should report him/her to the Federal Trade Commission. You can make a report online at
> RN.FTC.GOV/PLS/DOD/WSOLCQ$.STARTUP?Z_ORG_CODE=PU01

What if you owe the money, but the debt collector has the facts wrong? You acknowledge owing $200 – but the collector is demanding payment of $845? You have the right to contest the accuracy of the debt collector's information. The law requires the collector to provide forms to you and to assist you in filling out the forms.

Once you have submitted a written notice that you contest the accuracy of the collector's information, the collector has 30 days to investigate. If the collector decides that you are correct, the problem must be fixed and a corrected statement must be sent to anyone who got the false information.

If the collector decides that the information was correct, the collection efforts can go forward. If the investigation has not been completed in the 30 days allowed the collector must 1) stop all collection efforts, 2) presume that your information is correct, and 3) send the corrected information to anyone who got the false information.

The Car Lemon Law

When you buy a new car, you expect it to work flawlessly. What are your legal rights if your new automobile is a lemon?

Your legal rights are contained in the manufacturer's warranty as modified by Texas law. Car warranties vary in coverage, but they must meet the minimum standards set by Texas law. If your car spends too much time in the shop for repairs, even warranted repairs, you may be protected by the "Lemon Law[40]."

A car dealer cannot require you to waive your rights under the provisions of the Lemon Law, and any attempted waiver is void.

You qualify for protection—

- If your car is repaired for the same problem four or more times within the first year you own it; or

- If your car spends more than 30 days in the shop (for any combination of repairs) during the first year you own it. But even so, the dealer gets credit against the 30 days for any days he provides a "loaner" car that is similar to yours.

You must establish that the defects have significantly impaired your ability to use the car and have reduced the market value of the car. These conditions are easily met when a major problem like engine trouble recurs.

When all the law's conditions are met, your first step should be to mail the dealer a "notice of non-conformity." The notice tells the dealer that the car has not met the warranty standards. If the trouble is not fixed, you have the right to either:

- Have your car replaced with a similar vehicle; or

- Obtain refund of your purchase price, less an allowance for the use you received from the car.

If the dealer resists, you should then get help from the Texas Motor Vehicle Commission in Austin. The Commission can hold a hearing, and might order the dealer to replace the car or to refund your money.

If the Commission's help is desired, you must start the proceedings before you have owned the car for 18 months or within 6 months of the end of your warranty. Otherwise, they cannot assist you.

Internet Resource:
The Texas Motor Vehicle Division has produced a video to explain the law, how to bring a complaint, and how to handle a hearing under the law. It is available free online at WWW.DOT.STATE.TX.US/MVD/LEMON/LEMONLAW.HTM along with a complaint form that you can use to start the process.

PROTECTIVE SERVICES

I was contacted by a 66-year-old widow who was under extreme stress. Her home had been broken into several times and items of property were stolen. She had been beaten. She lived in fear of opening the door. Her drug-addicted son was responsible.

If you are a witness to or have cause to believe that there is abuse, exploitation or neglect of a senior, you have a legal obligation to report the events to Adult Protective Services (APS), part of the Texas Department of Family and Protective Services. All reports are confidential and state law provides immunity from potential civil or criminal liability arising out of your report.

APS was created in Texas in 1981. In 2004 (the most current year in which statistics have been compiled) APS investigated 61,342 reports of possible abuse. They confirmed 44,694 reports as actual events. This number is up from 2001, when 40,559 cases were determined to be actual events of abuse.

Elderly or Disabled Adults

Protective services are available to anyone 65 or older or to anyone over 18 with a mental, physical or developmental disability. The definition of "disability" is liberal, so if you are not sure whether a person qualifies, it is best to call anyway. APS' mission is to protect these persons from abuse, neglect and exploitation.

Abuse, Neglect and Exploitation

A large portion of the reports to APS involve "neglect." Neglect occurs when an elderly person is without the goods or services necessary to prevent physical harm, mental anguish or mental illness even though there is a responsible caretaker.

Many other cases involve reports of "abuse" involving intentional injury, unreasonable confinement, intimidation, or cruel punishment of an elder.

The rest deal with "exploitation:" illegal or improper acts of a caretaker who uses the elderly person's resources for the caretaker's own personal benefit.

Reports to APS

Any report that you make to APS is legally confidential. The caseworkers will not even disclose the information in court unless ordered to do so by the Judge. Telephone reports may be made anonymously, but online reports identify you by your Email address. Even so, online reports are still confidential.

> Internet Resource:
> Report abuse of a senior online at WWW.TXABUSEHOTLINE.ORG
> Or phone the APS Hotline at 1-800-252-5400

You have more than a moral obligation to report suspected abuse, neglect or exploitation to APS. Failure to make a report is a "Class A" misdemeanor[41] punishable by:

- A fine not to exceed $4,000;

- Confinement in jail for a term not to exceed one year; or

- Both the fine and confinement.

To commit the crime of "Failure to report," you must have cause to believe that an elderly or disabled person has been abused, exploited, or neglected or is in the state of abuse, exploitation, or neglect. You must then knowingly fail to report the information to APS.

I am not aware that anyone has been charged, prosecuted or convicted of this crime. I suspect that it is not meant to capture innocent bystanders; rather, it is another trap for the person who is actually committing the abusive acts. By law, they must report themselves... and failure to do so is a misdemeanor.

When you do make a report to APS you are immune from civil liability for releasing the information about the abuse. You are protected by law even if you release information you obtained at work – like a bank teller reporting suspicions that a customer is being exploited.

Response to a Report

Upon receiving a report, APS is required to investigate within 24 hours. If it determines the elderly person really needs protection, APS then determines what services are needed, how the services will be paid for and if the elderly person wants the services.

State law gives APS the tools it needs to act. With prior court authorization, it can enter a home (along with a police officer) to conduct its investigation. It can seek an emergency order for protection of an elderly person if that person needs protection but lacks mental capacity to accept or to reject the services. It can also seek injunctions against any person who attempts to interfere with the providing of its services to an elderly person who has consented to the services.

If you witness questionable acts or know someone who may be abused, neglected or exploited, it is your duty to call Adult Protective Services.

PROTECTION AS A VOTER

The Texas Secretary of State has proclaimed that Texas leads the nation in its efforts to increase ballot accessibility for all voters, including elderly and disabled voters. State law requires all polling places to be accessible. The standards for what constitutes an accessible polling place include: a) all polling places must either be on ground level with a street entrance or be accessible by an elevator with at least 36-inch wide doors, b) curbs and stairways must have permanent or temporary ramps, and c) entrances cannot be made inaccessible by gravel, automatic gates, or other barriers that block access to the polling place.

In addition to making the polling place accessible, Texas law requires:

- That a friend or aide may assist a voter in reading or marking a ballot;

- That all polling places have voting equipment that accommodates those with vision or hearing deficits, limited dexterity or strength, or low mobility. The law requires a Direct Recording Electronic device (DRE) at each polling place to enable paperless, computerized voting to maintain secrecy;

- That a person may vote from their vehicle curbside if that person is physically unable to enter the polling place. The Secretary of State recommends that if you need to use this option, you call ahead so election officials will expect you. Call 800-252-VOTE or your local voting office;

- That early voting be available at convenient neighborhood locations to avoid the long lines and crowds that may be present on election day; and

- That voting by mail be available for those who are ill, disabled or 65+ (or who expect to be away from home on election day and early voting days). Voting by mail used to be called "absentee voting" but those restrictions were legally lifted to make the process available to a wider group of voters.

PROTECTION AGAINST CRIME

Although criminal laws are enforced by the State (through the various police forces, District Attorney's offices and Courts) and not by individuals, they do afford extra protection for the Elderly.

Various Texas laws define "elderly" in different ways. The Bill of Rights says that an elderly individual is anyone 60 or older. The legal definition for Adult Protective Services and under the Texas Penal Code says that only persons 65 or older are elderly.

Several criminal statutes have already been discussed on earlier pages. They include:

- Misapplication of Fiduciary Property (page 18);

- Assisted suicide (page 77); and

- Failure to report (page 157).

Several other statutes criminalize certain actions against seniors or enhance the punishment when the action is against a senior. They include:

Injury to a senior

Under the Texas Penal Code a person commits a crime if through an action he intentionally, knowingly, recklessly, with criminal negligence or by omission causes an elderly individual bodily injury or serious mental deficiency, impairment, or injury.

Notice that it can be either an "act" – that is, doing something – or an "omission" – that is, not doing something, that gives rise to the crime. But an omission that results in injury to a senior is only criminal conduct if the person who failed to take the action either:

- Had a legal or statutory duty to act and failed to act; or

- Had accepted responsibility for protection, food, shelter, and medical care for an elderly individual (and the law says that "responsibility" is "accepted" if that person's actions, words or conduct would lead a "reasonable person" – meaning a judge or jury – to conclude that responsibility was accepted).

Intentional or knowingly violating this law is a first-degree felony. Recklessly violating the law is a second or third degree felony, depending on the harm done.

If a caregiver fears this law and wants to avoid committing a crime, the caregiver can withdraw from providing care to the elderly individual. The caregiver can either:

- Notify the elder, in person or in writing, that the caregiver is no longer responsible. The written notice must give all the information required by this law; or

- Notify the Texas Department of Family and Protective Services that the caregiver is no longer responsible.

Fraud Against or Theft from a senior

It is a crime in Texas to cause another person, by deception, to sign any document affecting property or services or the pecuniary interest of any person with intent to defraud or harm the person. Likewise, it is a crime to steal property belonging to another person. When the injured party is elderly, the punishment is enhanced. For instance, fraud or theft that causes $500 to $1500 in damage is ordinarily a class A misdemeanor, but when the victim is elderly the same act is a state jail felony.

Sexual Assault

In Texas, it a crime for an employee of a long-term care facility and one of its residents to engage in sexual conduct. The law presumes that the patient has not given consent for the sexual conduct, which creates grounds for charging the employee with criminal assault. In this context, a "long-term care facility" includes any nursing home, adult day care, assisted living center and mental health facility. The only legal exception is if the employee and patient are married.

PROTECTION AS A DRIVER

A driver's license is precious because it provides independence. But independence must be weighed against other precious essentials: life and safety.

What if a person can no longer safely drive a car? Perhaps it is a specific illness that causes troubles – like a diabetic who might "blackout" for short periods if blood chemistry is out of balance. Maybe it is old age – slower reflexes, poor vision. Is driving a risk worth taking?

A car can be dangerous if used incorrectly. The adage that "driving is a privilege, not a right" is generally true. In order to drive, a person must have a driver's license. In order to get and keep a valid driver's license, a person must meet the requirements of Texas law.

The Texas Transportation Code regulates issuance and revocation of a driver's license. A driver's license may be revoked if:

- A person is found by a court to be incapacitated. If Guardianship is granted over a ward, the Judge can take away the ward's driver's license; or

- A person is, in the opinion of the Department of Public Safety (DPS), incapable of safely operating a motor vehicle; or

- A person fails to provide medical records or has failed to undergo medical or other examinations as required by a panel of the medical advisory board.

Texas Medical Advisory Board

The Medical Advisory Board was created to assist DPS with physical or mental disability decisions. The Board can call together local panels of medical experts to review medical records and examinations. Based on this study, the local panels advise DPS on a driver's mental or physical abilities.

How do they find out about a driver's disability? When a driver apples for license renewal, he/she is supposed to reveal to the DPS any medical condition that might hamper his or her ability to drive safely. This may be used against the driver later. Also, a physician who feels a patient is incapable of safely operating a vehicle can make a report to DPS or to the Medical Advisory Board. That report is legally not a breach of the patient-physician privilege, because public policy seeks to protect the community from unsafe drivers.

If the panel decides the driver's disabilities make his/her driving unsafe, the license can be revoked or suspended. The panel can require the driver to submit to a medical examination. Refusal to submit to a required examination is grounds for revoking the driver's license, whether or not there are any physical disabilities that make his/her driving dangerous.

The final say in the revocation process comes from the local Justice of the Peace or Municipal Judge. If all the evidence indicates the person's driving is dangerous, the

Judge will revoke his/her license. The safety of pedestrians and other motorists take priority to any driver's convenience.

Convincing a person to stop driving can be a very difficult battle. If you feel your spouse or parent is no longer a safe driver, you might consider these strategies:

- Discuss your fear of personal liability. The senior may not care about putting himself at risk, but may think twice about putting you and others at risk.

- Talk to the senior's insurance company to see that he/she has adequate liability coverage. Texas law requires minimum insurance levels, but may be wise for him/her to have higher coverage amounts. The cost will be pricey, but driving has always been expensive.

- Suggest that the senior enroll in a defensive driving course for his/her own safety. Either his/her driving skills will improve, or the realization will emerge that he/she cannot safely handle big city traffic.

- Offer some reasonable transportation alternatives. The family can team up to drive when and where he/she wants to go. You can look into public transportation, taxi service, neighborhood organizations, or moving to an assisted living facility that offers transportation services. Your local area agency on aging can provide details of other transportation services available in your area.

Remember: when it comes to driving, there is more at stake than independence. Health and safety – of the driver, people sharing the road, and pedestrians – must come first.

PROTECTION AS AN EMPLOYEE

Both Texas and Federal law ban discrimination in the workplace based on age. However, the law has very detailed stipulations that can limit its scope. There is a heavy legal burden on anyone who wants to claim age discrimination exists.

Civil Rights Division, Texas Workforce Commission

In Texas, the Civil Rights Division of the Texas Workforce Commission (formerly an independent panel called the Texas Commission on Human Rights) handles employment discrimination claims. In House Bill 2933 passed in 2003 by the Texas legislature, the Commission on Human Rights was abolished and its powers were transferred to the Texas Workforce Commission.

Employment discrimination is outlawed—whether based on sex, race, religion, disability or age. However, age claims are available only if the employee is age 40 or older. Younger people cannot claim age discrimination. Additionally, the law applies only to companies with 20 or more employees.

An employee cannot be forced to retire due to age unless the employee is an executive of the firm and has a guaranteed pension of at least $27,000 annually. If this cushion exists, the employee can be forced to retire starting at age 65.

If you feel you have been discriminated against based on your age, (for instance being passed over for job promotions you feel you deserved) you have the right to complain to the Texas Workforce Commission. You can do so in person in Austin, by phone to 1-888-452-4778 or by mail.

The process begins when you fill out an "intake questionnaire" and file it with the Commission. They will then review it to decide if a claim exists. If they feel there has been discrimination, they will prepare a complaint form for you which you must sign before a notary and return to them within 10 days. It must be filed within 180 days of the time of the alleged discrimination, or the Commission will dismiss it.

Equal Employment Opportunity Commission

The federal Age Discrimination in Employment Act (ADEA) also bans arbitrary age discrimination in hiring, firing, paying, and promoting employees age 40 or older. It bans discrimination in providing fringe benefits like pensions and health insurance, and regulates mandatory retirement age rules. It applies, however, only to companies that had 20 or more employees during a portion of the prior year.

The Equal Employment Opportunity Commission (EEOC) is charged with enforcing this law. Charges must be filed with EEOC within 180 days of the alleged discriminatory act. You can get their help in person, on the web, by mail or by telephone.

Internet Resource:
The Equal Employment Opportunity Commission website is found at WWW.EEOC.GOV. You can phone them at 800-669-4000 (or for a TDD call 800-669-6820).

PROTECTION WHILE VOLUNTEERING

Seniors are ready volunteers. Be it AARP, your local Senior Center, RSVP or helping the community or a neighbor, seniors are among the first to volunteer.

Emergency Medical Assistance

The best interest of the public is served when citizens are ready and willing to help in an emergency. Texas law is designed to protect volunteers who provide help when someone is having a medical emergency[42].

A person who makes a mistake while rendering emergency medical care bears no liability for that mistake, so long as:

- The mistake was not willfully or wantonly negligent; and

- The aid was rendered "in good faith;" and

- Even though the person giving aid may have been legally entitled to payment, in this instance there was no expectation of being paid.

If you are a licensed medical professional and expect to be paid for the emergency services, you are not legally immune. Hence, no volunteer protection is granted under this law to professional emergency room personnel, to someone who represents a business that hopes to be paid for the services, or to an admitting physician in the hospital.

Public policy, supported by the law, is clear: volunteers are encouraged to step in and render aid when a stranger collapses. Even though this law exists, caution is due; use your best judgment and call 911 immediately if you observe a medical crisis.

Non-Profit Agencies

The Texas Charitable Immunity and Liability Act[43] is meant to encourage volunteerism. People who are worried that their volunteer actions will be repaid with a lawsuit and liability find relief in this law.

The Act protects volunteers at a non-profit agency from liability if something goes wrong – but only if the agency and volunteer meet all the legal qualifications.

Under the law, a "volunteer" is someone who works for an organization without being paid (except for expense reimbursement). This specifically includes a medical professional who is working without pay for a charitable organization. On the other hand, an "employee" is not a volunteer because they are paid by the organization. If an officer or director is paid, that person is an employee; if unpaid, that person is a volunteer.

Volunteers are legally protected and immune from civil liability for any act or omission, even if it results in someone's death, or injury, or in property damage so long as:

- The mishap occurred while the volunteer was "acting in the course and scope" of his duties for the organization; and

- The volunteer was acting "in good faith." Good faith means "honest pursuit" of the activities the organization was created to provide.

If the volunteer is providing licensed medical services, the patient must sign an agreement acknowledging that the medical care is being provided for free, and waiving any recovery for damages if something goes wrong.

Volunteers are not protected from liability if:

- An injury results from a volunteer's intentional, willful or wantonly negligent act; or

- An injury results from an act done with conscious disregard for the safety of others.

If the mishap occurs while the volunteer is operating a vehicle then the volunteer is legally liable, but only up to the level covered by existing insurance. Texas law requires all vehicle operators to have liability insurance with the following limits: $20,000 for injury or death of one person, $40,000 for injury or death of two people, and $15,000 for property damage arising out of any one accident.

These protections apply only if you are volunteering with an agency that meets certain criteria. Most tax-exempt organizations under the Internal Revenue Code qualify (though the law does specifically exclude fraternities, sororities and secret societies).

The organization must also have adequate liability insurance. Texas law requires the organization to carry liability insurance that covers $1,000,000 for personal injury and $100,000 for property damage. If it fails to do so, then the organization and its employees do not have immunity (but the volunteers are still safe).

Federal Volunteer Protection

The United States Congress got on the protection bandwagon when it passed the "Volunteer Protection Act of 1997[44]." As a federal law, it currently offers protection to any volunteer who may be liable, and restricts the recovery rights of any plaintiff who files a lawsuit. Additionally, if state law offers more protection to a defendant, the state law will apply.

Under the federal law, a volunteer cannot be sued unless the volunteer is:

- Acting outside the scope of his or her responsibilities;

- Engaging in "willful or criminal" misconduct;

- Not properly licensed to perform the actions that caused the injury; or

- Driving a vehicle. (Note that Texas law does protect volunteers who are driving if the volunteer has adequate insurance. Texas limits liability to the amount of the insurance policy. If there is no policy, there is no limit.)

A volunteer is still liable for any act that is otherwise criminal (including violent crime, international terrorism, any hate crime, a sexual offense, a violation of civil rights or any crime involving intoxication or drug use.)

Make sure the organization with which you volunteer meets all the legally required conditions. When it does, you are legally protected.

Internet Resource:
Want to volunteer and not sure where to start? "Senior Corps" is part of the Corporation for National Service, and feeds into RSVP, Foster Grandparents, Senior Companion Program, seniors for Schools and others. Find more at
WWW.SENIORCORPS.GOV

Chapter 5: Family & Marital Issues

Texas is only one of nine states that use the community property system, along with Arizona, California, Idaho, Louisiana, Nevada, New Mexico, Washington and Wisconsin. Each of those states has local variations; the systems are not identical. The rest of the states are called "common law" states, where the property system is descended from the British system of separate ownership.

COMMUNITY PROPERTY

Texas' community property laws descended from our state's Mexican history. Almost all assets you acquire during marriage are community property. Almost all income you receive during marriage is community property. An asset is presumed to be community property unless there are "clear and convincing" facts which legally show it is separate property.

The opposite of community property is "separate property."

- Any items you owned before you got married are your separate property and remain separate throughout your marriage;

- Any items you acquire after marriage through gift or inheritance are separate property;

- Any recovery you are awarded for a personal injury is separate property (except money to replace lost income that would have been community property); and

- You and your spouse may agree that certain items are separate property via a binding written contract.

One feature of community property is far from obvious: any interest earned on separate property is, by definition, community property unless the spouses agree in writing that it will be separate.

The legislature has done a fast flip-flop on this issue. Before September 1, 2003 the statutory rule just what I said above – interest earned on separate property is community property unless the spouses agree in writing that it will be separate. But from September 1, 2003 until September 1, 2005 the law was changed so that all new earnings generated by the separate property were separate property under all circumstances unless the spouses agreed that it would be community. Then the legislature changed its collective mind[45], and after September 1, 2005 the old rule was re-established. For example:

> You have a certificate of deposit you owned before you married. The CD itself is separate property. The interest from the CD is community property that is silently commingled into your CD. At some point, it becomes difficult to tell where the separate property ends and the community property begins.

> In contrast, you have a certificate of deposit you owned before you married which is separate property. You and your spouse agree in writing (using a Prenuptial Agreement or a Spousal Partition Agreement) that the CD will remain your separate property and that the income it earns will be your separate property. Now, the interest from the CD is separate property and there is no commingling with the community estate.

On the other hand, when you own a separate asset that grows in intrinsic value, the growth usually remains separate property. Capital growth must be distinguished from income produced by a separate asset. For example:

> You have some shares of stock you owned before you married. Growth in the value of the stock is intimately part of the stock, and that growth remains separate property under most circumstances. If the stock was worth $10 per share before you married and is now worth $12 per share, the $2 of growth remains separate property.

There is an exception to this capital growth rule. If the separate property's value goes up because of the personal efforts of its owner, the increase is community property. For instance, if you own a separate property house, an increase in its value could be either community or separate property depending on the cause of the growth. If the value goes up simply because the market is good, then the increase is separate property. But if the value goes up because of the owner's personal efforts (like repairs or improvements) then the value increase is community property.

One other category of property exists: an "equitable interest" in the separate estate of the other spouse, or in the community estate. This was devised by the legislature primarily as a method to divide values in a divorce. For example:

> David is unmarried and buys a house, with a mortgage. Later, he marries Rebecca. They both work, and she pays half the mortgage payments for five years. Then they get divorced. The house is still David's separate property, but Rebecca has an "equitable interest" roughly equal to the contributions she made to the mortgage. She can be compensated for that contribution.

What if David and Rebecca enter into a premarital agreement so they will not have community property, but Rebecca still makes payments on David's house? Now, her "separate estate" has an equitable interest in the house, and she can be compensated if they divorce. But the house remains David's separate property, and the divorce ends Rebecca's homestead rights.

Conversion to Community

The Texas Constitution allows spouses to convert separate property into community property[46]. This has only been true since January 1, 2000 – before that date, there was no legal way to switch separate property into community property, except through "sloppy bookkeeping" that forced the presumption that an "unidentified" asset is a community asset.

The agreement must be written, must be signed by both spouses and must identify the property that is being converted. It does not need to have other "consideration" – that is, no "swap for value" is needed to make the conversion legal. Finally, the agreement must specifically point out that it is a conversion. Without a specific reference to the conversion, the law will presume that any transfer creates separate property of the receiver.

One more point: both spouses must be aware of the legal effect of the conversion. The law provides a disclosure statement, and when it is included both spouses are presumed to understand the legal effect of the agreement.

Presumed Community Conversion?

Texas law has a broad presumption that any asset held by either spouse is community property, unless clear evidence establishes that it actually belongs to only one spouse as separate property. Can one spouse unintentionally "stumble" into converting his separate property into community property? For example:

Husband's mother dies, leaving him $300,000. He invests the money in several CDs, in both his name and his wife's name. Are the funds his separate property, or has he converted them into community property? The legalities in a situation like this can be difficult to unravel. It is clear that when he received this inheritance, it was legally his separate property. If he had invested the funds in his name only, there would be no question that it remained his separate property (except for the new interest earned, which is community property). However, he would have to prove that the funds in this joint account were traceable to his inheritance to overcome the presumption that the funds are community property.

There are two possible legal consequence of putting the money into the joint account with both names: 1) that adding wife's name made her an owner, or 2) that adding her name was simply a convenience and did not change the ownership at all.

The Texas Probate Code contains several provisions that deal with joint accounts. One of them states that a "joint account belongs, during the lifetime of all parties, to the parties in proportion to the net contributions by each … unless there is clear and convincing evidence of a different intent." Under this provision, it would be the wife's burden to prove that husband affirmatively intended to give half the money to her.

The Texas Court of Appeals, in its decision in "In the Matter of Case[47]," looked at a very similar situation. It decided that the provisions of the Probate Code apply. The funds belong to husband as separate property unless wife can prove that he intended to make a gift. His intentions legally control the outcome.

There has not been a court decision yet that says the only way a person can express his intention to convert separate property into community property is by following the new constitutional amendment.

MANAGEMENT OF COMMUNITY PROPERTY

Texas property law has some management features that are unfamiliar to most people. Community property falls into two management divisions:

- "Joint management" community property exists whenever assets are commingled into a joint account or titled in both names. Both spouses have equal rights to control or to spend the assets.

- "Sole management" community property exists when an asset is maintained in one spouse's name alone. That spouse then has the sole right to control or to spend the asset.

A salary check, for instance, payable to you only and deposited into a bank account with your name only, is your sole management community property. Even though the spouses own it equally, they do not have equal management rights.

If you have a sole management asset, your spouse has no control over it. However, if you get divorced, or when you die, your spouse will obtain control over his/her share. You can dispose of your half in your Will to anyone you desire.

Under the Texas Family Code, your share of any community property is not subject to a liability that arises from an act of your spouse, except under a few circumstances. One is if your spouse incurred the debt while acting as your agent. Another is if your spouse incurred debts for "necessaries" like food and shelter.

Any sole management community property held by one spouse is not liable for the contractual liabilities of the other spouse (like credit cards) so long as the holder is not a party to the contract. However, if the other spouse commits a tort (like causing an injury in a car accident) then all the community property of both spouses, whether joint management or sole management, is subject to the liability.

COMMON LAW MARRIAGE

Common law marriage is really called "informal marriage." If you claim that you are married to someone, you must have proof. Generally, your marriage license is that proof. If you did not go through the formal process of obtaining a marriage license and having a wedding, then the public does not know the legal status of your relationship.

What proof is needed? You must establish that you have both agreed to be married, have lived together in Texas as husband and wife, and have told other people that you are married. No specific amount of time needs to pass to create an informal marriage. Both spouses must be 18 or older. The marriage begins the first day that all these legal conditions are met.

You can also use written proof. You may file a "declaration of informal marriage" with the county clerk. They have the form and provide it to you. It must be signed and must be sworn to by both the husband and the wife.

Does a couple who are informally married have to get divorced if they break up? Technically, the answer is "no." If one "spouse" wants to make the type of claims typically made in a divorce, then Texas law says he/she has two years from the date of separation to prove the marriage existed. It is legal to wait beyond two years, but then there is a presumption that the couple was not married – hence, any divorce would be more difficult.

The Texas Supreme Court has ruled that trial courts should be careful about implied agreements to be married. They want a fairly obvious and mutual agreement. It may not be enough to show that just one of the couple said the marriage existed. The court also looks at acts to back up words. For instance, if the "husband" pays the "wife's" medical bills or takes on some other obligation that only married couples usually assume, that act supports an implied agreement to be married.

Technicalities aside, if you've been in an informal marriage that has ended, you should strongly consider going through a formal divorce to close out any lingering legal issues.

PREMARITAL AGREEMENTS

When a senior considers marriage, more often than not it is really remarriage. A second marriage raises many concerns. Unlike youngsters who are just starting out in life, seniors have commitments to honor—perhaps children, perhaps significant savings, and certainly treasured memories.

Although the love and companionship that can be found in a second marriage are of immeasurable value, so is devotion to your first family. You should go into a second marriage with your eyes open, aware that you are empowered to address the issues and find solutions before marrying.

Discussing financial issues may be perceived by your fiancé as offensive. If it is, get on with it now. Certainly it is better to find out you have different attitudes toward money and family before you are legally married. He/she may feel the same worries as you. If you're going to be married, you'll want to find positive ways to discuss important issues. The discussion is certainly not one of the more romantic components of your relationship, but it is a vital component.

Your discussion might include the practical issues such as: Where will you live? Who will pay living expenses? What debts exist? When you take a vacation, will you pay or will expenses be split? Will you pay for the other's nursing home bill if that day arrives?

The discussion should also introduce several legal issues. Will you allow a community property estate to be created? Will investment income be community or separate property? Is your fiancé's estate taxable?

Seek full resolution and mutual understanding of those questions before marriage. The discussion may lead you closer to marriage, or may teach you that this person is not the person you should marry.

If you both feel that marriage remains a good choice, your next step is to see an attorney about a premarital agreement. You may be tempted to settle upon a loving, trusting verbal understanding. Don't. It would be non-binding, and would fall apart under pressure after the honeymoon ends. You need a loving, trusting written contract that will be legally binding.

You can agree to keep your estates separate. In the contract, the two of you can agree on how to pay living expenses, what assets each of you own and what happens when the marriage ends. The premarital agreement can go so far as to avoid the creation of community property altogether.

You can agree to do away with the confusing rules regarding income and growth of capital assets. Essentially, you are legally allowed to set up your own system of legal ownership, even though it is completely different from regular Texas law.

Once you have determined that certain assets belong to you – and are neither affected nor changed due to the new marriage – then you can choose how to manage and how to dispose of the assets. You can declare in your Will or in a living trust who your heirs will be. Estate administration is simplified because your assets are clearly identified in the premarital agreement and your heirs are clearly identified in your Will or trust.

Partition

If you failed to make a premarital agreement, the door is not locked. Even a couple that has been married for years can convert community property into separate property. The legal tool is called a "partition agreement" because the existing community estate must be split.

The Texas Family Code allows you and your spouse, in a written partition agreement signed by both of you, to convert some (or all) of your community property into separate property. You may record the agreement with your county clerk, a practice I strongly encourage.

The partition process may be done by the two of you at any time during your marriage. It can include property that is currently community and property that might become community in the future.

Fraud Not Allowed

The partition is not valid if it is done to "defraud" a preexisting creditor of one of the spouses. Also, one of the spouses may later challenge the validity of the agreement by proving that:

- The agreement was not signed voluntarily, or

- The agreement was "unconscionable" when it was signed and that before signing, the challenger did not know and was not provided with a fair and reasonable disclosure of the assets and the debts of the other spouse.

You should hire an attorney to draw up the agreement and to review your Wills to be sure they conform to your new pattern of ownership.

DIVORCE

... and your Will

Under the Texas Probate Code, divorce alters your Last Will and Testament. Any provision giving any assets to the former spouse is void. Also, any provision making the former spouse Executor is void. This happens automatically when the divorce decree is signed.

Will provisions leaving assets to a spouse do not become void until divorce is final. If you die before the divorce is final, your spouse still inherits. If you are in the process of getting an unfriendly divorce, you should modify your Last Will and Testament immediately to remove your spouse.

If the divorce is on friendly terms, and you still want to devise something to your ex-spouse, you must make a new Will after the divorce was granted.

... and your Living Trust

Until recently, State law did not address what happens to the assets inside a living trust when the spouses who set it up divorce. Now, the Texas Probate Code[48] states that divorce or annulment of a marriage voids any provision in a living trust that provided benefits to the former spouse. Those funds are treated as though the former spouse disclaimed their benefit, meaning that items will pass as though the former spouse had already died. Also, any appointment of the former spouse as Trustee is voided by the divorce.

... and your Power of Attorney

Divorce also affects your durable power of attorney. Texas law voids any powers given to your ex-spouse the moment a divorce decree is signed. If you are getting divorced, you should proactively change your power of attorney no later than the moment you file for divorce. Don't wait for the decree to be issued, or your spouse can still use the power of attorney to wipe out your finances. (Of course, with the fiduciary duties now owed by an agent to a principal being open to enforcement in criminal court, your spouse would be sadly mistaken to abuse his/her fiduciary duty).

... and an Incapacitated Spouse

What about divorce when one of the spouses is incapacitated and under a Guardianship? Even people with mental impairment can divorce under our "no-fault divorce" law. It is enough for one spouse to claim that discord or conflict of personalities has destroyed the legitimate ends of the marriage and that there is no reasonable expectation of reconciliation.

Divorce signals not only the end of marriage; it is also the end of the financial partnership. The real problem when one spouse is incapacitated is whether he/she can adequately defend property interests. If a guardian has been appointed, the guardian can protect the ward's interests. In the case of Stubbs v. Ortega[49], heard in the Court of Appeals in Fort Worth, the wife had Alzheimer's disease and was under Guardianship. Her husband was abusive, so her guardian sued him for divorce. The husband claimed it was against public policy to allow an incapacitated person to get divorced.

The court decided that although it has been public policy to "foster and protect marriage and discourage divorce," this does not bar an incapacitated person from obtaining a divorce. Under state law, a person with mental illness has all the rights, benefits, responsibilities, and privileges guaranteed under the law, including domestic rights. The court allowed her guardian to petition for divorce on her behalf, and it was granted.

The 2001 legislature added another twist. If there is no guardianship, but there is a community administration under which the well spouse is managing the community property, then the probate court must be informed of any divorce suit brought by the well spouse. At that point, the probate court can choose to remove the community administrator, appoint a guardian, and can even hear the divorce case as a matter incident to the administration.

GRANDPARENT'S RIGHTS

When your child gets a divorce, you and your grandchildren may be innocently caught in the crossfire. You do have legal rights as a grandparent, but they are limited. The US Supreme Court, in its year 2000 decision in Troxel v. Granville[50] said, "…the interest of parents in the care, custody, and control of their children—is perhaps the oldest of the fundamental liberty interests recognized by this Court." The parent-child relationship cannot be interfered with lightly, not even by the grandparent.

The Texas Court of Appeals ruled in 2003 that the Texas grandparent rights statute is constitutional only if interpreted in a way that is consistent with the Troxel decision[51]. The parent's power can only be interfered with when there is a compelling reason, and the only allowable compelling reasons are 1) if the parent fails to care adequately for the child, or 2) if denying access to the grandparent would significantly impair the grandchild's physical health or emotional well-being. The burden of proof is on the grandparent.

As a consequence of those court decisions, the legislature updated the Texas Family Code in late 2005. Grandparent rights were expanded by allowing not only access to the grandchild, but also "possession" of the grandchild (which means the grandchild would live with the grandparent, not just visit). Grandparent rights were limited by requiring the grandparent to prove that "denial of possession of or access to the child would significantly impair the child's physical health or emotional well-being".[52]

A grandparent can intervene and make a request for access or possession in a lawsuit originated for that purpose, may intervene in an existing divorce matter, or may request modification of a divorce that was already concluded. Seeking assistance from an attorney with extensive family law background is wise. Discuss legal fees and court costs up-front to avoid surprises.

To bring an action, the grandparent must prove that the parent is the "biological or adoptive parent" of your grandchild. If you are the step-grandparents from a second marriage, the Court cannot help you unless your child officially adopted the grandchildren after marrying their natural parent. You must also prove that your child (the parent) is either:

- In jail for the last three months; or

- Has been ruled incompetent; or

- Has died; or

- Does not have actual or court-ordered possession of or access to the grandchild (in other words, you cannot piggyback on your child's access to the grandchild).

The most recently reported Texas grandparents' rights case, In re Keller[53], dealt with a grandfather wanting visitation of his 21-month-old granddaughter. His son, the granddaughter's father, had died and her mother refused visitation. Though the trial court granted visitation, the appeals court reversed that decision, holding that to "protect parents' fundamental rights under the Due Process Clause," the courts must "presume that a fit parent acts in the best interest of his or her child." The burden of proof is on the grandparent to overcome that presumption.

A PARENT AS A DEPENDENT

As reader, you may not be the grandparent looking down the generational ladder at your descendants. You may be a child looking up the ladder to your progenitors, providing support and assistance to your parents.

There is no law in Texas that requires a child financially to support a parent. Nonetheless, it is a widespread and loving practice. There are few rewards other than the knowledge that you have done right. One possible legal reward, however, is a tax deduction.

The Internal Revenue Code lists five conditions that must be met before you can claim your parent as a dependent.

- The parent must receive over half his/her support from you. Note that the "fair market value" of the lodging you provide to them counts as part of the support. Keep close track of your expenditures to be sure this condition is met;

- Your parent must be U.S. Citizen, a resident alien, or (if you are a U.S. taxpayer who lives in Canada or in Mexico) can live with you in Canada or in Mexico;

- Your parent must not file a joint income tax return for the tax year you want to claim the dependency deduction;

- Your parent's gross income during the tax year must be less than the exemption amount for that tax year. For this test, your parent's gross income does not include that part of his/her social security that is tax-free; and

- Your parent can be treated as a dependent even if he/she does not reside in your home (so long as that parent meets all the other four required conditions).

If your parent passes all of the tests, then you may legally deduct the exemption amount on your tax return. The amount changes from year-to-year. If your parent does not meet any one of the tests, then you cannot take the dependency deduction.

If he/she passes all the tests or if he/she passes them all but #4 (dealing with income) you can still deduct any medical expenses you paid on your parent's behalf. This deduction for medical expenses can be, at times, more valuable than the dependency deduction.

Medical expenses can only be deducted if insurance did not reimburse the expense. Also, the total medical expenses claimed on your return will have to exceed 7.5% of your adjusted gross income to be deductible.

When trying to reach the 7.5% threshold, you can add together medical costs you paid for yourself and for your parent. You can include the cost of transportation essential to medical care, premiums for health insurance, hospitalization insurance, and membership fees for group health plans and HMOs. To help, you should keep close track of all payments for physician, hospital, nursing home and dental care.

Chapter 6: Planning Your Estate

Having an estate plan should be as common as having a bank account. You open a bank account because it creates security, provides a way to control your finances and lets you plan for the future. You make an estate plan for the same reasons. But if you don't create your own plan, the state has one all set up for you... without knowing who and what is important to you, and without asking your opinion.

INTESTACY: THE STATE'S PATTERN

If you have not acted to make a Last Will and Testament, you are "intestate." For many years, Texas law was inconsistent with the pattern most people would select for themselves. However, in the early 1990's section 45 of the Probate Code was amended to make the law more closely match the most common expectations.

That Texas law says your spouse inherits your half of the community property if you die intestate. Most married couples want all their assets to go to the surviving spouse; the kids can wait until both parents have died. The law is now consistent with this desire (except for the "second family" exception discussed below, which is still like the former law in that the children are heirs even when there is a surviving spouse.)

You may be saying to yourself, "Well, the pattern the state set up for me sounds pretty good. Why shouldn't I just use it?" The answer lies not in the results, but in the legal process your family must endure to get to those results.

Using a Will, the legal procedures known as probate can be quite simple. However, if you die intestate the odds are that the legal procedures will be very lengthy and expensive. You may have the same heirs either way, but they have to spend more money to prove they are your heirs if you fail to provide a Will.

Preplanning streamlines the procedures, saves money and identifies your heirs and what they will receive. If you don't yet have a Will, you should make one.

The Second Family Exception

Texas law since 1993 allows your spouse to inherit from you even if you do not have a Will. One exception was carried forward from the old law: if you are married for the second time, your kids from the first marriage inherit your half of the community property instead of your spouse. For example

> Greg and Abby are married and have three children. Greg dies, and several years later, Abby marries Sam. They are married nearly 20 productive years and accumulate substantial wealth. Abby dies intestate – without a Will. As a result, her three children inherit her ½ of the community estate. Sam must be content with the remaining half.

The only ways to defeat this legal exception are to make a Will or a Trust that gives explicit instructions to the contrary, or to rely on other non-testamentary transfers like Rights of Survivorship.

Your "Default" Will

If you decide not to make a Will, here is a sample of the "default" Will state law has written for you. Does it do what you want?

> To my dear Spouse:
>
> I did not make a Will. If all of the children are the product of our marriage, then I leave to you my entire community estate. You may have to go to Court to establish your rights.
>
> If I have any kids from previous marriages, I leave my half of our community property to those children. You have to get by on the half of the assets you already owned, and you may have to manage them jointly with those children.
>
> I give all of my Separate Property real estate to the children, none to you. I give 2/3 of my Separate Property personal assets (like mementos, heirlooms, and investments) to the children and 1/3 to you. You all can fight over who gets which specific asset.
>
> If you and the children die before me, I give everything I own to my "heirs at law," who may be our grandchildren or my parents or my siblings. They may have to go to court to decide who gets what.

In conclusion, you and the children must start a confusing and expensive legal process. Instead of seeing my lawyer for a Last Will and Testament to make an easy transition after my death, I accept state law as my "Will."

Signed: Your Spouse

I'll say it again: The only way to defeat this legal pattern is to make a Will or a Trust that gives explicit instructions to the contrary, or to rely on other non-testamentary transfers like Rights of Survivorship. You must pre-plan to avoid the state's pattern.

COMMUNITY PROPERTY SURVIVORSHIP AGREEMENT

Spouses are now legally empowered to use a Community Property Survivorship Agreement (CPSA) to automatically pass their community property to the survivor without probate when one spouse dies. A properly written, signed, and filed CPSA simplifies the complex tasks faced by a widow or widower. A Will is still necessary to cover issues that the survivorship agreement cannot address.

Other tools you can use to help avoid intestacy include setting up assets as "survivorship" property, making gifts while you are living or using a funded living trust. Proper use of these tools might eliminate the need for probate.

Historically, our community property system thwarted attempts by married couples to create survivorship arrangements for their community property. When one of the spouses died, title could only pass to the survivor through the Last Will and Testament. The CPSA law changed that pattern.

A CPSA is a nontraditional approach to estate planning. It automatically passes your community property to your surviving spouse, without the need for probate. Its legal foundation is very reliable: the Texas constitution was amended in 1987 to allow the process, a statement that both the legislature and the voters desired this law. The current Probate Code contains exact parameters for the procedure. It is as reliable as any law can be, if you follow the proper procedures.

Formalities

The community property survivorship agreement is a contract between you and your spouse. Both spouses must sign the agreement, which should be prepared by an attorney. You must then file it with the county clerk. If you own real estate in more than one county, you should file the agreement in both counties.

You can file your CPSA with your County Clerk by mail or by hand. If you mail it, you may want to send it via certified mail to confirm delivery. Most clerks charge $16 for the first page you are filing and $4 for each added page of the same document, but check with your clerk to verify. The clerk will retain the original for a few weeks then mail it back to you.

No standard document has been printed commercially for distribution. You need to see your attorney, or obtain it through the Internet.

> Internet Resource:
> You can obtain a CPSA from the Legal Documents Store at WWW.PREMACK.COM (click on "legal documents").

Procedures

Probate of a CPSA is not ordinarily necessary. The agreement passes title to community property without any further action. The statute says that: "An agreement between spouses creating a Right of Survivorship in Community Property that satisfies the requirements... is effective without an adjudication." It works to keep your estate out of court – most of the time – but it is not necessarily absolute.

After the death of a spouse, the survivor can optionally apply to the court for an order stating that the agreement satisfies the requirements of law. Then, if a dispute arises, the probate court can guarantee validity of the agreement. The Judge will need to see the original agreement, so keep it in a safe place and let someone else know its location. Once an order is signed, anyone who should deliver property to the survivor may do so without hesitation.

In a very few instances, stubborn and out-of-date title company examiners refuse to accept a CPSA after the first spouse dies. This is frustrating, since they are ignoring well-established Texas law. Typically the worst thing they will ask for is an "affidavit of heirship" to bolster the spouse's claim to legal ownership. The surviving spouse can challenge the title company; can even obtain a court order forcing the title company to accept the CPSA. But because it is less expensive to give in to their demand for an affidavit of heirship, the economy of the situation leans against court action to enforce the CPSA. My discussions with the legal staff at Texas' largest title insurance company indicate that each situation is reviewed independently. If the CPSA complies with state law, it should be accepted as a valid title transfer.

Who Should Use a CPSA?

Most married couples with assets below the estate tax exemption amount can consider a CPSA. Be aware, however, that there are circumstances where a CPSA is not appropriate and a Will is necessary for depth of planning. A CPSA cannot accomplish the following tasks:

- It cannot pass title to any separate property. However, recall that an amendment to the Texas Constitution allows spouses to convert separate property into community property.

- It cannot name a "backup" heir if there is no surviving spouse;

- It cannot pass assets to someone other than the surviving spouse; and

- It cannot reduce estate taxes if your estate is larger than the exemption amount.

If those exceptions do not apply to you, then a CPSA may be a good tool to help you avoid probate. When properly written it streamlines procedures, it is straightforward and it will save you time and money.

LIVING TRUSTS

There are several kinds of trusts. Some can be set up to help others while you are alive and some to help others after you die. One type, the "living trust" is set up to help you during your lifetime and then to help others after you die. It helps solve your own estate and probate problems. It may also help you achieve other commendable goals while you are living and able to enjoy the benefits.

A living trust is a contract to manage your assets and to protect you if you become disabled. A living trust is typically revocable and amendable, so you can change it when you need to.

A living trust has three important internal positions:

- The "Grantor" establishes the trust, provides assets to the trust, and determines the trust's goals. The grantor can revoke or amend a living trust unless that right is given up when the trust is first created.

- The "trustee" manages the trust and its assets on a day-to-day basis. You select a trustee (typically, you select yourself) who acts as legal owner and manager of the assets.

- The "beneficiaries" receive the trust's bounty. A typical living trust names its grantors as beneficiaries. The beneficiaries are entitled to the use and enjoyment of the trust's assets. When you name yourself as beneficiary of our own living trust, you continue to have access to the funds in the trust and to use the trust's other assets (like your home and car).

Why would you want to set up a living trust? Here are some common goals:

- To help avoid probate;

- To save estate taxes;

- To help manage your assets while your are well and if you become disabled; and

- To assist and to provide for your loved ones.

Let's look at each of those goals in more detail to see exactly what they mean and how they can be accomplished.

Avoiding Probate

One requirement of a well-functioning living trust is that you transfer ownership of the bulk of your assets to the trust. This is called "funding" the trust. Why is it necessary? A trust can only manage the things it owns – and if you become disabled the trust needs to manage your assets. Also, if you die, the trust helps avoid probate for assets that are registered in its name.

Probate may still be needed if you leave assets outside the trust (perhaps you acquired them after it was set up and forgot to transfer them to the trust.) A Will is still needed to dispose of the incidental personal items you possess.

Should you use a living trust to avoid probate? Cost can be a determining factor, and varies depending on your choice of attorney and the complexity of your plans. Here are two scenarios, using hypothetical cost estimates:

ONE: Husband and wife have a home, a CD worth $65,000, some savings and a car. They are debt free, and want all assets to pass to the surviving spouse when one dies. Attorney written Wills should cost them between $150-250. Someday, probate may cost about $2,000. On the other hand, a living trust could cost $1,500 out-of-pocket today. This couple might decline a living trust in favor of Wills, and allow the estate to go into probate.

TWO: Husband and wife have a home, stocks, investments, a Car and real estate worth $1,220,000. One spouse is a few years older than the other, and they are anxious about possible illness. A living trust may cost this couple around $3,000. Wills would cost about $1,200 and probate could cost from $2,000 - $6,000 down the road. This couple is likely to select a living trust to avoid probate, instead of using Wills.

Hence, the potential cost of probate is often the determining factor. Remember that probate in Texas is often simpler and less expensive than its general reputation would have you think.

One additional warning: some lawyers write living trusts that say, "When I die, the assets in this trust should pass to my estate" or "under my will" or "as part of my testate estate." This choice, while legally allowable, means that your estate must go to probate. The trust does nothing after you die. Instead, your Will must be probated and the trust assets are given to your Executor. There are not many good reasons for making this choice in your trust – except that from the lawyer's perspective it produces another fee for doing the probate. If your lawyer suggests it, carefully question the reasons.

Remember also to make your decision on the Trust versus Will question based on unbiased input. Some attorneys and insurance agents offer free seminars. Often they have only one goal: to sell you a living trust. They don't care about the legal alternatives that may be more suited to your needs. They won't give you a valid comparison. Seek balanced advice by going directly to a CELA or to a CPA.

Saving Estate Taxes

If your estate is large enough – in 2006, larger than $2 million – then your living trust can save estate taxes by including a shelter trust. This can only be set up while both spouses are living, then when one spouse dies the trust assets are split into two separate trusts. This method eliminates federal estate taxes on up to $4,000,000 in 2006-08.

If you are widowed or single, you automatically receive the maximum federal credit available. Your living trust will not give any greater tax savings than you are already entitled to receive. You may need to focus on other tax saving techniques. These might include an Irrevocable Life Insurance trust, a charitable trust, and lifetime gifts to family members.

Note that these tax savings can be accomplished with a Will also. The main advantage of using a living trust is the avoidance of probate plus tax reduction, instead of just tax reduction.

Managing Your Assets

When you establish a living trust, you are typically its beneficiary and its trustee. But you may want to allow someone else to be the trustee, or at least have a standby trustee waiting in case you need help.

Perhaps the day will come when you feel overly challenged by management of your assets and want assistance. Perhaps your spouse has died, leaving you alone and in charge for the first time. Perhaps you have been informed of an illness, and want to plan an orderly transition. Or maybe you are retiring and plan to travel a good part of the year, and you need someone at home to guard the nest egg and to pay your routine expenses.

Because you have selected a standby trustee, management of your assets is not interrupted if you decide to shift control. The alternate trustee continues to handle your business affairs as a fully capable manager. Investments continue without interruption, payments are made on time, and your expenses are managed. Your trustee would pay all your medical bills and provide for your continuing health care.

In this way, your living trust continues to protect you and your assets. As its beneficiary, you remain entitled to all of the income generated by the trust, and remain entitled to benefit from the trust assets if you are disabled.

Providing for Your Loved Ones

A living trust can be written so that part of it mimics a Will – that is, it can contain instructions for the distribution of your assets after your death. You can provide benefits to your heirs, and you can also choose to provide benefits to someone while you are alive. With a living trust, you have considerable flexibility. For example:

Jack and Betsy have been married 48 years. Jack has always handled the family finances, but he hasn't been doing so well lately. The doctor fears Alzheimer's disease may be slowly disabling Jack.

Jack and Betsy decide to set up a living trust and to transfer their home, CDs, stock, savings, and cars to the trust. They select their son Wesley to act as trustee. Their goal: to be sure that Jack's illness does not reduce their income or ruin their reputations. Additionally, they want Betsy to be cared for as long as she lives, and they want their granddaughter's college education to be encouraged.

As trustee of the living trust, Wesley can invest the assets conservatively to protect the principal and to generate income. He will then apply the income to pay Jack's medical bills and Betsy's living expenses.

As Jack becomes less capable, there is no freeze on assets. Their son continues management without interruption. If Jack was still in charge, bills would be left unpaid and investments left unattended. Betsy would be in real trouble, especially if Jack's signature was required on something. She might be unable to access their savings, and be forced to start Guardianship proceedings over Jack. But the living trust has made these difficulties vanish.

After several years pass, Jack dies. There is no probate since all their assets are titled to the trust. The trust continues for Betsy's benefit. Betsy's period of mourning and depression has no effect on the finances, since Wesley is still managing all funds.

When Betsy dies, there is also no probate since the assets are still titled to the trust. The trust continues in Wesley's capable hands, providing a college fund for their granddaughter. When she is out of college, Wesley is permitted to terminate the trust and to distribute the remaining funds as instructed in the trust made years earlier by his parents.

Jack and Betsy's foresight in setting up the living trust helped them avoid ruin during Jack's illness, provided for Betsy's continued security, helped pay for college for their granddaughter, and ultimately released the funds to their heirs. This all happened without a moment in court, as a private and confidential process.

Funded v. Unfunded Trusts

If you decide to use a living trust, your assets can be transferred two ways:

- You can change title to your assets the same time the trust is established (a "funded" trust); or

- You can put in only enough to start the trust's existence (an "unfunded" trust.) Sometimes this is also called a "stand-by trust."

An unfunded trust is less dependable than a fully funded trust. If your goal is to avoid probate, and to do so your trust must own your assets at the time of your death, an unfunded trust may fail you.

With an unfunded trust, you must have a strategy to move your assets at a future date. This is usually done with a durable power of attorney. Here's how it works:

You set up an unfunded trust—putting perhaps $100 into a new bank account under the trust's name. At the same time, you create a durable power of attorney, authorizing your agent to "dump" your estate into the trust if you become ill. The agent must be relied upon to follow your instructions, and must act quickly since the agent's authority ceases when you die.

If your agent acts too slowly, or if your death is rapid, there is not enough time to transfer your assets into the trust. All financial powers of attorney legally terminate when you die. If you die unexpectedly, the unfunded trust provides no significant benefits. The agent would have needed several weeks to move your assets into the trust.

If you die before the agent finishes moving your assets to the trust, then the trust fails to manage your assets and fails to keep your estate out of probate court. You still own the assets when you die, so probate is necessary. The standby trust was meaningless and wasteful.

On the other hand, using a funded trust is a more certain strategy. With it, you create the trust and see that your assets are transferred at that time. There is no reliance on an agent, nor is there a risk that your death will be too sudden for your agent to respond and "dump" assets into the living trust.

Using a funded living trust is a particularly effective way to avoid the confusion that results when you own real estate in more than one state. Typically, if you reside in Texas yet own land in another state, then you must probate your Will in both places. By removing the asset from your testamentary estate (that is, allowing it to pass to your heirs through the terms of the trust instead of the terms of your Will) you can avoid multiple probates.

Choosing the Trustee

Selecting the proper trustee is the key to a successful living trust. Your trustee is the manager of the trust assets, and is the person who must follow the instructions laid out in the trust. When you create a trust and give it ownership of assets, the trustee is owner of the "legal title" – that is, has control over the assets. As such, this type of control is very different than naming someone as agent under a durable power of attorney, and is consequently more reliable.

Being Your Own Trustee

With a living trust, you may be your own primary trustee. What is the benefit? As your own primary trustee, there is little practical difference between before and after the trust was established. You own legal title to the assets (and as beneficiary you also own the "equitable title") so you retain full control.

So long as you are healthy, you can continue to be your own trustee. But should you become ill, or simply desire management assistance, a well-written trust instrument will provide for an alternate trustee to assume your duties. The transition is "seamless"—there is no need for court intervention or legal process to hand over control.

You can also elect to turn over control from the beginning. If you do, you must select several persons to serve as trustee in sequence. The goal is always to have a trustee you have chosen, and never be left to rely on the courts to appoint a trustee for you.

Selecting your trustee and alternates must be done carefully. Choose someone you trust deeply, who has good business sense, and who desires to assist you. The emotional component should not be overlooked: your trustee becomes your caretaker and your watchdog. For this important role, you should select someone with whom you will be comfortable.

Bank Trust Departments

Are you required to have a Bank act as trustee? No. An individual can easily manage the trust for you. However, a Bank may offer some advantages:

- Professional management;

- Support staff; and

- Increased income that may result from the investment opportunities open to the Bank.

Many people worry that involving a trust department will be either too expensive or too intrusive. Those are valid concerns. However, if your trust is written with adequate safeguards and if you carefully select the institution that will be your trustee, you should be all right.

Banks do charge a fee for their services, while individuals often act as trustee without drawing a fee. Each Bank's fee structure is different, but is usually based on a percentage of the assets in the trust.

Ask for their fee structure before you hire a trust department. Most of them charge based on the size of your estate. For example, an estate of $300,000 may pay a 1.5% annual fee for trust services at one bank, and but only 1% at a different bank. Rates vary at different institutions and so does the level of personal attention you will receive.

Trust Department as Backup

You do not have to activate the trust department's services immediately. You can name yourself as the initial trustee, and the trust department as backup. Then, they will only become active (and only charge a fee) after you become disabled or upon your death. You can choose the timing of the bank's involvement and choose the degree of management they are to offer.

Your trustee, whether a Bank or an individual, has very specific legal rights and duties spelled out in the Texas Trust Code. These provisions can be adjusted in the living trust agreement to fit your desires.

Your living trust provides unique planning alternatives. If the goals we've discussed match your goals, you should consider a living trust.

High Pressure Trust Sales

Have you thought about attending a free seminar on living trusts? Let me give you a few extra things to think about while you re-read that advertisement.

Controls on Attorneys

The State Bar of Texas, which is charged with enforcing the Disciplinary Rules that all Texas lawyers must follow, publishes guidelines on advertisement of living trusts. They require that without objective substantiation "a lawyer may not advertise that a particular approach to a legal problem ... is superior" when compared to other "accepted and appropriate approaches" to the same problem.

Specifically, the Bar says ads touting the exclusive use of living trusts can be misleading, and may create unjustified expectations among consumers. Look at an ad that ran in a major newspaper a few years ago (before the estate tax exemptions went up) and compare it to the guidelines:

> The ad states, "with a living trust . . . if you are married and your estate is worth less than $1.2 million, there will be no federal estate taxes to pay." It goes on to say "without a living trust (even if you have a will) . . . if you're married and your estate is over $600,000, without proper tax planning your family may owe federal estate taxes of 37%-55%."

Looked at from a narrow perspective, both of these statements were true. But the State Bar warns that a lawyer may NOT advertise that "The use of a living trust in and of itself will reduce or eliminate estate taxes..." that "Estate tax savings can be achieved only by use of a living trust," or that "The use of a living trust will achieve estate tax savings that cannot be achieved using a will."

The ads lead you to believe a living trust ALWAYS saves taxes. They ask you to believe absence of a living trust (even with a will) results in high estate taxes. In truth, either a Living Trust or a Will can provide exactly the same estate tax relief. To do so, either document must contain a tool known as a "shelter trust." If a living trust does not also contain a shelter trust, it will not save any taxes. The solution to estate tax woes does not lie solely with living trusts as the advertisers wish you to believe.

Another tactic used by advertisers is that "probate could take months or years, and probate fees could be substantial." In contrast, a living trust transfers your estate "quickly without the expense of probate." Again, both these claims are often true.

However, the State Bar points out that it is misleading to say that probate "is always lengthy and complicated," or that probate "should always be avoided." I've handled many situations where probate was simple and cost effective. I've handled the opposite, where probate was complex and expensive. A living trust might save time and money, or it might waste time and money—it depends on the specific situation.

The State Bar rules conclude that lawyers may offer free seminars on estate planning in general, and may advertise that a seminar will discuss the advantages of living trusts. To be fair, I must point out that I often advocate the benefits of living trusts. I've handled many situations where the effort of creating, funding and maintaining a living trust saves time and money. But I believe that a living trust is not the sole solution to tax and estate problems. Every person has unique attitudes and unique problems, and needs exposure to a unique set of solutions.

Beware Biased Advice

One size does NOT fit all. When a salesman makes his living selling widgets, he wants to sell you widgets. But your lawyer isn't supposed to be a salesman; your lawyer is supposed to be a professional. A living trust might be right for you, or it may not. You'll never know if you listen to someone whose goal is to sell you a living trust. Your lawyer should find out what best fills your needs, not sell you whatever makes the most profit for the lawyer.

Direct Trust Sales by Non-Attorneys

If you are like thousands of other seniors, you have received fliers from an estate planning company telling you to come to their free seminar. The flier says that some new laws took effect on January 1 "that could make it a felony to gift money, property or hold accounts in joint tenancy."

In fact, there were no such law changes. The flier is misleading and you should regard it as trash. It is similar to a postcard many seniors received claiming that "As of January 1, even with a will your estate and assets will go through probate when you pass away." There were, in fact, no changes to Texas probate law of that type.

These "estate planning" companies are not licensed to practice law in Texas. You might think, "Great, if they are not lawyers they'll be less expensive." In fact, these illegal operations often charge higher fees than licensed attorneys. They also avoid the controls imposed on licensed attorneys who bear professional liability for errors. Licensed attorneys are typically insured for malpractice, and answer to the State Bar for ethical breaches. The companies that put out these fliers are not subject to those rules, nor to any regulation. Lawyers are not perfect, but we are educated in our field and are well regulated.

These companies use a salesperson to gather your information. Typically, the sales representatives are insurance agents – good at the important job of selling insurance, but not qualified to give legal advice. They then pass your information on to a "trust mill" in another state, and return the forms to you. Often, you agree to have an attorney "represent you" by reviewing the documents. Don't be fooled by this arrangement – that attorney never meets you, never assesses your unique needs, and provides you no service. On the other hand, that attorney gets a lot of business from the trust mill and is under pressure to rubber stamp all their documents.

The people who sell only trusts, and nothing but trusts, have one aim: to sell you a trust. As such, they may not tell you about other viable options. Other options include, for instance: durable power of attorney, Joint ownership with Right of Survivorship, or a Last Will and Testament.

I strongly advise you to stay away from non-attorney trust sales. While your goals may be fulfilled with a living trust, don't ever jump to conclusions as to what is right for you. See a certified legal advisor to compare and contrast the costs and benefits of a living trust versus other planning techniques. Always aim to achieve your goals with as simple and cost effective an approach as possible.

Internet Resource:
Many State Attorney General's offices have taken action against "strong-arm" trust sales. Read an article by the State Bar of Texas at
WWW.TEXASBAR.COM/TEMPLATE.CFM?SECTION=ELDER_ISSUES&CONTENTID=8
366&TEMPLATE=/CONTENTMANAGEMENT/CONTENTDISPLAY.CFM
Or one by the State Bar of Michigan at
WWW.MICHBAR.ORG/PUBLIC_RESOURCES/TRUST_KITS.CFM

Generic Trust Forms

I'm sure you have seen the packets in bookstores with a trust form for ten or twenty dollars. You need to ask yourself these questions: how long and hard did I work to save my assets? Do I really feel safe trusting the management and disposition of all my hard-earned assets to a $20 generic form?

The generic form may be missing many important provisions. For instance, it may omit provisions relating to section 11.13j of the Texas Tax Code. The omission could put your homestead tax exemption at risk, which could cost a whole lot more than $20 to fix. The generic form may omit clear instructions on when an alternate trustee takes over management. Such a shift in control could be triggered if you become disabled, so the trust must have a clear definition of disability. The generic form may omit clear provisions relating to distribution of assets when you die.

Additionally, the generic form will not include the other legal documents that should accompany a living trust (like a pour-over Will and a Durable Power of Attorney). A short generic form is never enough to address all the complex issues of planning your estate with a trust. If you are really curious, buy the form and take it to your attorney or a bank trust officer. They can look at the generic form to highlight the things it does right and the things it fails to do.

Your Attitude toward a Trust

Various responsibilities you have when you create a living trust can be viewed as negative – or can be viewed simply as part of the peace of mind in having a living trust. It depends on your attitude.

Some people may feel that the complexities of having a living trust are drawbacks. Some may find the same complexities to be beneficial.

A fully funded living trust requires you to transfer ownership of your assets out of your name into the name of the trust. Ownership of assets must be registered with the trust itself (perhaps making you feel that you are losing control of your assets). However, you are allowed to be the trustee of your own living trust (which means that so long as you are competent, you are the manager of the trust).

A fully funded living trust must be dealt with regularly for the rest of your life. It is the active owner of your resources, and you are its beneficiary. When you want money, you must deal with the trust. When you sell an asset you must deal with the trust. When you receive income, you must deal with the trust. Many feel that this is a very light burden, but some people never get comfortable with the new style of asset management. In reality, it is not much different than you would handle things without the trust – still balancing your own checkbook, paying your own bills and making your own investment decisions.

A living trust eliminates probate if it owns your assets when you die. However, if you leave a single stock certificate, a single bank account, or a single plot of land outside the trust, probate may still be necessary. Of course, certain items may never become part of the trust at all – like your IRA or a life insurance policy. The type of item that already has a designated beneficiary typically stays out of probate as well.

> Internet Resource:
> The Federal Trade Commission has some good advice and resources to help you decide when a living trust would be appropriate for you. Find it online at WWW.FTC.GOV/BCP/CONLINE/PUBS/SERVICES/LIVTRUST.HTM

Documents Accompanying a Living Trust

If you prepared a living trust, it becomes the foundation of your estate plan. As important as it becomes, you still need several other legal documents to help round out your plan. These include:

A Pour-Over Will

This type of Will says, essentially, that any asset not owned by the trust when you die is willed to the trust. It is called "pour-over" because it is designed to gather any assets not yet in the trust and "pour them over" into the trust's ownership. The pour-over Will should be written to be ready for probate – even though it is your hope to avoid probate, you want it to be ready just in case. For example:

> Margie decided to create a living trust so that her son could receive her estate without probate. She was very careful about putting all her assets under the name of the trust.

Several years after the trust was established, her good friend Liz asked Margie for a loan. Wisely, Margie declined to give Liz any of her own money. But the friendship called for some action, so Margie offered to cosign a loan for Liz at the bank. The bank was happy to extend the loan if Margie would deposit $10,000 as collateral. This Margie did, but made that new deposit in her own name, not the trust's name.

All would have gone well but for Margie's sudden illness and death. When her son went to the bank to get the $10,000 – showing his credentials as successor trustee of her living trust – the bank insisted that he probate her Will before it would turn over the money. He probated her pour-over Will, and the money was funded into the trust.

If Margie had made only her trust (and not a pour over Will) her son would have had a terrible time getting his hands on that $10,000. Because her attorney recommended a pour-over Will to complement the trust, her mistake was no more than an inconvenience.

A Durable Power of Attorney

Again, the trust is your legal foundation. But it cannot do everything for you. If you become disabled, the trustee can manage any assets that belong to the trust. But the trustee cannot handle your personal affairs that are unrelated to the trust. For that, you need a durable power of attorney. For example:

Don set up a living trust and set about funding it with his assets. He also signed a durable power of attorney to his son Brian. About a week after he signed the trust, Don had a minor stroke. While the doctor saw to his recovery, Brian used the power of attorney to finish what Don had started. He changed the bank accounts, brokerage account and house over to the trust. Although Don recovered, his trust would not have accomplished its goals had Brian been powerless to convey assets.

Another example:

Don's living trust is in great shape, fully funded and operational. Don has another minor stroke, and while he is in the hospital he gets a letter from the IRS about last year's taxes. Brian can use the power of attorney to hire counsel for Don, get information from the IRS and try to settle the tax problem for his father. Without the power of attorney, Don would be on his own at a vulnerable moment.

Advance Medical Directives

Just a quick reminder: while you are thinking about the issues and making the plans, be sure to include a Medical Power of Attorney and a Directive to Physicians. While these have no real relationship to your living trust, they do round out your plans and shouldn't be overlooked.

Homestead Protection

If you put title to your house in a trust, will the house be exposed to liabilities, or does it still have a homestead's protection? There is a debate over this in the legal community. Some say that since the trust is revocable your homestead continues to be exempt from creditor's claims. Some say the house will be at risk because the trust has become owner.

Perhaps the most conservative solution is to convey your home to the trust, but to retain a "life estate." When you do so, you are considered to be the homeowner and it will definitely be protected from creditors. However, immediately upon your death it will belong solely to the trust. Hence, you avoid probate and your home is protected from creditors.

Revoking a Living Trust

Most living trusts end automatically, as scheduled by the trust's creators, sometime after the trust creators have died. But from time to time, the situation that you thought called for a trust may completely change. You may decide to do away with your trust ahead of schedule.

If you want to revoke your trust, you must first verify that you left that door open when you created the trust. If you gave up the right to revoke the trust – that is, you made it irrevocable – then you cannot shut it down. Otherwise, the trust document itself should recite the steps you must take to revoke it. This is generally done by signing a written statement that declares the trust ended.

After you sign the revocation statement, you need to "un-fund" it by taking the trust's name off your assets. Do this by contacting your bank, broker and other financial institutions. They may require a letter of instruction, and the whole process could take several weeks.

As you revoke the trust, you must decide on a new and appropriate form of ownership for those assets. You also need to be certain you have an alternative plan – probably a new Will – to identify your heirs.

GIFTS TO INDIVIDUALS & NONPROFITS

Any time you wish, you may give away all or any part of what you own. Frequently, gifts are given to children or to grandchildren. Although no special reason is needed, you might give one of your children extra money to pay back a loan or you might give your grandchild money for college tuition. But whenever you make a gift, for whatever reason, you must think about federal gift tax.

Annual Exclusion

You have an annual IRS gift tax exclusion of $12,000, as indexed. You may legally give any person up to $12,000 in any year without even thinking about the gift tax effect.

The exclusion covers an unlimited number of recipients. If you have three children and six grandchildren, you may legally give each of them up to $12,000 (for a total of $108,000) without worrying about gift taxes. You can do this one time each year if you want.

Indexing of Exclusion

The annual exclusion was set at $10,000 in 1981. In mid-1997, Congress passed an update rule: starting with 1999 the annual exclusion was indexed for inflation. It uses the same cost of living allowance (COLA) that is used to calculate increases in Social Security checks. It took several years before the exclusion actually increased, because it must be rounded down to the nearest $1,000.

The COLA went up by 2.5% in 1999, so the gift tax exclusion might have been $10,250 but due to the rounding down to the nearest $1000 it stayed at $10,000. In 2002 the first actual increase bumped the exclusion up to $11,000 and it took until 2005 for the exclusion to hit $12,000.

Tuition & Medical Care

Tuition and Medical expenses are special exceptions. The amount you give for these purposes can be unlimited, and does not even count against the $12,000 annual limit if you follow special rules.

You can make a tax-free tuition gift for anyone, whether they are in your family or not. However, you have to pay the tuition directly to the school or pay the medical bill directly to the medical facility. You cannot gift the money to your children or grandchildren expecting them to pay bills directly. If the funds are put in any hands other than the school or medical facility, gift tax may be due.

For gifts of tuition, the student must be attending a "real" school – it must maintain a full time faculty and have regularly enrolled students. The money can only be for tuition. Any gift you give to help pay for room and board, transportation or entertainment will count against the $12,000 annual gift exclusion.

Another way to help pay tuition is to buy US Savings Bonds. Although this type of gift does count against the $12,000 annual limit, the bonds can be cashed without paying income taxes under certain conditions.

You would gift the savings bonds to your children, with the understanding that they will be held until tuition bills for the grandkids are due. The income tax break is available only if the bond owner was age 24 or older when the bonds were issued. The tax exclusion is valid only for the student's parent or the student. As a grandparent, you cannot cash your own bonds and exclude the income.

Do not gift savings bonds that are older than December 31, 1989. The law behind this tax break applies only to newer bonds issued after that date. Other restrictions apply, so talk to your tax advisor before you make a move.

While we're on the subject, I'll mention two more tax breaks to help educate your grandchildren. First, education IRAs became legal on January 1, 1998 and were expanded in 2001 and renamed "Coverdell Education Savings Accounts". Contributions are non-deductible and limited to $2,000 per year, but the accounts grow tax-free. Money can be withdrawn for college or for K-12 education, and withdrawals are tax-free.

Second, "529" plans for college education were also expanded in 2001. To make 529 plans even more attractive, the Texas legislature has rendered them legally exempt from execution – that is, the money in a 529 plan cannot be seized to pay your debts, even if there is a court judgment against you. Thus, 529 plans join other exempt assets like the homestead, life insurance and retirement accounts.

Though authorized by federal law, 529 plans are created by the states and are typically administered under contract by a financial institution. The Tax Act of 2001 expanded 529 plans, and all 50 states now offer them. Each state's plan is different and you may need a financial counselor to advise you on the right one for your needs.

What are the advantages of a 529 plan? First, like an IRA, the earnings and growth are not subject to income tax. Surpassing the IRA, a 529 also allows tax-free withdrawals so long as the money is spent on qualified educational expenses. Thus, there can be zero income tax from the day the education account is established.

Second, any funds you contribute to a 529 plan are removed from your estate for federal estate tax purposes. Once removed from your taxable estate, it will not be subject to federal estate taxes. This is true even though you retain certain powers over the funds. For instance, you have the right to reclaim the funds -- but if you do, you must pay the income taxes, pay a 10% penalty, and the funds are back in your taxable estate.

Third, you can switch the 529 over to another beneficiary. If, for example, your granddaughter's college costs less than expected so there is money left in her 529, you can switch it to your grandson (or to a future born grandchild).

Fourth, you can contribute in an accelerated fashion. Federal law allows you to contribute 5 years worth of your $12,000 gifts (that is, $60,000) in a single year. You can double that if grandmother and grandfather both make identical contributions. By doing so, you could set aside $120,000 for a grandchild's college fund instantaneously.

529 plans have other pros and cons. If you would like even more details, visit my website at www.Premack.com for additional internet based information. Talk to your financial advisor to see if a 529 plan or savings bonds will work as a gifting strategy for you.

Internet Resource:
Read more on savings plans for your grandchildren's education at
WWW.COLLEGEBOARD.COM/STUDENT/PAY/ADD-IT-UP/395.HTML

Split Giving

Your annual exclusion can be combined with your spouse's exclusion to double the amount you can give away in a year without gift tax. This is called "split-giving." It requires the approval of your spouse and the filing of a gift tax return. For example:

> You are in your second marriage and have your own rather substantial estate. You also have three children and six grandchildren from your first marriage. On your own, you could give each one of them $12,000 each year. Your second spouse likes your family but has no intention of giving them any gifts. You can ask your spouse to consent to a "split gift" so that you utilize the $12,000 that your spouse could have given to your family. You give them that extra $12,000 from your own money, for a total tax-free transfer of $24,000 to each of them. This costs your spouse nothing at the same time that it increases the amount you can transfer tax free.

Lifetime Exclusion

If you give an individual more than $12,000 in a year (or $24,000 if you are splitting the gift with your spouse) you must file a gift tax return. Will you owe any tax? It is typically your choice whether to pay the gift tax or not. If you don't want to pay it, you can claim part of your $1 million lifetime gift tax exclusion. For example:

> You have a rent house that you want to give to your daughter. It is worth $65,000. You can deed it over to her in a single year. You'll have to file a gift tax return showing that the first $12,000 was tax-free, and that the next $53,000 was taxable. You can then choose whether to pay the resulting tax, or to reduce your $1 million lifetime exclusion to $947,000.

Basis Warning

Be warned that the recipient of a gift keeps the same basis as the donor. If you give away something that has capital appreciation, the recipient will owe capital gain taxes when the item is sold (just as you would have). But if the recipient inherits the item, the step up in basis rules apply and can eliminate, or at least greatly reduce, the capital gain tax.

IRREVOCABLE TRUSTS

So far we have only examined arrangements that are revocable. The choice to make a trust *irrevocable* must be made very deliberately. Once you start an irrevocable trust on its course, you cannot stop it until it reaches its destination. That may be in just a few years – if the trust is for a grandchild's education – or may be decades away; it depends on the purposes you set for the trust.

You might establish an irrevocable trust as an estate tax-saving tool. The trust could receive a gift from you, which reduces the size of your estate. You save on estate taxes because there is less for the IRS to tax. Giving assets to an irrevocable trust allows you to direct the use and application of the assets after they are shifted to the trust. For example:

> You want to give $12,000 to your grandson for his education but you fear he will spend it on fast cars and beer. You decided to give the gift to an irrevocable trust, and ask your attorney to write the trust so that it will only pay money for educational expenses. If your grandson wants the benefit, he'll have to go to school. He can get a job and use his own money to buy beer (if he still wants to).

There is a technical tax problem, however. If you give money to your grandchild directly, it is thereafter under his control (and out of your control entirely). But if you give money to a trust, your grandson does not control it (rather, he has a "future interest" while it stays under the trustee's control). Federal tax law does not allow a "future interest" to use the annual gift tax exclusion. Hence, if you give $12,000 to an irrevocable trust, you may owe gift tax on the transfer. To get both advantages, estate-planning lawyers came up with an alternative called a "Crummey trust."

Crummey Trust

The word "Crummey" refers to a 1968 lawsuit between the Crummey family and the IRS[54], in which the IRS lost. The Crummey trust uses a "limited right of withdrawal" to get around the future interest problem.

Under the Crummey rules, if a trust allows its beneficiary a window of opportunity to take some money out, then the future interest becomes a present interest. The opportunity is structured as a 30-day right to withdraw the greater of $5,000 or 5% of the trust's principal.

Once this right exists, you hope that the beneficiary will elect not to use it. It is fair to warn the beneficiary that use of the withdrawal power may eliminate your desire to give the trust any more money next year.

Using a Crummey trust, you can put that $12,000 gift into trust for your grandson, and still not pay a gift tax on the transfer. It is as though the gift was given directly, even though the funds remain under the trustee's experienced guidance.

Irrevocable Life Insurance Trust

In a large estate, owning life insurance poses an estate tax paradox: every dollar of new insurance increases the size of your estate and therefore increases your estate tax. Buying $100,000 new life insurance increases your taxable estate by $100,000. Assuming your estate is already larger than the exemption amount, your tax increases due to the purchase of that new life insurance.

In this situation, an Irrevocable Life Insurance Trust (ILIT) can help control the size of your estate. Using an ILIT keeps the new life insurance from being included in your taxable estate. Since the new insurance, once owned by an ILIT, does not increase the size of your estate, the estate taxes do not go up. All of the insurance proceeds are available to benefit your family. For Example

If your estate is valued at $2,200,000 and you are single, the gross estate tax will be about $90,000 (in year 2006). If you buy life insurance of $100,000, you can get caught in a loop. Now your estate is $2,300,000, and you'll owe about $135,000 in estate tax (again, calculating this based on year 2006 rates). Your tax went up by $45,000. Do you thereby purchase another $45,000 of insurance to cover the new tax? If you do, your estate goes up to . . . well, you get the idea.

To get off the loop, you can buy the insurance in an ILIT. This keeps the value of the insurance out of your estate. However, you must live with restrictions on your access to the insurance. You must irrevocably give all ownership rights in the insurance, including the right to borrow against the cash values.

What if you already have a life insurance policy? You can move it to an ILIT, but it will remain in your taxable estate for the next three years. If you put a brand new policy into an irrevocable life insurance trust, it never becomes part of your taxable estate.

Typically, an ILIT is also structured to be a Crummey trust. You give the trust an annual gift, and the beneficiaries have a limited right of withdrawal. This makes the gift exempt from gift taxes (so long as it is below the annual allowable amount). The trustee then uses your contribution to pay the insurance premiums when they come due.

After your death, the insurance proceeds are paid to the ILIT. This money can be used to purchase assets from your estate so there will be liquid dollars available to pay the estate tax. Your family can be the trust's beneficiaries so they end up with your assets. The government gets less tax and your assets are preserved.

Charitable Trusts

The Internal Revenue Code was not designed only to collect government revenues; it is also a primary vehicle for social reform. Allowing you to reduce your taxes by sending money to a charity encourages and motivates charitable behavior. No gift tax is charged when you donate to charity, and the charity does not pay income tax on your donation.

Income Tax Effect

In their most basic form, charitable gifts are quite simple. For example, when you give $1,000 to the Alzheimer's Association you take a $1,000 deduction from your income tax. In the 28% bracket, you eliminate $280 of income tax that year.

Your overall charitable deductions in a single year cannot, however, exceed one-half of your "contribution base", which is defined by the IRS as your "adjusted gross income" (income after deducting IRA, Keogh, or SEP contributions) computed without considering any net operating loss carry-backs.

If, for example, you had $80,000 income and made a $7,000 Keogh contribution, your "contribution base" is $73,000. Half of that, or $36,500, is your maximum allowable charitable income tax deduction for that year.

You may recall that Congress modified the limits for a short time in 2005 in response to the crisis produced by hurricane Katrina (the Katrina Emergency Tax Relief Act). One of its provisions – intended to encourage charitable gifts as a disaster relief measure – allowed cash gifts made to charity between August 28 and December 31, 2005 to be deducted from the donor's 2005 tax return up to 100% of adjusted gross income. The tax law returned to the regular limit of 50% for 2006 and beyond.

Estate Tax Effect

You can reduce the size of your estate by making a direct charitable gift. Reducing the size of your estate also reduces the amount of estate tax that may someday be due. For example, if you give $30,000 to charity, the following happens:

> If you are in the 28% bracket, you save $8,400 on that year's income tax. You reduce the size of your estate by $30,000, and after your death, the estate pays less estate tax. Tax savings depend on the overall size of your estate. The most you will save is 46%, so a $30,000 gift can reduce estate taxes up to $13,800. Because of income tax and estate tax savings, your $30,000 gift actually costs you only $7,800 (2007 figures).

Ways to Give

There are various ways to donate to a charitable organization:

- Give cash, which makes valuation of your gift very easy.

- Give personal property or real estate. The value of this type of gift is more difficult to define, and you may have to pay for an appraisal to substantiate your tax deduction.

- Give life insurance, which multiplies the power of your dollar. If you give a charity $30,000 that is the whole amount they receive. But if you buy life insurance using the $30,000 to pay a single premium, the charity will receive the entire death benefit that should greatly exceed $30,000.

- Give your charity a more loosely defined benefit, like the income or the "left-overs" (remainder) from an investment when you die. This can be accomplished by using charitable trusts or pooled income funds.

Because it may be unsettling to you to give away enough of your asset base to reduce significantly your taxes, more complex methods of giving have been devised so you can retain certain benefits at the same time you are helping a charity. Some of the more complex techniques follow.

The Pooled Income Fund

When you make a gift to a charitable organization under this method, the organization pools gifts from a variety of donors and you receive interest payments on your donation for your lifetime. However, income paid to you by the fund is taxable just like any other income.

In the year you make the fund contribution, you get an income tax deduction for the value of the "remainder" (calculated using IRS provided figures). For example, if you are 62 years old and give a Pooled Income Fund $25,000 with guaranteed interest of 5%, the value of the remainder and your deduction is $12,007. In the 28% bracket, this results in tax savings of $3,362 the first year.

After your death, the charity keeps the principal of the gift. Your estate gets the added benefit of being smaller and therefore paying less tax. In the 46% estate tax bracket, this amounts to saving another $11,500. Overall, your tax savings are $14,862 and you were paid interest on the full $25,000!

Your gift to a Pooled Income Fund must be irrevocable. The charitable institution pays to have the Fund's legal charter created, so the gift should not have any extra legal fees. Many other donors contribute to the same Fund, and all the contributions are pooled.

Internet Resources:
Some examples of already existing pooled income funds can be found on the Internet. For example, the American Lung Association discusses its pooled income fund at WWW.WPG.CC/STL/CDA/ARTICLEDETAIL/1,1001,177-431,00.HTML and the Arthritis Foundation information is at 24.104.4.141/DONATE/PLANNEDGIVING/POOLED.ASP. Many other charities have similar pooled funds.

Charitable Remainder Trusts

These are similar to Pooled Income Funds, but are handled on an individual basis, not pooled with other donor's gifts. You make a gift to charity and receive income for life. You pay income tax on any income you receive. You may structure your trust income to be guaranteed or to fluctuate, and you can pick from any qualified charity whether they have a planned giving department or not.

You benefit by receiving a tax deduction when you make the gift, by potentially increasing your monthly income, and by reducing the size of your estate. You also benefit by reducing your future capital gain taxes. For example:

> You are widowed and have a $3,000,000 estate. Part of it is a piece of land your father gave you. It is worth $400,000 but your basis is only $20,000 because you received it as a gift. The land could be sold, but the capital gain tax would cost a fortune. In the meantime, it does not produce any return for you and you have out-of-pocket expenses to pay the real property taxes.

> You decide to create a Charitable Remainder Trust, and, being willing to part with the land, you donate it to the trust. The charity sells the land, but pays no capital gain tax (because it is a charity). The full $400,000 is invested in bonds returning 8%. The 8% return is paid to you. This is new cash flow of $32,000 each year that you did not previously have. While you must pay income tax on it, you still have more money than before.

> Now, you decide to establish an irrevocable life insurance trust and buy life insurance for your children's benefit. You qualify for a policy worth $400,000, and use part of that new $32,000 income to pay the premiums. When you die, the trust pays the $400,000 death benefit to your children without estate tax.

Your kids still get $3 million, the charity gets $400,000, and the government gets fewer estate taxes and fewer capital gain taxes. This is legal and encouraged and entirely beneficial to everyone involved.

Unitrusts and Annuity Trusts

With a Charitable Remainder Trust, you receive regular income from the donation. If the amount of your income fluctuates, it is because you chose to base your return on a percentage of the trust's ever-changing annual value. This is called a unitrust. If the amount of your income is fixed, it is because you chose to calculate your return as a fixed portion of the value of the gift. This is called an annuity trust.

If you make a gift of $25,000 to a unitrust promising to pay 5%, your income will vary. In the first year, the trust might purchase stock and bonds valued at $25,000. Your 5% is calculated against the value of the trust's principal, so you would get $1,250. In the second year, the stock market might go up so the trust principal might be worth $27,000. Then your 5% income would be $1,350 the second year. If the value goes down, so does your income.

If you give $25,000 to an annuity trust that is required to pay you 5% interest, your income will be constant. Each year, regardless of the value of the trust or the amount of its income, it would pay you $1,250.

For either type of Charitable Remainder Trust, you may deduct from this year's income tax the value of the remainder to be kept by the charity. However, the deduction amount differs for an annuity trust and a unitrust because the amount left over for the charity varies for each type.

The annuity trust tax deduction is the value of your gift minus the value of your annuity. If you are 62 and give $25,000 while keeping a 5% return, the IRS values your deduction at $16,000. In the 28% bracket, this would reduce your income tax the first year by $4,480.

The unitrust tax deduction is the value of the remainder, calculated using IRS provided figures. If you are 62 and give $25,000 while keeping a 5% variable return for life, the deduction is valued at $11,620. In the 28% bracket, that reduces your income tax by $3,254.

Charitable Lead Trusts

This is the exact opposite of the Charitable Remainder Trust and Pooled Income Fund. In a Lead trust, you make a gift to charity and the charity keeps the income instead of paying it to you. However, when the trust ends, the original gift amount is returned to you or to your heirs.

You benefit by getting an income tax deduction each year the trust is in effect. You also get the pleasure of assisting a worthy charity while retaining your estate for your heirs.

The amount paid to the charity may be a guaranteed annuity or a unitrust amount. The annuity is a fixed payment chosen by the donor for a certain number of years or for the whole lifetime of the donor. The unitrust amount is a set percentage of the original donation paid to the charity for a certain number of years or for the whole life of the donor. For example:

You create a Charitable Lead annuity trust. You fund the trust with $50,000 and require that the income of $5,000 be paid to the charity each year. Each year you would be entitled to deduct from your income tax the $5,000. In the 28% bracket, that is an annual savings of $1,400.

When you die, the trust would cease its payments to the charity and the $50,000 would pass to your heirs. Your estate tax is not reduced with this technique. If the managers of the charity are wise, they might use some of your annual contribution to buy life insurance payable to the charity when you die. If so, the death benefit would go tax free to the charity. Your heirs get the money, but so does the charity.

LAST WILL & TESTAMENT

Why do thousands of people avoid making a Last Will and Testament? Here are three possibilities:

- A Will reminds people of their mortality, which makes people feel uneasy;

- A Will reminds people that their personal or financial affairs are a mess, and they don't want anyone to know about it; and

- A Will makes people deal with and pay a lawyer, an experience many people would rather avoid.

There are serious reasons to put these concerns aside and prepare a Last Will and Testament. Here are some of the benefits of making a Last Will and Testament now:

- You get to choose your heirs. If you have no Will, Texas law determines who receives your assets when you die. Usually the heirs identified by the law are different from the heirs you would choose.

- Your heirs save time and money. If you have no Will, your estate is more likely to go through a complex, expensive and intrusive legal process. If you think your paperwork is an embarrassing mess now, planning for a Will gives you the perfect opportunity to get things organized.

- You can reduce taxes. If you have no Will your estate may be exposed to higher estate taxes. The Estate Tax is still our federal government's highest tax. There are many legal and ethical ways to reduce this burden. To avail yourself of many of them, a Last Will and Testament is the first step.

- You can show your family how much you care. If you have no Will, you may be creating family quarrels. No matter how well your children get along, your death will cause anxiety. Too often, this flares into disputes over family "treasures" or land. It separates brothers and sisters for decades. Your guidance at this stressful time, in the words of your Will, provides your family the direction it needs to stay together. Having a Will simplifies life for your survivors by defining who gets your assets when you die and appointing someone to administer your affairs.

The cost and effort it takes to prepare your Last Will and Testament today is inconsequential compared to the increased harmony it provides your family after you die.

Preparing a Last Will and Testament is neither expensive nor unsettling when you find the right attorney. Ask for a referral from your friends, your doctor or hospital, or your senior community center. Find a CELA in your area, or use the lawyer referral agencies listed in this Guide.

Three Texas Will Varieties

Texas allows three varieties of the "Last Will and Testament," each with its own technicalities: nuncupative, holographic and formal.

Nuncupative (Spoken) Wills

Based on a statute dating to 1879, the days of trail drives and gunfights, the spoken Will was designed for frontier days when written documents were not as common.

Many limitations are imposed on the spoken Will to increase its accuracy. Prized possessions (like a horse and saddle) should not be handled frivolously!

Hence, your spoken Will must be made during your last sickness while at home; if not at home, you must have been at another location for at least ten days before you can make a spoken Will, unless you are removed from your home due to sickness, then make the spoken Will and die before you return home.

Clearly, a cowpoke on a trail drive could not rely on a spoken Will to pass on his personal possessions. He wasn't at any particular location long enough to qualify.

Even if your location is correct, your spoken Will may give away no more than $30 worth of personal items unless three witnesses hear the Will spoken.

If six months pass between the date of speaking and the date of a Court hearing, the three witnesses must have written down what they heard (but must have written it down within six days of hearing it) for the Will to be brought into court at all.

A spoken Will cannot be used to pass ownership of land under any circumstances. The writers of the law felt that land was too valuable a resource to be entrusted to the spoken word.

Finally, when it comes time to "probate" a spoken Will, the people who could have inherited if the spoken Will did not exist must be notified and have a chance to contest the spoken Will.

The question is: why go to all this trouble just to give away $30 worth of personal property? The spoken Will, while still found in the law books, has little use in today's society. You should have a correctly executed holographic or formal Will.

Holographic Wills

For a holographic Will to be valid, Texas law requires that it:

- Be written entirely in your own handwriting,

- Contain the date on which it was written, and

- Be signed by you. Witnesses are not necessary.

Though handwritten Wills are valid, they are not efficient and can cause problems. Since you prepare your own Will, you initially save some attorney's fees. But eventually the inefficiency of a handwritten Will overcomes the initial savings and the overall cost rises.

Various factors make a handwritten Will less reliable and potentially more expensive than a formal Will:

If any part of the Will is not in your handwriting (for example, is typed or preprinted) the Will is not valid. Avoid writing it on preprinted letterhead or hotel stationery. Beware of "fill in the blank" Will forms that ask only for your signature at the end without witnesses; they will not be recognized as valid in Texas.

Since you are writing your own Will you must be cautious about mistakes or incorrect use of words. The "plain meaning" of your words is not always the legal meaning that will be attached when your handwritten Will is interpreted by the court.

Your handwritten Will is unlikely to contain legal "shortcuts" (that save time and money) which will be contained in formal wills written by professionals. Probate is likely to take much more time and be more expensive if courtroom probate is necessary.

With all of its difficulties, a handwritten Will is still better than no Will at all. If you do not currently have a Will, follow these easy steps:

Take a blank sheet of paper, and in your own handwriting identify yourself, give the date, and describe where you want your assets to go when you die. Sign the handwritten Will. Then call your lawyer for an appointment to make a formal Will.

Formal Wills

The third type of Will, the "formal Will," is most thorough. Generally prepared by an attorney, it must be dated, signed by the person making the Will, and signed by two witnesses who are fourteen or older.

Your formal Will should take advantage of the following valuable options:

Criteria for Selecting an Executor

When selecting an Executor, you should consider two main factors: experience and convenience. It is most important that your Executor be educated and capable of working with your attorney, your bank and your broker. He or she should have enough experience to understand your finances.

It is also important that your Executor have the time and availability to do the job. Now that your son has moved to California, do you have someone else who may find it more convenient to be Executor? If not, your California son can legally be your Executor.

Selecting Alternates

Realizing that you need to name one or more alternate Executors as backups becomes a challenge when there is no one you trust to do that job.

Who do you consider? First, you can look to the heirs named in your Will. You probably identified certain individuals or charitable organizations to receive your estate. Perhaps one of those persons is trustworthy enough to act as alternate Executor. Perhaps you could ask a representative of one of the charitable organizations to act as Executor.

Second, you can name a bank trust department to act as Executor. Though you don't want to establish a trust, and it is logical to assume a trust department would require a trust before they'll provide assistance, many trust departments recognize that acting as court appointed Executor is also a valuable service.

Independent Administration

Using the correct legal wording in your Will frees your Executor from detailed court supervision. This saves time and reduces attorney's fees. Look in your Will to see that this language appears: "My Independent Executor shall not be required to take any action in any Court in the administration of my estate other than the probating of this Will and the filing of any inventory, appraisement and list of claims required." Variations in the wording are allowable, and it is best if the Executor is referred to throughout your Will as your "Independent Executor."

Waiver of Bond

Unless your Will states otherwise, Texas probate law requires your Executor to purchase a bond (an insurance policy guaranteeing the Executor will act honestly.) The bond must be paid for from your assets. However, if you select an Executor you trust without reservation you can waive the bond and save the money.

Self Proof

When you die and your Will goes before the Judge, reliable proof must be presented showing the document offered is indeed your Will. There are three methods of proving a Will's validity:

- The first requires the witnesses to testify in court. However, people in our mobile society tend to move frequently; they may be living in Arizona when you need them. Transportation costs and compensation add to your costs.

- The second requires a handwriting expert (or two persons familiar with the signature of the Will's maker) to examine the Will. This can only be used if the original witnesses are not available. Someone familiar with the handwriting must appear before the Judge. If you use an expert, he must be paid, which increases costs.

- The third is best: a legal Self Proving Affidavit can and should be attached to your Will. You and the witnesses sign the affidavit at the same time you sign the Will, and the affidavit is notarized. After your death if the Will is presented to the Judge, the affidavit is complete proof. Because you preplanned, an inconvenient cost was eliminated.

Any Will you make may also have the following features:

- It should appoint an Executor, with alternate choices in case your first choice is not available;

- It should identify your heirs and alternate heirs if your first choices are not available;

- If you have minor children, it can appoint guardians for them;

- If any of your heirs are disabled or are minors, it can create a trust to protect them; and

- It can contain a plan to reduce or to eliminate estate taxes.

Carefully Identify your Heirs

Writing a Will allows you to identify your heirs clearly. You can include or exclude whomever you like. There is no legal requirement that you give an inheritance to anyone in particular. No one has the right to demand to be your heir; it is your choice entirely.

The best approach is to identify your heirs by name. If you have two children named Tom Smith and Sue Baxter, your Will can say "I give my estate in equal shares to Tom Smith and Sue Baxter." Little doubt remains about who they are.

Heirs are sometimes identified by "group" or by "class." Your Will might state that you leave your estate to your "children" or to the "issue of your children." In that case, identifying who belongs to those groups is vital, and naming the members of a class somewhere in your Will is a good idea.

A case out of Dallas[55] points out the potential problems:

> A woman (Kathleen) made her Will knowing that her son had adopted his stepdaughter (his wife's daughter from her prior marriage.) The adoption legally changed his stepdaughter (Martha) into his legal child.

> When writing the Will, Kathleen wanted to leave Martha out, so Sarah said that she left her estate to her son's "bodily issue." By using the phrase "bodily issue," Sarah meant to limit the inheritance to children who were the biological descendants of her son.

> After Kathleen died, Martha claimed to be the "bodily issue" of her adoptive father so she could get part of Kathleen's estate. The court, upon reviewing the law, decided that Martha should inherit. According to the Texas Family Code, an adopted child is treated just like a biological child.

Kathleen could have avoided the problem by defining terms in her Will. She could have stated, "Bodily issue does not include adopted children." She could have simply said, "I give no inheritance to Martha." Kathleen's opportunity to get it right has passed, but your opportunity is open. The more specific you can be, the more likely your wishes will be understood.

Adopted Children

As the above case points out, a person adopted into the family is treated by the law as though that person was a natural biological child of the adoptive parent. But in reality, that adopted child has two sets of parents: the ones who adopted her and the ones who gave her up for adoption. Can a child given up by the parents still be their heir, or does the act of giving up the child terminate the relationship?

Since the mid-1950's Texas law has allowed a biological child to inherit from a biological parent, even if that child was adopted by another parent (but only if the biological parent made no Will or other estate plan).

That law changed on September 1, 2005[56]. The new law reverses the old, saying that an adult who is adopted out may no longer inherit from an intestate biological parent. Distinguish between an adult who gets adopted out and a minor who get adopted out. When an adult is adopted by another family, the adult loses the right to inherit from the intestate biological parent. But minor children who are adopted under age 18 get the opposite treatment: they are legally allowed to inherit from the intestate biological parent and continue to have that right under the new law. The child's age on the date of adoption is the key rather than the child's age on the date the biological parent's death.

The best way to control who inherits from you is to name names. If you have an adopted child, you can include or exclude her by naming her. If you have given up a child for adoption, you can control who inherits your estate by clearly identifying your heirs by name. Silence creates a void that must be filled by state law, and state law's solution may not be the right one for you. Taking action is the cure.

Excluding Someone from your Will

The law gives you the absolute right to select your own heirs. Conversely, it does not give anyone the right to demand to be your heir. Even so, people have expectations that may be stymied by your Will. For Example:

> Your father has just dropped a bombshell: nearly 50 years ago he had an affair and you have a sister about whom you never knew. As the shock wears down, you grow concerned about his estate. Will this new relative make a claim against his estate? Can he put a clause into his Will to solve this problem?

Your father holds the key to the situation. If he dies intestate, then his daughter, whether a surprise or not, would automatically be entitled to part of his estate. If he makes a Will he can include or exclude whomever he wishes. He would be completely within his legal rights to give nothing to this daughter, or conversely, to include her.

Attorneys often recommended simply giving a person a dollar instead of leaving them out of the Will. I think that action is too simple. To leave someone out of your Will, it should say three things:

- First, the Will should acknowledge the existence of the relative. By acknowledging that the person exists, the person cannot claim that he/she was accidentally forgotten.

- Second, the Will should directly state that no part of the estate is given to that person. Doing so means that person does not inherit anything under the terms of the Will. The Will can also state that the person is disqualified from any inheritance rights she might otherwise try to claim under state law.

- Third, the Will should include a "no contest clause." This says, essentially, that any person who attempts to contest the Will should lose whatever inheritance they may have otherwise gotten. It also says that if a court, as part of a Will contest and not as a simple inheritance, decides someone is legally entitled to part of the estate, that person inherits only one dollar.

Including Someone Not Specifically Identified

What happens if someone should be included in your Will, but you did not know to mention that person? For instance, if you have a new grandchild after the date the Will is signed by you; do you want that grandchild included or excluded?

The best answer, of course, comes from asking yourself that question in advance and making your own specific decision. Then you can state in your Will, "I devise $__ to each of the then living children of my son." If your son has another child later on, you have included that new grandchild.

If you don't think about it in advance, the law has an answer, though under some circumstances the answer is vague. The legal term "pretermitted child" means a child who is born after the date your Will was written. Here's an example:

Betty has two children. Bob was born in 1955 and Sylvia was born in 1957. Betty wrote a Will in 1956 that left her estate to her husband, and if he wasn't alive then to Bob. In 1999 Betty's husband died, leaving everything to Betty. Then in 2002 Betty died. She never did update her 1956 Will, so there is no mention of Sylvia in it. According to Texas law, Sylvia is a "pretermitted child" who may be able to inherit along with Bob anyway.

In the case of Gorski v Welch[57] the court applied the Texas statute to allow a pretermitted child to receive a portion of the estate when not mentioned in the Will, or not provided for in the Will, or not otherwise provided for outside the Will in a manner intended to replace a Will-based inheritance. The court said that for a pretermitted child to receive part of the estate, "it must appear from the Will, interpreted in light of all the circumstances, that the failure to provide for the child... was accidental, or due to inadvertence or oversight."

Most of the appellate court cases on pretermitted children take a very conservative approach to recognizing inheritance rights. The statute requires a variety of factors to be proven before a pretermitted child will inherit. But if all those factors are proven and the child's right to inherit is legally established, then those inheritance rights should extend to the next generation as well.

For example, if daughter Sylvia was clearly established as a pretermitted child - but Sylvia died in 2001 (the year before mother Betty died), then Sylvia's children should be entitled to the same inheritance Sylvia would have gotten if she had outlived her mother Betty. Although the definition of pretermission is clear, the issue of whether those rights extend to the grandchildren through the children has not been ruled upon by a Texas appeals court.

It is, on the other hand, very clear that the concept of pretermission does not apply directly to grandchildren. For instance, if Betty's Will said "I leave everything to my two grandchildren Jim and Joe," and a year later a third grandchild named Julie is born, Julie is not automatically included as Betty's heir (even though Julie was born after the Will was made). The pretermission statute includes only Betty's the natural born or adopted children when granting inheritance rights, not her grandchildren. The grandchild's only hope is to receive by virtue of their parent's right to receive, so granddaughter Julie would be left out.

Illegal Heirs

State law says that two categories of people cannot be your heir, even if you want them to be. They are:

- The attorney who drafts your Will for you, or who oversees its creation. Also, any employee of the attorney or any heir of the attorney cannot be named as heir (because they'd just be the attorney's surrogate). However, if any of those persons are your spouse, are your ancestor or descendant, or are related to you within the third degree, then it is legal for them to be your heir. This stops a dishonest attorney from writing a Will for you that names that attorney as your heir.

- The witnesses to your Will. A formal Will needs two witnesses to be valid. If someone you name as an heir is also a witness and his/her testimony is required to prove the Will, then he/she cannot also be an heir. An exception: if the Will is self-proven, then the testimony of the witness is not required and he/she can still be an heir. Another exception: if the witness would also be an "heir at law" (under the laws of intestacy) then the witness can still inherit – but not more than he/she would have received if there was no Will at all. This is intended to encourage independent witnesses, who have no vested interest in the Will.

Changing your Will

Using a "Memorandum" or a Codicil

Is it legal to attach a list or memorandum to your Will that gives away specific personal and household items? The concept of attaching a handwritten memorandum to your typewritten will is very attractive. The idea could simplify the details actually stated in your will, and give you the flexibility to change the memorandum whenever you wish.

Texas law, unfortunately, does not favor the use of memorandums attached to Wills. There is no statement in the Probate Code which specifically authorizes the use of a memorandum. There are, however, two possible ways to use a memorandum in Texas.

First: you declare the memorandum does not actually modify your Will and understand that a court will not enforce your instructions if left in a memorandum. The memorandum becomes a "suggestion" to your Executor and heirs. To make your intentions clear, there should be an explicit section of your Will that says you intend to leave a memorandum. It should say that you understand the memorandum cannot change your Will, but that you request the Executor and heirs to follow your instructions anyway. If your Executor is a close friend or family member, the memorandum can then act as guidance to him. If the Executor is given broad powers to decide who-gets-what when it comes to personal items, he can look to the memorandum while doing his job. If the memorandum is ever challenged in court, it will lose. Also, you must make it clear that if no memorandum is attached to your Will when you die, the Executor is to presume that you destroyed it. You must also be certain that the memorandum deals only with personal effects, and not with real property. But when the limits are followed, this type of memorandum can play a small role in your over-all estate plan.

Second: you treat the memorandum as a codicil to your Will, being certain that all the proper formalities for creating a Will are followed. That is, the memorandum is entirely in your handwriting, dated, signed by you and specifically declares your intent that it act as a supplement to your Will. Or, more formally, that the memorandum be typed, dated, signed by you and by two witnesses and specifically declares your intent that it act as a supplement to your Will. This type of codicil can be dangerous, because it will be admitted to probate along with the Will prepared by your attorney… and it modifies that Will. Thus, it provides an opportunity for you to make a mistake that could throw off your whole estate plan. The best approach is to allow your attorney write up any memorandum that deals with any item other than personal and household effects.

Of course, you also have a third choice: avoid using a Memorandum and instead have your attorney draw up a formal codicil to your Will. This works well because your attorney should write the codicil to complement your Will, avoiding contradictions or confusion. Sometimes in this age of computers and word processors, your attorney may forgo a codicil in favor of making you a whole new Will with the changes you desire integrated directly.

Is a Letter to your Lawyer a Change to your Will?

The law is clear that writing a letter (or email or fax) to your attorney with instructions about how to change your Will is not, in itself, a legal change to your Will. The case Estate of Schiwetz[58] makes this very clear. Mrs. Schiwetz made a Will naming several family members as heirs. Some years later, she changed her mind and wrote her attorney four letters with instructions on changing her Will. For some reason, the changes were not formalized before she died.

Her Will was admitted to probate, and later the four letters were offered for probate by the people who would benefit from the changes. Eventually, the court held the letters did not express a direct intent to dispose of assets; they were nothing more than instructions to make a change to the Will. The court stated that, "Instructions or directions to attorneys to prepare a new will or codicil that carry out the designated changes are not themselves intended to be wills or codicils."

Thus, the original Will was left intact and all the instructions contained in the letters were not enforced. The proponents tried one other logical tactic: they alleged that one of the letters was actually a codicil signed by Mrs. Schiwetz. Her "signature" was at the top of the page, where she identified herself to her attorney. The court found that mere placement of a person's name on the page (even if in the person's handwriting) was not a "signature" unless it was "written with the intention and purpose that it should be or was the signature" of the person. In this case, the name was meant to identify the party, not to act as a signature.

Testamentary Trusts

A testamentary trust is a tool you can write into your Will to extend control many years into the future. This type of trust sits in your Will, waiting, until you die. Then it is activated to fulfill your goals. The goals a testamentary trust can fulfill are extremely varied. Here are a few of the more common uses:

- A trust for minors. Perhaps you want your estate to pass to your children when both you and your spouse have died. They are adults, so they can inherit directly from you. At the same time, you want your grandchildren to inherit if their parent (your child) should die first. If the grandchildren are young and inexperienced, you can leave their share in a testamentary trust. You select someone as Trustee and give explicit instructions about management and distribution of the inheritance. The grandchildren's inheritance can be used for college education, health care and to launch their adult lives.

- A trust for a spendthrift. Perhaps you have an adult child whose money-handling skills are awful. You decide that leaving your estate to him/her without any rules is the same as throwing it away – in six months your lifetime's hard earned savings will be gone. Instead of disinheriting that person, you can put his/her inheritance into a testamentary trust. Your rules for accessing and spending the money will help preserve it for many years, and will ensure that the beneficiary has some funds to rely on for the future.

- A trust for a disabled heir. You may have an heir who is physically disabled. Perhaps that person is even receiving Supplement Security Income benefits from Social Security that pay all medical bills. If you leave an inheritance directly to that person, the government benefit may be lost. Instead, you can leave funds to a testamentary trust tailored to meet the requirements of law, providing benefits to the heir while retaining the heir's government benefits.

- A trust to save taxes. The federal estate tax system includes an "exemption amount" designed to reduce your final tax bill. With testamentary shelter trusts built into the Wills of a married couple, they can double the amount of the exclusion.

Beware Will Forms and Software

A variety of Will forms and software packages are available for purchase at office and computer stores, both online and walk-in. You can go into many of the major office warehouse stores to pick up a blank form for a Will. They are fairly inexpensive and widely available.

Beware that the forms and software may not be written to comply with Texas law (even though they are sold here). They may also be confusing and difficult to use. For instance, in a review of three leading Will-writing software packages for MoneyCentral and CNBC, correspondent Ginger Applegarth wrote, "The problems I had reviewing this round of software would be laughable if they weren't so frustrating even to someone being paid to identify, buy, use and compare the products. At one point, I remarked to my assistant that I felt as if I were on Candid Camera and that Alan Funt was going to jump out of the closet and tell me it was all a joke." One of the leading products, Quicken Willmaker, only has a lease on the venerable Quicken name. The Willmaker program was published for a while by toy company Mattel, but is now published by self-help company Nolo Press.

Valuable or not, these software programs are protected by law in Texas. In 1999, in a lawsuit over the "unauthorized practice of law," the US District Court decided that certain Will writing software was illegal in Texas. The Judge said the software companies were attempting to practice law without a license. The state legislature responded very quickly to the Judge's ruling, and passed a bill specifically legalizing Will software, redefining the "practice of law" concept. They still require the software packaging to clearly and conspicuously state that the products are not a substitute for the advice of an attorney.

Going back to Applegarth, she concluded that, "you have to choose from a variety of products so difficult to use that you fear the result you want—a will—may not be any good," and "these packages are best used to prepare yourself for a trip to the lawyer."

Sometimes the software packages can do an adequate job. Each situation is different. Depending on your wishes, your planning documents can become quite complex. You must decide if using software instead of an attorney is worth the risk.

Pre-Printed Forms

Through the years, I have seen pre-printed Will forms that look very official. Often they are handed out by a charity seeking your donation, with a gift to the charity printed into the form. Besides the common sense warning that you shouldn't let someone else tell you where your money goes, many of these forms are legally defective.

The worst case involved a form that failed to provide for witnesses. It was typewritten, yet un-witnessed. Look back at the three varieties of legal Wills: a holographic Will must be handwritten; a typed Will must be witnessed. This did not satisfy either category; hence it was not a valid Texas Will (even though it looked very proper to the untrained eye).

Be cautious of Wills prepared by the Judge Advocate's office at a military base. While these are often well done, they are sometimes inappropriate. Why? The military attorney may not be licensed to practice law in Texas and may therefore rely heavily on forms recommended by others in the office. The result can be a poorly drafted inappropriate Will. The JAG will decline to prepare a Will with any type of trust – especially the type of shelter trust needed to avoid federal estate taxes. For that, you need to hire your own attorney licensed in Texas.

Can a Notary Write a Will?

No! Never rely on a Notary Public to prepare any legal document. Texas law states that a Notary Public may only notarize already prepared documents, administer oaths, and make certified copies of documents which cannot be publicly recorded (like letters or business accounts).

Notaries do not have any special training. They simply apply to the Texas Secretary of State, pay a filing fee and get a surety bond. This does not qualify someone to practice law.

Lawyers must complete college, three years of law school and must successfully pass the Texas bar examination before the Supreme Court will issue a license to practice law in Texas. A Notary is legally forbidden to practice law unless that Notary is also a licensed lawyer.

Some of the confusion comes from Texas' Mexican origins. In Mexico, a notario publico must also be a lawyer and must have a law degree. In Texas, it is illegal for the phrase "notario publico" to be used by a notary. It is misleading, and is considered a "deceptive trade practice" and a Class A misdemeanor.

If a Notary states or even implies that the Notary is an attorney (unless, of course, the Notary is in fact licensed to practice law in Texas) it is a Class A misdemeanor. Beyond that, if a Notary asks for or receives payment for preparing legal documents or for representing someone in a judicial or administrative proceeding, it is a

Class A misdemeanor. A second conviction of any of these deceptive acts is treated as a third-degree felony.

Lawyer Referral Services

Instead of buying software or relying on an untrained Notary, hire an attorney. If you don't already have one, ask your friends for a referral. If they don't give you any good leads, here is a list of the major Texas lawyer referral services available:

Internet (and Telephone) Resources:

Arlington Bar Association	817-277-3113
Central Texas Lawyer Referral	512-472-8303
Corpus Christi Bar Association	361-883-4022
Dallas Bar Association	214-220-7444
El Paso Bar Association	915-532-7052
Harris County Bar Association	713-236-8000
Jefferson County Bar Association	409-835-8438
Legal Hotline for Older Texans	800-622-2520
North Dallas Bar Association	972-424-6113
San Antonio Bar Association	210-227-1853
State Bar of Texas Lawyer Referral	800-252-9690
Tarrant County Bar Association	817-336-4101

The Martindale Hubble Law Directory is located at WWW.MARTINDALE.COM

The National Academy of Elder Law Attorneys maintains a nationwide membership list of attorneys who focus on the needs of the elderly. It is on the Internet at WWW.NAELA.ORG. Be sure to look for a Certified Elder Law Attorney.

Where Should You Keep Your Will?

Once you have properly created your Will, where is the best place to keep it? Opinions vary, and you must select the place that you feel is best. Here are a few options.

...at Home

If you keep your Will at home, be sure it is in a well-protected environment. You should consider buying a small fireproof box. They are available at the major office supplies stores. The biggest threats to your Will are 1) being destroyed by fire and 2) simply being lost. A fireproof box protects against both those risks.

…with Your Executor

You have selected a person to handle your affairs and named that person in your Will. You could give the Will to that person for safekeeping, and when you die that person will be ready to follow the instructions you left in your Will.

At first, giving your Will to your Executor may sound ideal. But consider these possibilities: What if you change your mind about who should be Executor? Are you comfortable asking for the return of your Will? What if that Executor dies before you do – are your papers safe in the custody of that person's relatives?

…with the County Clerk

Each county clerk's office can receive your Will and hold it for safekeeping. Giving your Will to the clerk is not the same as "filing" your Will (a Will is only filed when the time for probate arrives after you have died). Safekeeping simply means that the clerk holds your Will in a vault, and will only release it to you, to someone you specify, or directly to probate when you have died.

The biggest trouble with the clerk's safekeeping system is that no one thinks to look there. If you use it, you should inform your Executor and heirs that your Will is at the clerk's office.

…in a Safe Deposit Box

For many years, Texas law required a safe deposit box to be sealed when a renter died, until a properly appointed representative opened it. This law caused many people to avoid storing important papers in their safe deposit box.

But under current Texas banking laws, if you and another person have a joint safe deposit box and one of you dies, the bank must give the survivor access to the box and must allow any items to be removed from the box. It is no longer sealed.

Hence, a safe deposit box is a fine choice if there is more than one renter. It is not a good place if there is only a single renter. For example:

> Rhonda and Sam (who are married) have a safe deposit agreement with the bank that says they are "Joint Tenants." Under the former law, when Sam died Rhonda would have been locked out of the box. Under current Texas law, Rhonda has the right to open and empty the box without anyone looking over her shoulder.

What if you do not have another person as a joint renter? The bank may permit an examination of your safe deposit box – without a court order – by any of the following people after you die: (1) your surviving spouse or your parents, (2) any of your adult descendants, or (3) a possible Executor who presents a document that looks like a copy of your Last Will and Testament.

Under the above conditions, the box would be examined in the presence of a bank officer. Legally, however, the bank is only allowed to deliver specific items to certain people:

- Your Will can only be given to the Probate Clerk;

- Your life insurance policies can be given only to the policy beneficiaries;

- The deed to a burial plot can be given to the person who is examining the box; and

- Other items cannot be removed from the box until court authority is obtained.

PLANNING FOR YOUR PETS

The continued care of beloved dog, cat or other companion animal is a concern raised by a many pet owners. These animals bring you comfort, give love and can be as close to you as your family ever was. You don't want to abandon your animal friends.

Several situations may arise that require immediate care for your pets. Sudden illness may take you away from them. You may gradually lose the ability to care for them due to your own infirmity. Or you may die, leaving them alone.

You can plan to be certain they will not be abandoned. I suggest that any pet owner do the following:

- Arrange for a backup caretaker for your pets. You should always have someone who checks on your well being regularly. If they find that you are ill, they should know whom to contact to care for your pets.

- Leave written emergency instructions. Do your pets take any medications? Where is their food, and how much do they get? Who is their veterinarian?

- Be certain that you have a durable power of attorney in place. It would allow your agent to access your funds, and provide resources so your pets' caretaker can buy supplies and pay the vet.

- Mention your pets in your Last Will and Testament. While I do not recommend leaving your estate to your animals (which is of dubious legal validity anyway) you should consider their welfare. You can leave money for the care of your pets, but you have to leave it to a person – not to the pets themselves. One idea is to leave a sum of money to the caretaker on condition that the caretaker properly sustains the pets. Ask your Executor to be certain that the conditions are met.

In your Will, you can name a friend or a charitable organization to adopt your pets. A pet is property and can be bequeathed like any other property.

The veterinary school at Texas A&M runs a program that provides "red-carpet" care for your beloved pet if you die. It is an expensive alternative if you don't have any family to adopt your pet, and you don't want your pet euthanized. You can read more about it at WWW.CVM.TAMU.EDU/PETCARE/.

A Pet Trust

Texas law had no formal method to leave funds for your animals' care until 2006. Then the legislature passed an amendment to the Texas Property Code[59] allowing you to establish a trust for the care of your pets – but only pets that were alive during your own lifetime.

You could not, for instance, set up a trust for your dog and "any puppies born after" you die. The law says that the trust must end on the death of the pets you had while you were alive.

A pet trust can be established either inter vivos or in a testamentary fashion – meaning you can set one up in a trust or in a Will. For instance, if you have a living trust you can add a provision for the welfare of your pets during any time that you become disabled. Then the trustee of your living trust will have resources available specifically to care for your pets. If the pet care trust is contained inside your Will (a testamentary pet care trust) then it won't take effect until you die, so you would need some other plan to care for your pets if you become disabled.

The law allows you to identify persons to whom the funds will pass after both you and your pets have died. If you do not make the choice for yourself, then the funds will pass to your heirs at law. Clearly it is best to make the choice yourself.

What if you establish a trust in your Will and an "interested" person thinks that you were overly generous to the dogs, unnecessarily cutting into the money available to the human heirs? The code says that the trust funds may be "applied to a use other than the property's intended use under the trust to the extent the court determines that the value of the trust property exceeds the amount required for the intended use."

In other words, leaving a million dollars for the care of your dog can be challenged, and the excess funds that are not realistically needed for the dog can be distributed to the human heirs named in the trust instrument (or to your heirs at law if the instrument is silent).

FEDERAL ESTATE TAXATION

"In this world nothing is certain except death and taxes." -- Benjamin Franklin, 1789

Franklin's wit and humor is always enlightening. However, even he could not have anticipated the complex twists in our modern estate tax system. The estate tax system is anything but certain since passage of the Economic Growth and Tax Relief Reconciliation Act of 2001 in which Congress *appeared* to repeal the estate tax.

The 2001 Tax Act

The 2001 Tax Act became law on June 7, 2001. Only a small part of it actually addresses estate taxes, significantly reducing those taxes over the next decade. And the estate tax is indeed repealed starting on January 1, 2010.

Don't blink. Oops, you missed it. Twelve months later, it's baaaaack, just like it never went away. Worse, just like it would have been if the 2001 Tax Act had never existed. The last thing the Act provides is certainty, and I suspect that Franklin would have found the situation humorous – or horrifying!

You can rightly view the 2001 Tax Act as a significant yet temporary reduction in estate taxes. That reduction is based on two features of the law. First, the top estate tax rate is reduced in 2002 from 55% to 50%. Each year following, the tax rate comes down by 1% until it freezes at 45% from 2007 until 2009. In 2010, the federal estate tax rate is zero – but twelve months later it's back to 55%.

Second, the exemption amount is being increased dramatically. The exemption amount was formerly called the "unified credit" – but Congress had to rename it because the gift tax system and the estate tax system are no longer "unified" under the 2001 Act.

For several decades, the federal estate tax and federal gift tax rules used the same tax rates, tax deductions and tax credits. The only real difference between an estate tax and a gift tax was the timing: you can only make a gift while you are living, and you can only incur an estate tax after death. Under the 2001 Tax Act the systems are again separate. Since they are no longer unified, the law couldn't use that word in its description; hence the estate tax cut-off point is called the "exemption amount" and the gift tax cut-off point is called the "lifetime gift exemption."

It is also important for you to realize that the Estate tax and Gift tax are completely separate from the Income tax. The items taxed and the tax rates are different. Some similarities do, however, exist:

- Income tax, Gift tax and Estate tax are all collected by the IRS;

- Income tax, Gift tax and Estate tax all require a return to be filed under certain circumstances;

- Income tax, Gift tax and Estate tax all allow certain deductions to adjust the pool of items being taxed, and all allow certain credits to reduce the amount of tax paid; and

- All three tax systems are very complex.

Unlimited Marital Deduction

The Unlimited Marital Deduction eliminates estate and gift taxes on ALL transfers to your spouse. When you die, your half of the community property plus all of your separate property are part of your taxable estate. Before the IRS figures out how large your taxable estate is (and how much tax they can collect) you are allowed to deduct the value of anything you are leaving to your spouse. For example

> Joe and Norma, married for 46 years, have acquired a joint estate of $2,500,000. When Joe dies, he leaves his entire half to Norma. She does not pay any tax on the transfer because the Unlimited Marital Deduction eliminates the tax.

The Unlimited Marital Deduction is automatic. You need make no specific mention of it in your Will. Just the fact that you leave an asset to your surviving spouse (as long as it is a no-strings-attached, outright inheritance) invokes the tax-deferral granted through the Unlimited Marital Deduction. A bequest to your surviving spouse that has conditions (like a gift to a testamentary trust) does not qualify for the marital deduction unless certain rules are followed.

There is no dollar limit on the marital deduction. If you leave everything to your spouse, your estate pays NO estate tax. That sounds so simple, that one is tempted to look no deeper. Don't be mesmerized by the unlimited marital deduction. It is not a tax reduction; it is only a tax deferral. Remember, someday that surviving spouse will die – and then there is no unlimited marital deduction. Tax time has arrived, unless the remaining estate is smaller than the exemption amount.

Exemption Amount

The 2001 Tax Act's largest immediate estate tax impact was to exempt many "medium" size estates from the entire estate tax.

The Exemption Amount eliminates estate or gift taxes on the first million dollars of assets passing to anyone other than your surviving spouse. The amount of this tax break has not been static. Although it was stuck at $600,000 from 1987 until 1997, Congress started increasing it with the passage of the 1997 Tax Reduction Act.

But Congress was stingy in 1997, and they scheduled the credit to increase slowly – starting with a meager $25,000 increase in 1998. They planned for the credit to top out at $1 million in 2006.

Table 5: Comparison of Exemptions			
Year	The 1997 Tax Reduction Act's Unified Credit	The 2001 Tax Relief Act's Exemption Amount	One Proposal in Congress
1998	$ 625,000	--	
1999	$ 650,000	--	
2000	$ 675,000	--	
2001	$ 675,000	--	
2002	$ 700,000	$1,000,000	
2003	$ 700,000	$1,000,000	
2004	$ 850,000	$1,500,000	
2005	$ 950,000	$1,500,000	
2006	$1,000,000	$2,000,000	$5,000,000
2007	$1,000,000	$2,000,000	$5,000,000
2008	$1,000,000	$2,000,000	$5,000,000
2009	$1,000,000	$3,500,000	$5,000,000
2010	$1,000,000	No tax	$5,000,000
2011	$1,000,000	$1,000,000	$5,000,000

Then Congress passed the more generous 2001 Tax Act. This increased the tax break to $1 million starting on January 1, 2002 – shaving four years off the earlier schedule. They passed additional scheduled increases through 2010.

In 2010, there is no exemption because there is no estate tax. Shockingly, on January 1, 2011 the law reverts to the much tinier exemption they passed in 1997, and to the much larger maximum tax rate of 55%.

Most of the examples in this book use an exemption amount of $2 million. For later years, you can use the table to see the applicable exemption.

Avoiding Estate Taxes

Every individual – single or married – is entitled to one exemption amount. That means that a married couple has two exemption amounts: husband has his $2 million exemption and wife has her $2 million exemption (in 2006 to 2008). Sounds good, but many couples completely fail to use both exemptions – a multimillion-dollar tax break is just wasted because the couple assumes that the Unlimited Marital Deduction is enough to eliminate the tax. They don't realize that the estate tax is just deferred by the marital deduction.

Don't let that happen to you! The key to proper use of both exemptions by a married couple is for both spouses to coordinate them to avoid estate taxes. By carefully combining the exemption amount and the unlimited marital deduction by using a shelter trust, every estate smaller than $4 million can legally eliminate estate taxes (in 2006-08).

Shelter Trust

A married couple has the opportunity to shelter two exemption amounts from estate tax. This technique is called a "shelter trust," and also goes by the names "A-B trust," "Bypass trust" or "Federal Credit trust" depending on who you talk to.

Case 1: The Wrong Way

Jack and Alice have assets of $3,350,000. They have Wills leaving all assets to the surviving mate. When Jack dies, the Unlimited Marital Deduction eliminates the estate tax on the transfer. Alice now owns the entire $3,350,000 as her own estate. Later, when Alice dies, the first $2 million is exempt, and the excess ($1,350,000) is subject to estate tax at 46%. The gross tax due is $636,000. Hence, about 19% of the overall assets are paid in taxes.

Case 2: The Right Way

Jack and Alice's Wills contain "shelter trusts." When Jack dies, assets up to but not exceeding the value of his exemption amount ($2 million) are left to a trust for Alice's benefit. The rest of his estate goes to her directly. His exemption amount eliminates the estate tax on the transfer to trust, and his unlimited marital deduction eliminates tax on the excess. When Alice dies, her taxable estate does not include the trust assets, so it is $1,350,000. Alice's own $2 million exemption means that there is no estate tax at all. The shelter trust saved $636,000 – pretty good!

A married couple can ask their attorney to write a shelter trust into their Wills or into their living trust. If in the Wills, it most certainly goes to probate. If done in the living trust, this shelter trust technique can both reduce estate taxes and eliminate probate.

It is vital for you to realize that this technique for using the exemption amount is a true reduction of taxes. If is not automatic (contrasted to the unlimited marital deduction, which is automatic but only defers taxes instead of reducing them).

While both spouses are alive, they must create legal documents that contain shelter trusts. Without planning while both spouses are living, the exemption amount of the first spouse to die is wasted. Unfortunately, too many couples rely on the "simple" pattern of Case 1. They pay high estate taxes, not knowing that the legal opportunity existed to reduce the estate tax.

Using the exemption amount in both estates can save considerable money. Federal estate tax rates are the highest of any federal tax. It makes sense to reduce the tax in any way the law allows.

'QTIP' Planning

If you are in a second marriage, with children from the earlier marriage, you may have conflicting goals. You may want to protect your children, and may also want to provide benefits to your second spouse. (If you don't want anything to go to your surviving spouse, then you'd better review the section in this book on premarital agreements and on spousal partition agreements starting on page 172.)

This is especially meaningful when your new spouse has children by a prior marriage. You may be wary of leaving your estate to your spouse because the "other kids" may benefit instead of "your kids." On top of it all, you want to keep estate taxes low.

How can you satisfy all these contradictory desires? One approach is to leave your assets in a trust for your spouse with a requirement that when your spouse dies, the assets must go to your kids. This way, your second spouse is cared for as long as he/she lives and your children receive your estate when both spouses die. The trust keeps your stepchildren at arm's length.

If your estate is large enough to owe estate tax then you must be sure that this type of trust follows the QTIP rules. "QTIP" stands for Qualified Terminable Interest Property. "Terminable" means that ownership stops with the passage of time or on some particular event (like the death of your spouse.) However, "qualified" means that the gift is legally estate tax free anyway.

An ordinary inheritance received by a spouse (that is, one that is not terminable) is tax-free due to the unlimited marital deduction. A terminable transfer does not get to use the unlimited marital deduction. A terminable transfer causes gift or estate tax to be due. However, the "qualified" in QTIP means that the transfer does qualify for the unlimited marital deduction. Hence, a qualified terminal interest property bears no estate tax when the first spouse dies.

To be "qualified," the transfer must follow these rules:

- The spouse must receive all income from the assets, payable at least annually;

- No one may have a "power of appointment" (the ability to give away the property); and

- The Executor must notify the IRS that the assets are being treated as QTIP assets.

For example:

Ron and Gail each have children from earlier marriages. Ron wants to protect Gail (his second wife) but wants his kids to get his assets when Gail dies. Ron makes a Last Will and Testament placing enough assets to care for Gail into a QTIP trust when he dies. The QTIP trust pays all its income to Gail, at least annually. The trust preserves Ron's estate so that when Gail dies, the assets pass directly to his kids. Ron's trust is a "terminable interest" because Gail's benefit ends when she dies. But it is "qualified" since Gail gets the income her whole life. The assets pass without estate tax and both the wife and the children have been protected.

Non-Citizen Tax Avoidance

The rate of estate tax paid by U.S. citizens and non-citizens is identical, but non-citizens cannot claim the same estate tax deductions as citizens. Citizenship has its privileges; one privilege is the unlimited marital deduction.

Using the unlimited marital deduction, married citizens can defer all estate taxes until both spouses have died. Non-citizens who reside in the U.S. are not entitled to use the unlimited marital deduction. Congress feared that if estate taxes for non-citizens are deferred until the second death, the non-citizen would leave the U.S. in an attempt to avoid estate taxes.

If that happened, then only the assets that were actually left inside the U.S. could be taxed. Hence, the Internal Revenue Code is structured to prevent the loss of revenue by imposing restrictions on non-citizens.

Resident aliens do have three planning options to help reduce estate taxes:

- Resident aliens can use the exemption amount to eliminate or lower estate taxes. If the estate is less than $2 million (for years 2006-08) then this rule alone is enough to eliminate estate taxes.

- Resident aliens may create a Qualified Domestic Trust (QDT) as part of a Last Will and Testament. Under section 2056 of the Internal Revenue Code, when you use a QDT you can defer estate taxes using the marital deduction like a citizen. But when the non-citizen spouse dies, estate taxes are payable. At least one trustee of the QDT must be a U.S. citizen or a domestic corporation. The non-citizen survivor may use any income generated by the trust funds. The original assets put into the QDT when a spouse dies cannot be withdrawn by the non-citizen survivor except under special conditions.

- If you don't have strong personal reasons for maintaining your alien status, consider becoming a naturalized U.S. citizen.

Another privilege of citizenship is the free step-up in basis. If you are a non-citizen, the step-up is limited to $60,000. Compare that to the limits allowed to citizens, discussed in the next section.

Step-Up in Basis

"Basis" is the dollar figure the IRS uses when determining capital gain tax on the sale of a piece of property. Your basis is akin to your investment in an asset. For example:

> You bought 200 shares of stock in 1950 for $8 per share. Your basis is $8 per share (unless it is adjusted for depreciation or other reasons). You sell the stock now for $70 per share. Your taxable gain is only that part of the sale price that was more than your basis (that is $70 - $8 = $62 gain.)

When you inherit an asset, what is that asset's basis? You might think that the heir would have the same basis as the original owner. Not so. The heir is allowed legally to increase the basis to the fair market value of the asset on the day the owner died. Using the stock example above:

The fair market value of the stock on the day the owner died was $70. As heir, your basis in the stock is reset to $70. If you sell it the next day for $70 per share, you pay no capital gain tax.

This can add up to significant savings when applied to many assets, and is referred to as a free step-up in basis.

Although the 2001 Tax Act was generally intended to reduce taxes, several of its provisions actually increased them. Step-up in basis is a good example; a new and different system begins on January 1, 2009. The capital gain tax will be imposed on some inherited assets after January 1, 2009, whereas before the 2001 Tax Act those assets were free of capital gain tax.

Between now and December 31, 2009 the current rules still apply. Starting on January 1, 2009 only the first $1.3 million of inherited assets will receive the basis increase, except that the surviving spouse gets an additional $3 million step up. For example:

> Assume Joe's estate is $2.5 million made up of stock. He has held much of that stock for decades – the tax basis is only $300,000. Joe is single. If Joe dies in 2007, his estate will owe about $245,000 in estate taxes (which is a major reduction from the $680,000 that would have been owed if he died in 2001). Since the new step-up in basis rules don't apply until 2009, his children may treat the entire $2.5 million in stock as having a basis of $2.5 million (if they sell it for that value, there is no capital gain tax).

> If Joe dies in 2009, there is zero estate tax, but his kid's basis in the stock will be $1.3 million. If they sell it for $2.5 million, they owe a 15% capital gain tax on the profit (2,500,000 – 1,300,000 = 1,200,000 profit * 15% = $180,000).

> What if Joe dies in 2011? In that year, estate taxes go back up and the basis limitation is left in place. So in 2011, the estate tax will be $680,000. If they sell they stock, capital gains will be another $180,000. The government will collect $860,000, which is actually a tax increase compared to what Joe's family would have paid before the 2001 Tax Act.

The 2001 Tax act throws some more complications into the mix. The step-up must be allocated on an item-by-item basis. That doesn't make any difference if the entire gain is less than the allowance ($1.3 million for anyone or $4.3 million for a surviving spouse). But if the gain is more than those limits, the Executor is required to designate which assets receive the step up, and to what extent. It will be a difficult accounting task that will increase the expense of estate administration.

Due to the 2001 Tax Act, various items are no longer eligible for the step-up, no matter what they are worth. This includes anything that the decedent received as a gift during the last three years of life. It also includes several uncommon items, like stocks in a foreign personal holding company or foreign investment company.

Before the 2001 Tax Act's changes to the basis rules that start in 2009, the step-up rule provided an added benefit in community property states: when a spouse died, the survivor got to step-up the basis in all the community property. Although the language in the law is ambiguous, analysts are interpreting it to continue to extend the step-up in basis to all the community property up to $4.3 million. Beyond that, there is no step-up on basis after 2009.

Texas Inheritance Tax

The *estate* tax you have been reading about is imposed by the federal government. The state of Texas also imposes a death tax, but it is called an *inheritance* tax. These two tax systems have a vital interplay.

The inheritance tax allows Texas to grab some of the funds that would be saved because of section 2011 of the Internal Revenue Code. That section gave a credit on the federal estate tax for the amount of state inheritance tax paid. Texas law forces you to claim that federal credit then swoops in to grab 100% of that credit.

Notice the phrase "gave a credit" – as in past tense? The 2001 Tax Act phased out the section 2011 credit, effective in 2005. The Texas legislature has not yet responded to this federal restructuring of our inheritance tax. A bill was considered in the 2005 legislative session, but did not come out of committee. Hence, Texas inheritance tax has been gutted and no one will pay it until the legislature comes up with a tax scheme that is de-coupled from the section 2011 credit.

What is Next?

Predicting what Congress will do is dangerous. But they have left the estate and gift tax system in a position where it is very difficult for individuals to make concrete plans for the future. The House voted in 2005 and early 2006 simply to make the tax reductions they passed in 2001 permanent.

The Senate did not agree, and was debating a different approach. Then in June 2006 the House voted to allow a $5 million exemption amount (indexed for inflation), to eliminate the 2010 repeal of the estate tax, to eliminate the changes to capital gain taxes. The Senate has not responded in kind as an election looms ahead. Be sure to check my website (WWW.PREMACK.COM) where I'll be sure to report any changes to the system.

Chapter 7: Responding to a Death

Someone you love has died. As survivor, you may feel agony, fear, abandonment, guilt, relief, despair… probably all of them at different times. Certainly you feel overwhelmed. At this time of vulnerability, decisions must be made, the family must be notified and the funeral must be held.

This guide deals with the issues a surviving family member, particularly a surviving spouse, may face *before* contacting an attorney about the probate. Then Chapter 8 discusses probate and other legal actions the survivor should consider.

LOCATION OF THE DEATH

Home Death

Due to the availability of hospice care, more families are experiencing the death of a loved one at home. The Hospice Foundation of America calls hospice a "special concept of care designed to provide comfort and support to patients and their families when a life-limiting illness no longer responds to cure-oriented treatments." Hospice attempts to provide pain management and comfort care, without either delaying or promoting death. This acknowledges a trend in modern medicine to recognize death as an inevitable outcome in certain situations.

Pre-Need Legal Documents:

As discussed earlier in this book, the family can arm itself with several legal documents:

- An out of hospital Do-Not-Resuscitate (DNR) order can be used in the home to avoid any attempt by EMS to resuscitate the deceased;

- A Directive to Physicians and a Medical Power of Attorney can be used to enact the patient's wish that life sustaining treatments be withheld or be withdrawn, allowing death to arrive without medical intervention; and

- An Appointment of Agent to Control Disposition of Remains.

Who Should be Called?

When the death occurs at home, there are several options on who to contact:

The Hospice

If the death is expected, perhaps hospice has been arranged. If your hospice nurse is already on the scene, then the death is an "attended" death and you may be able to avoid a call to the police or to EMS. If not, call your hospice to report the death and follow their advice.

The Police

If the death was natural and expected, they will fill out a report and contact the funeral home. If the death occurred under unusual circumstances, they will investigate and call in the local medical examiner, who may transfer the remains to the medical examiner's office. The goal is to determine the cause and manner of the death. A Medical Investigator may investigate the scene of death and interview witnesses and medical caregivers. If the Investigator determines that the case belongs in the Medical Examiner's office, an autopsy may be the next step. If an autopsy is not indicated, the Medical Examiner may collect body fluids and tissue for toxicology analysis.

EMS

No matter how well prepared a caregiver may be, the actual death often elicits a call for emergency medical personnel. This is when the survivor should be armed with the DNR order, the Directive to Physicians and a strong opinion that the body should not be disturbed. EMS often transports the remains to the hospital, where a physician examines the body and certifies the cause of death.

The Funeral Home

If the death is expected, the survivor may simply call the funeral home if pre-arrangements have been made. The funeral director will arrange for the body's transportation, for a final examination and certification of the death. If there are no prearrangements with a funeral home, it is entirely appropriate to do some comparison shopping. A rushed choice is an expensive choice. There should be no rush to remove the decedent's remains. Family members may want to pay a final visit within hours of the death.

Nursing Home Death

If a nursing home resident's death is sudden, it may occur at the nursing home. Otherwise, as the resident's condition slowly worsens, the nursing home may transfer the resident to the hospital prior to death.

Nursing homes do not generally have a place to store a resident's remains. They do not want to leave the body in the room for an extended period, especially if it is a semi-private room. The survivor may be pressured to contact the funeral home quickly for transfer of the remains. If this is the case, find out if the body can be moved to the coroner's office for temporary storage while a funeral home is selected. Again, a rushed choice is an expensive choice.

Hospital Death

Death in the hospital is often referred to as an "attended death." The circumstances are known, the causes well documented. Often the physician will certify the death and release the body to the funeral home directly from the hospital's morgue.

If a person dies in a hospital and an attending physician is unable to certify the cause of death, the manager of the institution is required to report the death to the local justice of the peace. At that point, an inquiry is made regarding the cause of death.

Organ Donation Issues

Did the decedent arrange for organ donation or whole body bequeathal? Read more about organ donation cards and the willed body programs earlier in this book.

No Declaration = Family Decision

If the decedent did not sign a donor card then someone in the family must give written permission if a donation is to happen. A medical professional who is specially trained will approach the family to request the donation. Texas law establishes an order of priority to authorize the donation: 1st the surviving spouse, 2nd the decedent's adult child. 3rd either of the decedent's parents, 4th an adult brother or sister, 5th the court appointed guardian (if any), and finally, anyone else authorized to dispose of the body.

If permission comes from a family member and there are others of the same or a higher priority, then an effort must be made to contact those people and make them aware of the proposed gift. Also, the statute prohibits the donation if the decedent ever expressed opposition to anatomical gifts.

After the Anatomical Gift

Once the organs are removed, the body is delivered to the funeral home and prepared for burial or cremation as directed by the family. Donation does not disfigure the body, so an open casket viewing is still possible if called for by the family's religious practices.

Autopsy

Autopsy is not required in every death. Surviving family members may ask for an autopsy, or the state may require it under certain circumstances.

Elective Autopsy

The family may be asked for permission to perform an autopsy. The statute gives a priority list for who is may give the authorization: first, the surviving spouse; second, an adult child; third, the guardian of a minor child; fourth, a parent; fifth, the decedent's guardian; and finally, any next of kin. Note that the persons who may authorize an autopsy and the persons who may authorize organ donations are somewhat different. The spouse always has first priority. But for autopsy, the guardian weighs in ahead of the siblings.

An elective autopsy may cost $2,000 to $4,000, and the family member who authorizes it must agree to pay for it. However, health insurance may under certain circumstances pay for an autopsy if they see a need for one. All accident and sickness policies in Texas contain a clause authorizing an autopsy in the insurance company's discretion.

If the cause of death is unknown or not clearly determined, an autopsy can alert the family to health risks they can anticipate and avoid. Perhaps the autopsy will find a genetic component to the death.

Legally Required Autopsy

When the death occurs under circumstances that indicate unnatural causes or when the coroner suspects there might be a disease that poses a threat to public health, an autopsy can be performed. The Texas Department of Criminal Justice (state prison system, if the decedent was an inmate) or the local Justice of the Peace can authorize an autopsy even without family consent.

If a person dies an unnatural death (from a cause other than a legal execution), if a body is found and the cause of death is unknown, if foul play is suspected, if suicide is obvious or suspected, if the death was not attended by a physician then the local Justice of the Peace is legally required to conduct an inquest.

If a doctor who attends the death is unable to certify the cause of death, the doctor must report to the Justice of the Peace to request an inquest. The inquest must happen quickly, at the place the body is found or at the place of death. The JP can hold the inquest at any other reasonable location. A body may be disinterred for an inquest. The JP decides, based on advice of the Medical Examiner or a physician, whether an autopsy in needed.

AGENT TO CONTROL DISPOSITION OF REMAINS

When a person dies, Texas law strongly favors any steps necessary to honor that person's wishes regarding burial or cremation. Any instructions you issue in your Will must be followed, but the Will is often overlooked until after the funeral. A better choice is to preplan your own funeral and have arrangements made already. Also, the Texas Health & Safety Code[60] allows you to create a document called an *Appointment of Agent to Control Disposition of Remains*. This is a special power of attorney that takes effect at the moment of death, which is very unusual for a power of attorney. In contrast, normal durable powers of attorney end at the moment of death.

In your Appointment of Agent to Control Disposition of Remains you can appoint an individual in whom you have great confidence to see to your funereal arrangements. If your family is not your top choice, you can call on a close friend. You can appoint alternate Agents in case your first choice is not available. And you can give very explicit and legally binding instructions, including the requirement of cremation or for a traditional funeral.

You may need to have an attorney help draw up the Appointment of agent to Control Disposition of Remains. The law requires it to contain specific clauses and wording to be valid, and it must be signed by you and by your agent, and must be notarized. Don't do it by hand.

> Internet Resource:
> If you have no other source, the Appointment of agent to Control Disposition of Remains is available at WWW.PREMACK.COM and click on "Legal Documents".

OBTAINING A DECEDENT'S MEDICAL RECORDS

By law, a person's medical records are confidential. They can only be released under certain circumstances (and the circumstances can vary widely). If you want to see the medical records of a decedent, it is obvious that you can no longer get permission from the decedent. Thus, there are three valid approaches to obtaining the medical records of a decedent. You could:

- Obtain a copy of the death certificate from the vital statistics department (of the city in which the death occurred, or if the death occurred in a rural area, from the Dept. of Health in Austin). The death certificate lists one or more causes of death. It does not go into great detail, but may give you what you need. Death certificates will only be released, however, to a short list of qualified people;

- Ask the Executor of the estate (named in the Will and appointed by the Probate court) to obtain the records for you. Medical information can be released in Texas to the patient's legally authorized representative, and an Executor fills that legal role. If the decedent did not have a Will, you can consider applying to the Probate court to become "administrator" of the estate and will then be entitled to see the medical records; or

- Look for any outside source of the medical records. Was the decedent party to a lawsuit in which the medical records were an issue? There may be records at the courthouse that include portions of the medical file. The District Clerk's office keeps track of this type of lawsuit.

If your desire to obtain the medical records is based upon the desire to file a negligence claim against a medical provider, the Texas Medical Liability and Insurance Improvement Act[61] must be followed. It says that a request for the medical records of a deceased person must be honored if it is authorized in writing by a parent, spouse, or adult child of the deceased.

You also need to be aware that the laws on medical malpractice claims impose the obligation to notify the medical provider before you file suit, and limit who can start the suit. You would need to see a qualified personal injury attorney who handles medical malpractice or wrongful death claims for help.

FUNERAL ISSUES

Paying for a funeral is often the first financial decision that must be made upon the death. The first rule is: honor the decedent's wishes. These may be expressed in the Will, but most Wills do not go beyond instructing a "decent burial" or the like, and are often left unread until after the funeral. Look for a Pre-need arrangement, or an Appointment of Agent to Control Disposition of Remains.

Too often, the decedent will have expressed no preferences about the funeral. This may be a good time to call upon the family's religious traditions as a guide to the appropriate funereal practices.

Emotional Vulnerability

The funeral industry, while subject to disclosure regulations, is also aware of the emotional vulnerability of many of its customers. As a survivor who needs to set up a funeral, be wary of the following vulnerabilities:

- The funeral home décor, while on the surface intended to honor the dead, may intimidate the living. You may be off-balance from the death, and that lack of balance may be with you at the funeral home.

- The salesperson (called a "funeral director") may use flattery. "Given your position in the community, I'm sure you'll want…."

- The salesperson may use guilt. ("I'm sure you want the best for your …")

- The salesperson may use examples that do not apply to your situation. ("When your husband arranged his aunt's funeral, this is what he chose.") But is it what he wanted for his funeral?

- The salesperson may call on religious or community "tradition." Is it tradition, or simply the canned package the funeral home prefers to offer?

Remember that most funeral directors are caring people, trying to do their job and help you during a difficult time. Try telling them that if you were to spend equal to the amount you care, you would overspend. Try to stay reasonable. Acknowledge your deep loss and your desire to honor your loved one, but remember that finances are important to you as survivor.

Price Lists

Federal regulations require the funeral home to provide a general price list, a casket price list and an outer-container price list. The same regulations allow the funeral industry to add a "funeral director's professional services" fee to the bill. This covers overhead and general expenses for the funeral home, and cannot be declined. As such, the survivor should never worry that the funeral home may be poorly compensated if an inexpensive casket is selected. They get their money.

Internet Resource:

Texas regulates the funeral industry. You can learn more from the Texas Funeral Services Commission website at WWW.TFSC.STATE.TX.US

The Federal Trade Commission enforces federal regulations regarding funeral sales and services. They publish an excellent Consumer's Guide, available on the web at WWW.FTC.GOV/BCP/CONLINE/PUBS/SERVICES/FUNERAL.HTM

The Texas Department of Banking regulates the licensing and sale of prepaid funeral contracts. They have provided answers about these contracts online at WWW.BANKING.STATE.TX.US/SAUDITS/PFCQ.HTM

Government Assistance

Social Security

A one-time payment of $255 is due to the surviving spouse if he or she was living with the beneficiary at the time of death, or if living apart, was receiving Social Security benefits on the beneficiary's earnings record. Being apart for medical purposes (one spouse in a nursing home) is not "living apart." If there is no surviving spouse, the payment is made to a child who was eligible for benefits on the beneficiary's earnings record in the month of death.

Military/VA

An honorably discharged veteran may be interred in a national cemetery. The plot is provided free, as is the grave opening and closing, and a simple grave marker. An honor guard and an American flag may also be provided. This saves significant money for the surviving spouse.

In addition to veterans, the following categories of decedents are also eligible for burial in a national cemetery: (1) a Commissioned Officer of the National Oceanic and Atmospheric Administration, (2) a Commissioned Officer of the Regular or Reserve Corps of the Public Health Service, (3) United States Merchant Mariners who served during WWII, (4) The un-remarried surviving spouse of an eligible decedent, even if that decedent is not buried in the national cemetery, (5) a minor child of an eligible decedent, subject to certain conditions.

Eligible veterans who are buried in a non-governmental cemetery may still qualify for a free grave marker. Make the request using VA form 40-1330.

Internet Resource:
You can get information about national cemeteries from the National Cemetery Administration, part of the Department of Veterans Affairs. The website is WWW.CEM.VA.GOV

Cremation Issues

Many people desire cremation. They may have a variety of reasons, including the desire to save money. Cremation can cost as little as $800 with the right arrangements. Several cremation "societies" exist, some for-profit and some non-profit. They take the place of the traditional funeral home by contracting for low cost and no-frills cremations.

Internet Resource:

The Neptune Society website: WWW.NEPTUNESOCIETY.COM

The Funeral Consumers Alliance: WWW.FUNERALS.ORG

The Internet Cremation Society: WWW.CREMATION.ORG

Cremation does not require the purchase of a casket, and funeral directors are forbidden to say otherwise. A container is required, but cardboard is often the most appropriate choice.

Strictly interpreted, Texas law requires the cremated remains to be buried in a cemetery or placed in a columbarium. "Columbarium" means a durable fireproof structure containing niches used to contain cremated remains. In practice, the "ashes" are often scattered (although no law specifically allows scattering, no law penalizes it either). Creative (but highly expensive) scattering options exist. For instance, a company called Space Services, Inc. (Celestis) based in Houston will launch ashes into space. On a more realistic note, a surviving spouse may retain the urn at home, or scatter the ashes privately in the countryside or in a body of water.

Cremation can be motivated by environmental concerns as well. Burial space is at a premium in many places. The body may also contain harmful toxins, especially if chemotherapy shortly preceded death. Cremation is a cleaner alternative than burial in those instances.

DEATH CERTIFICATES

Although the death certificate is a legal document, its use in certain court or legal proceedings is restricted to providing proof that the death has occurred. The actual cause of death, as indicated on the death certificate, may not be accurate to the degree necessary in court – other evidence may be needed to establish accurately the cause of death for a wrongful death case or a criminal proceeding.

The vital statistics office can only issue copies of a death certificate to qualified parties. Other than designated personnel who deal with vital statistics, access to the death certificate is restricted for 25 years to immediate family members. For qualified individuals to obtain information from the government they must provide verifiable proof of their relationship to the deceased.

The process of obtaining the death certificate is often transparent to the surviving spouse. He/she answers a few questions at the funeral home regarding the date of birth, parentage and work history of the decedent. The funeral director forwards that information to the hospital or physician who will be certifying the death. Once the doctor enters the cause of death and signs the certificate, the vital statistics office issues death certificates. The survivor has already paid for them at the funeral home, and typically receives them in 2 weeks or less.

The certifying physician has the duty to document accurately the cause of death. While physicians should recognize the potential legal aspects of death certificates and be careful when wording the cause of death statement, their focus is on the medical cause of death. The primary reason the death certificate can only be issued to qualified parties is protection of the privacy of the family and the dignity of the deceased. The family may not want an "embarrassing" cause of death to become public.

This is ironic, as the survivor will be asked to deliver a copy of the death certificate to the bank, the broker, the insurance company and others. Although they are not primarily interested in the cause of death, it is on the face of the certificate. Confidentiality is destroyed when the certificate is used in this fashion, but financial institutions will not accept any other proof of death.

Texas law calls on physicians to certify the death and to release the death certificate to the funeral director within 5 days from the time of receipt of the death certificate. If a physician unduly delays the processing of a death certificate, he/she may be charged with a Class C misdemeanor. If an autopsy or other situation delays the completion of the death certificate beyond the 5 day time limit, the Department of State Health Services recommendation is that it be marked as "Pending Autopsy" or "Pending Further Investigation" and be sent on to the funeral director.

Although Registered Nurses and Physician's Assistants are able to pronounce death, in certain cases, they are not authorized to appear as certifiers on the death certificate.

In some cases, as with emergency room admittance, the pronouncement of death may be made, noted on an intake chart or other patient information form, and the death certificate generated later with the pertinent information transcribed by medical support personnel to the death certificate form. For instance, in some emergency-room admittance situations, the physician may need to pronounce a person dead whose name is not yet known to hospital personnel. The final certificate may be generated later, when the decedent's name and more information are known.

GATHER THE DOCUMENTS

The survivor should gather the original legal documents of the decedent and other vital information. This may include, among other things:

Table 6: Document Checklist

	Last Will and Testament		Family Limited Partnership Agreement
	Codicil to any Will		Military discharge papers (DD Form 214)
	Body Bequeathal Contract		Pension Survivorship Rights
	Pre-need Funeral contract and burial instructions		Life Insurance Policies
	Cremation Society membership		Irrevocable Life Insurance Trust
	Family address & phone numbers		Health Insurance Policies
	Social Security number		Auto Title
	Pension documents for any survivorship payments		Deeds to Real Property
	Memorandum or list regarding the distribution of personal effects		Real estate appraisal from the local tax appraisal district
	Living Trust Agreement		Residential Leases
	Amendments to Living Trust		Mortgages/Liens against Real Property
	Prenuptial Agreement		Home equity loan or reverse mortgage papers
	Postnuptial Partition Agreement		Notes Receivable and Payable
	Conversions to Community Property under Family Code §4.102		Judgments of Record
	Community Property Survivorship Agreement		Active Litigation files
	Last year's 1040 and identity of tax preparer		Buy-Sell Agreement
	Stocks, bonds		Partnership Agreement
	List of bank deposits		Password lists for computer access
	Credit cards and most recent statements		List of annuities
	Automatic drafts against bank accounts (for insurance premiums, etc.)		List of subscriptions (newspaper, magazines)
	Utilities (internet, telephone, electricity)		

Secure the Computer

The decedent may have left a computer at home. The surviving spouse may not be familiar with either the operation of the computer or the information stored on it. Vital financial data may be stored in programs like Quicken™ or Microsoft Money™. If your lawyer has either of these programs, you may save many hours of data tracking by providing a copy of the data file to your lawyer.

Other important data may be in computer storage. Is a family tree recorded on the hard drive? It may help you determine the identity of the heirs. Is there a computer address book, with phone numbers and email information?

If the surviving spouse in not computer literate, he/she may need to find someone to help close out any subscription agreements the decedent has entered. Does the survivor need or want to continue the decedent's Internet access agreement? Is there a second phone line or a cable modem that should be closed out?

At the least, the computer hard drive should be "wiped" clean by someone with computer skills before it is donated to charity, otherwise disposed of or given to a family member.

> Internet Resource:
> If you have no use for the computer, someone else will. Here is a directory of organizations that accept used computers for charitable and educational purposes:
> WWW.EPA.GOV/EPAOSWER/HAZWASTE/RECYCLE/ECYCLING/DONATE.HTM

NOTIFICATIONS

Family

An obvious but important step is to notify the family. The surviving spouse may have children who are already on the scene, and they can be very helpful making phone calls to siblings, grandchildren, nieces and nephews and close friends. The family address book is a necessity here.

Obituary

The funeral home will ask if an obituary is desired. Obituaries are voluntary. Some families feel that a public obituary is a proper tribute to a loved one. Some run several hundred words. Some families feel that an obituary would violate their privacy, or that it is too expensive. The obituary has no legal significance and is not an official notice of the death. A short obituary without a photo is adequate, unless more is desired by the family.

Power of Attorney

If another family member, other than the surviving spouse, holds a durable power of attorney for the recently deceased principal, the agent should be informed immediately about the death. Pursuant to the Probate Code, acts performed under a durable power of attorney are valid after the principal's death if the agent did not have actual knowledge of the death and was acting in good faith. Such an action might contradict the surviving spouse's wishes, so he/she must impart that "actual knowledge" to the agent quickly.

Clergy

After notifying the family, the next call is often to the clergy. The family's religious beliefs are both intensely relied upon and challenged at the time of death. Religious traditions important to the decedent and surviving spouse should be honored by contacting the family's house of worship. The clergy may be deeply involved with the funeral, offering suggestions to honor traditional religious practices and meeting with the family to prepare a eulogy.

Social Security

The Social Security Administration recommends that, as soon after the death as possible, a family member:

- Promptly notify Social Security of the beneficiary's death by calling SSA toll-free at 1-800-772-1213. The funeral home may offer to make this call for you, and there is no harm in the initial call coming from them. But the surviving spouse should still call SSA soon thereafter to be sure that survivor's benefits are properly processed.

- If monthly benefits were paid by direct deposit, notify the bank or other financial institution of the beneficiary's death. Request that any funds received for the decedent for the month of death and later be returned to Social Security. The bank will electronically return the funds.

- If benefits were being paid by check, do not cash any checks received for the month in which the decedent died or thereafter. Return the checks to Social Security by mail as soon as possible.

Survivor's Benefit

If the survivor is already receiving SS benefits on his/her spouse's earnings record, then upon the initial phone call to SSA they will change the payments to survivor's benefits.

If the survivor is already receiving SS benefits – but on his/her own earnings record – then the survivor must apply for survivor's benefits. The initial phone call to SSA is often enough to get this started as well. For this step, SSA asks for a copy of the decedent's death certificate. The survivor will get only one check, but it will be based on the bigger earnings record.

The surviving spouse receives full benefits at 65 or older or reduced benefits as early as age 60. A disabled widow or widower can get benefits at ages 50-60. The survivor's benefit may be reduced if he/she also receives a pension from a job where Social Security taxes were not withheld (this impacts many retired government employees).

Internet Resource: The Social Security website is at WWW.SSA.GOV

Office of Personnel Management

OPM handles the retirement and death benefits for all federal employees and retirees. To report a death, they can be reached at 1-888-767-6738.

If the decedent received benefits through the OPM, they will ask for his/her full name, date of death, retirement claim number and Social Security number. They will start the process of activating survivor's benefits, and may mail claim forms to be completed and returned.

The surviving spouse is entitled to a monthly survivor's pension only if the decedent so provided upon retirement. The vast majority do so provide. A lump sum payment, covering the benefits earned from the first of the month through the date of death may also be payable to the surviving spouse.

Claim for Federal Employee Group Life Insurance benefits should also be started with a phone call to 1-888-767-6738.

Internet Resource: OPM is online at WWW.OPM.GOV

Military Survivor Assistance Office

If the decedent was retired from the military and receiving a pension the surviving family should call the Survivor Assistance Office. Look on discharge papers (DD Form 214) and for the annual pension statement for military ID numbers and pension details. Here are some contacts:

- Army Retirement Services Offices - WWW.ARMYG1.ARMY.MIL/RSO/RSO.ASP?RSO=TEXAS

- Air Force Retiree Services Branch - ASK.AFPC.RANDOLPH.AF.MIL/AFRETIRE/

- General Department of Defense retirement pay issues: 800-321-1080.

Other Pension Administrators

The surviving spouse will have information on other pensions the decedent received. If he/she is not sure of the data, ask to see last year's 1040 tax return. A 1099 should be appended that identifies the company and gives account details for the decedent.

Life Insurance Companies

Each policy owned by the decedent must be located. The issuer should be contacted so the claim paperwork can be started. There is no need to wait for receipt of the death certificate; a phone call to the claims department will initiate the process. They will mail claim forms to the beneficiary. This way the survivor may receive the claim forms and the death certificates at about the same time.

The insurance company must pay the claim either 1) on receipt, or 2) not later than two months after due proof of death and the right of the claimant to the proceeds. The Texas Department of Insurance has imposed additional time constraints: a company must acknowledge the claim and start investigating it within 15 days of receiving written notice of the claim. Once the company has all necessary information, it has another 15 days to notify the claimant in writing if it will accept or reject the claim. If a company cannot meet these deadlines, it must send a notice explaining why it needs more time. The company then has 45 days to either approve or deny the claim. If a company rejects the claim, it must explain why. If the company agrees to pay the claim, it must send payment within five business days.

The survivor should also review credit card agreements, loan documents and mortgages regarding credit life insurance. The decedent may have paid premiums so that upon death, a specific debt would be paid by credit life insurance.

Tax Appraisal District

If a homeowner was receiving the 65-plus exemption and died, leaving a surviving spouse under age 65, the surviving spouse can continue the exemption so long as he/she is 55 or older. The younger spouse must also become owner of the house after the death (usually the house is community property, so the surviving spouse already owns ½ and gets the other ½ via probate or another legal process), and must reside in the home. The survivor must apply with the local appraisal district to continue the exemption. Some districts find out about the death and send a letter along with an application for exemption, and some do not reach out. If that is the case, the survivor should contact the appraisal district to obtain the application, fill it out, and submit it as soon as possible.

ASSETS AND ACCOUNTS

Many assets pass to survivors through non-testamentary designations. This might include a living trust or may include bank account arrangements like pay-on-death or right of survivorship.

If you, as survivor, know that you are on an account with the person who died, you can ask the bank (or the broker) for a copy of the account signature card. It is actually a contract, and will show whether you are entitled to become owner of the account due to the death. If so, you'll need to give a death certificate to the financial institution and they should release the funds to you.

Legally, there are a limited number of ways to classify bank accounts. The Texas Probate Code clearly identifies the options. The law provides a "Uniform Single Party or Multiple Party Account Form," but in my experience the banks rarely use it, preferring their in-house forms. With the many bank ownership changes of the 1980's and 1990's, you may find that the documentation is not clear. Particularly with the elderly, who may have opened an account "three banks ago," the signature card may be a mess or may be unobtainable.

Brokerage Accounts and Dividend Reinvestment Plans

When an account is held with an out-of-state institution (as are most Dividend Reinvestment Plans) the institution's internal paperwork is vital. It must clearly indicate a right of survivorship or a pay-on-death designation; if it does not, the institution is likely to demand letters testamentary. This may be good for the law firm you hire to help with probate, but may be frustrating to you if you expected immediate access to a fund.

Automobiles

Only in mid-2000 has Texas made it easy to put a car title into right of survivorship. This is evidenced by a separate right of survivorship agreement on record with the Department of Transportation or, for titles issued after about 2002, is actually pre-printed onto the title (but its activation is not automatic; it must be signed by both spouses before it has effect). If so, title can be transferred to the survivor by presentation of the title and death certificate to the local tax assessor-collector's office.

If the title lists both names but there is no right of survivorship, the tax assessor-collector will ask for Letters Testamentary, an Order Admitting Will to Probate as Muniment of Title, or an Affidavit of Heirship to a Motor Vehicle.

> Internet Resource:
> Affidavit of Heirship to a Motor Vehicle is available for free download from The Premack Law Office website at WWW.PREMACK.COM (select "legal documents").

Community Property Survivorship

Probate of a Community Property Survivorship Agreement (CPSA) is not necessary. Current law provides that the agreement is effective to pass title to the community property without any further action. However, the law does provide a method for "proving" the validity of the agreement in a dispute: the surviving spouse may apply to the courts for an order establishing that the agreement is valid and meets the requirements of the law. This requires the survivor to produce the original agreement in court – but it is on record with the County Clerk, so a certified copy will suffice if the original is lost.

The survivor may sell any community property which he/she obtains in survivorship, but must wait six months after the date of decedent's death. The purchaser is assured good title if the CPSA was on record with the County Clerk.

Title companies were initially reluctant to issue a policy based on a CPSA. My experience in the last several years has been generally positive as CPSAs become more widely used. In a very few instances, stubborn and backwards title companies shy away from approving a CPSA (even though they are approved in the Texas

Constitution and are authorized in the Texas Probate Code). When that happens, the survivor has the option of either 1) insisting that the law be followed by obtaining a court order forcing the title company to accept the CPSA, or 2) cave in to the title company's position, generally submitting an Affidavit of Heirship to satisfy their underwriter.

Checks Payable to Decedent

If dividend checks or other payments made out to the decedent arrive in the mail, the surviving spouse has two options:

- He/she can return the payment, requesting that a new check be issued to the "estate of decedent;" or

- Since money in hand is hard to turn away, and if the surviving spouse is the sole heir, the payment can be deposited to an account that bears the decedent's name. Since the decedent is not available to endorse the check, the best course is to endorse it as "deposit only to account #___." Banks will almost always receive funds, even if hesitant to pay them out.

IRA Funds

The question has never been "will the IRS get a chunk" of a decedent's IRA; rather, it is "*when* will the IRS get a chunk?" The combination of income tax and estate tax on a large IRA can be devastating. If the surviving spouse is the IRA beneficiary, he/she can rollover the IRA into his/he own IRA, deferring income tax. The survivor can also defer estate tax using the unlimited marital deduction. This does not solve the tax problem, it just delays it.

The surviving spouse must contact the IRA trustee, probably a bank or a brokerage. He/she will need to supply a copy of the death certificate. The trustee will process the IRA rollover in-house.

In mid-2001, the IRS changed its regulations regarding minimum distributions from IRAs. These regulations try to simplify distribution of IRA assets to surviving beneficiaries when the IRA owner has died. The owner is supposed to designate a beneficiary – that beneficiary must be specified before December 31 of the year after the owner's death. Usually it will already be clear, but the delay allows for some estate planning flexibility if an IRA goes through probate.

The IRA funds must be withdrawn, and income taxes paid on the withdrawal, under these rules:

- For a surviving spouse – withdrawals must be made based on the surviving spouse's statistical life expectancy;

- For non-spouses – withdrawals must be made based on the remaining statistical life expectancy of the designated beneficiary as of the year after the IRA owner's death; and

- If there was no designated beneficiary – withdrawals must be based on the IRA owner's remaining statistical life expectancy as the IRS would have shown it in the year of his/her death.

Trust Assets

With a living trust, it is likely that the surviving spouse will be the successor trustee. This minimizes the procedures that are required, as there will not be a change of ownership. The trust may simply continue for the surviving grantor's benefit.

If the survivor is not named as the successor trustee then authority for management of the assets will vest in the person who is named as successor trustee. That successor will need the original trust agreement and a certificate of death in order to access the various trust assets.

If the living trust contains shelter trust provisions (to utilize fully the estate tax exemption amount of the first to die) then the trustee will have to re-title appropriate assets to fund the shelter trust. While the trust agreement should contain clear instructions to carry out the funding, you may want to call upon your Certified Elder Law Attorney to assist with the process. If it is the same attorney who drew up the trust, he/she will know and be able to advise you in carrying out the intent.

Homestead Occupancy

Texas homestead laws have a large and varied impact on homeowners. One very important right, but one that is often overlooked, is the surviving spouse's right to "occupy and use" the homestead.

The surviving spouse's homestead occupancy right continues after the other spouse dies. The surviving spouse always has the right to continue to occupy the homestead for life or until abandonment. Even if your spouse's Will gives his/her community property half of the house to someone else (maybe one of the children), that new half owner cannot exercise any dominion over the house. For example

Adelia and Humberto are married, but they live in a house Adelia owned years before their marriage. Her Will leaves the house to her son from her first marriage. When

Adelia dies, her son becomes the owner subject to Humberto's homestead rights. Humberto can continue to live there, by virtue of his homestead occupancy right even though he is not the owner. He does not pay rent or anything of value to Adelia's son. When Humberto subsequently dies, or when he voluntarily decides to leave the house, his homestead rights end. Adelia's son can then take possession and handle the house in any way he feels is appropriate.

Due in part to the strength of the surviving spouse's rights, he/she also has legal responsibilities. One of them is to pay the property taxes in full and in a timely manner. As far back as the 1920's our courts ruled that "It is certainly according to equity and good conscience to require the survivor to pay current taxes…[62]".

Additionally, Texas law requires the surviving spouse to keep the property in good repair and to pay the interest portion of any mortgage that may exist. The trust or its beneficiaries must, by law, pay the principal portion of any mortgage and pay for insurance on the property.

Occupancy of a home an easy concept: if the survivor lives there, she occupies the house and her rights continue. But what about the idea of "using" the house? Is the survivor "using" the house if she moves to some other location and rents the house to someone else?

That issue was addressed in a 1976 case handled by the Texas Court of Appeals in Waco[63]. In it, the father died leaving his land and home to his children, and the wife had the legal right to "occupy and use" the premises. She moved out due to poor health, and rented the home to her brother.

The court applied the legal rule that "a temporary renting of the homestead will not terminate its homestead character if no new homestead has been acquired". The wife had moved out involuntarily due to poor health. She claimed that she wanted to return to the home, and she did not claim any other property as her homestead. The court decided that she was still "using" the home under these conditions, and denied the children's claim.

Homestead occupancy and use rights can be waived in a premarital agreement. This may be something important for anyone pondering a later-in-life marriage.

CLEANING OUT AN APARTMENT

If a person who lives in rented quarters dies and an Executor is appointed by the court, the Executor is responsible for cleaning out the apartment. Speed may be necessary so that rental payments are not prolonged.

If, however, the estate is small and it is unlikely that probate will be necessary, then pre-planning by the renter can create a clear line of authority. Texas law allows the renter to give the landlord the name, address, and telephone number of a person to contact in the event of the renter's death. At the same time, the renter can sign a document authorizing the landlord to: 1) give the contact person access to the apartment, 2) allow the contact person to remove personal possessions, and 3) allow the contact person to claim refund of the security deposit.

The same law allows a landlord to put all the renter's personal items into storage (and to deduct storage costs from the security deposit). When the contact person makes a request for possession of the deceased renter's personal items, the landlord is legally required to turn them over to the contact person.

The contact person needs to act promptly to claim the personal items because the landlord may legally dispose of the possessions if: 1) the landlord mailed the contact person (by certified mail, return receipt requested) a written request that the property be removed, 2) the property was not removed within 30 days of the postmark date, and 3) no one else contacted the landlord to claim the property.

What does it mean to "dispose" of the property? The landlord does not have to account for it in any way, even if it is still in storage, or if it has been thrown out, destroyed, or even if it has "disappeared" – which covers a lot of ground. Can the landlord just keep it, claiming it has "disappeared"? The law says the landlord has "no responsibility" for the property if the renter had been provided with a copy of the 1999 law.

On the other hand, if the renter does designate a contact person as the law allows, and the renter provides a copy of the 1999 law to the landlord, then the landlord is liable to the renter's estate for any violation of the law.

However, the law allows the lease agreement to contain an entirely different procedure for removing, storing, or disposing of property in the apartment of a deceased renter. Thus, before you go through preparing the notice and obtaining a copy of the law, carefully read your lease agreement. If you are not sure how to interpret the lease, visit with an estate planning or elder law attorney to be sure your rights are protected.

REVIEW OF SURVIVOR'S DOCUMENTS

The survivor should review his/her own planning documents. The decedent may have been the survivor's only named agent in a durable power of attorney or a

Medical Power of Attorney. If so, the survivor has some thinking to do about a new and trusted representative.

The survivor should review his/her Will to reflect any new dispositive instructions. Perhaps the decedent had a different attitude about a particular heir, and now that he/she is gone the survivor desires to drop that heir (as the decedent can no longer find offense in the act). Perhaps the decedent was named as the survivor's sole Executor. Again, the survivor should quickly select a new Executor and sign an updated Will.

The survivor should also reconsider any "right of survivorship" arrangements. All the rights of survivorship between the decedent and the survivor should have performed their function, leaving the survivor as sole owner of various assets. The survivor can, if he/she wishes, now add the children or any intended heir to various assets to enable non-testamentary transfer upon the survivor's death. Pay attention to the fact that non-testamentary transfers take priority over any contradictory statements in the survivor's Will; thus, an effort should be made avoid contradictions.

Certain legal arrangements may have been rendered irrevocable upon the decedent's death. Sometimes revocable grantor trusts become irrevocable on the death of a grantor (by agreement of the parties). These arrangements must be reviewed and understood by the survivor.

Though a death has occurred and the survivor's life will forever be different, the sun continues to rise and to set. Eventually the survivor will regain equilibrium. Then it is time to begin a new chapter, cherishing the past while looking to the future. Part of that is being certain that your own plans are in order and that the people who will outlive you will have as easy a time, legally, as you can possibly arrange.

Chapter 8:   Settling an Estate

What is Probate? When is it necessary? What can be done to reduce the chances of needing probate? Why does it even exist?

Probate is the process of proving that a Will is valid, and handling any business left untended by the decedent. Generally, probate involves an Executor who must gain control over the estate, pay the debts, pay the taxes, and distribute the remaining assets to the proper heirs.

The term probate is also used to describe the procedures used when a person dies without having a Will. Typically, the probate procedures for an intestate estate (no Will) are more complex than those in which there is a Will. Without the evidence provided in your Will, probate may involve the additional complexity of a "proceeding to determine heirship."

The Texas Probate Code requires that most types of probate must be started within four years after someone dies. After that, the courts will not approve an application for probate that seeks to issue letters testamentary to an Executor.

Ownership of assets passes instantly to your heirs when you die. The trouble is that neither the public, nor your bank, nor your broker nor the person buying your house knows the identity of your heirs. Evidence is needed to identify your heirs. Probate provides that evidence by establishing the validity of your Will or by determining the identity of your heirs when there is no Will.

When does a Will need to be probated, and when can you skip the whole process? The answer depends on what assets and debts exist, and how they are legally titled. For instance, if the person who died owned only a checking account and a certificate of deposit that were both held jointly, with rights of survivorship and had no debts, then probate is probably not necessary. The surviving account holder can simply claim ownership using a copy of the death certificate.

On the other hand, if the person who died was sole owner of a home, was sole owner of a bank account and a few stock certificates – which is not too unusual a scenario – then probate is probably necessary. No one has automatic ownership of those items, so probate is used to establish the legal identity of the new owner and to transfer title.

Thus, the need for probate depends primarily on these factors:

- The estate's complexity in terms of debt and obligations of the decedent;

- What the estate owns (not how much). Assets that rely heavily on paperwork to show ownership—like stocks & bonds, real estate, and bank accounts—tend to force an estate into probate. Why? Because the people who process the paper-work are protected from certain risks if they deal with a duly appointed Executor;

- The heirs' desire for clear and unquestionable title to assets; and

- Efforts at avoiding probate by preplanning.

TYPES OF PROBATE

Probate is often confused with preparation of a federal estate tax return. Probate is a Texas-based, local process. Needing probate does not automatically mean that you'll need to file a federal estate tax return with the IRS. On the other hand, when an estate is large enough that a federal estate tax return becomes necessary, then it is almost certain the estate will also go through probate.

Probate is rarely the nightmare experience it is rumored to be. In fact, the term "probate" covers six basic legal procedures ranging from extremely complex to simple:

- Dependent Administration is the most complex probate procedure. It may be necessary when a person dies without having a Will, or when a person fails to simplify the process through instructions in his/her Will. In this method, the es-tate's manager is called an "Administrator", receives "letters of administration" as credentials, and must get prior court approval for most actions. This often operates hand-in-hand with a proceeding to determine heirship.

- Independent Administration is a simpler probate process than Dependent Administration. It is called *independent* because the Executor may act in most instances without prior court approval by following the instructions in the Will. The credentials an Executor receives from the court are called "letters testamentary". This is contrasted with Dependent Administration.

- Muniment of Title may be used when there are no debts to be paid. A court order acts as evidence that ownership has passed through the terms of the Will. In this procedure, no Executor is appointed and no letters testamentary are issued.

- A Small Estate Affidavit may be filed if the estate is smaller than $50,000, has no debt and has only a homestead as real estate. Again, no Executor is appointed and no letters testamentary are issued. This does, however, require appearance before a judge.

- Finally, an Affidavit of Heirship might be filed with the county clerk. This process has the advantage of being inexpensive, and the disadvantage of being unreliable. No court approval is issued, no letters testamentary are issued, and the affidavit does not have to be accepted as proof of title.

Internet Resource:
Need to find a Texas Probate Court? Look at the Texas Judiciary Online site at WWW.COURTS.STATE.TX.US/TRIAL/PROBATE.ASP

SUMMARY OF THE EXECUTOR'S ROLE

Even though the Will identifies an Executor, that named person is not legally Executor until appointed by the court. Prior to being officially appointed, think of that person as the "pending Executor."

The Executor's official role begins with selection of an attorney. Although it is legal for a pending Executor to act without a lawyer "pro se," most people would rather let an experienced attorney assist them through the system. Select an attorney with experience in probate matters. Either ask your friends for a reference, call your local Bar Association or the Texas Bar Association, or find a local attorney who is a member of the National Academy of Elder Law Attorneys.

The attorney will help the pending Executor select an appropriate probate procedure. This includes Dependent Probate (where there is no Will, or the Will requires the highest level of supervision), Independent Probate (where the Will appoints an

Executor to act without court supervision), and Muniment of Title (where the Will is used to transfer ownership without an Executor's appointment).

The attorney will draw up an "Application for Probate" and file it, along with the original Will, with the probate clerk. About two weeks after filing, the attorney and pending Executor will appear before the probate Judge for a hearing. If all goes well (that is, there is no contest and the Will is not faulty) then the Judge will sign a court order admitting the Will to probate, officially recognizing the Will's validity. Since the Application for Probate included a request for appointment of the pending Executor, the court order will officially activate the Executor's powers. The clerk will issue "letters testamentary." Depending on which probate procedure was selected, other legal steps may be required by law as well.

The letters testamentary are used by the Executor as credentials. If a bank or broker holds some of the estate's funds, they will allow the Executor to access to the funds upon presenting a copy of the death certificate and a letter testamentary. The Executor uses the funds to pay debts and taxes of the estate, and when all debts are paid, distributes the remaining assets to the heirs named in the Will.

The Texas Probate Code has been modernized and usually says *personal representative* instead of *Executor*. They are the same thing. Most lawyers continue to use the word Executor. Also, a female Executor can be called an "Executrix," but the distinction is legally meaningless.

Can the Executor Live Outside Texas?

Texas law favors using a Texas resident as your Executor. However, it is perfectly legal to have an Executor who is not a Texas resident. The pending Executor must sign a document appointing a "resident agent" – someone in Texas who can accept delivery of legal documents on his behalf. The document must be filed with the probate and approved by the Court. Then the non-resident is treated exactly like a Texas resident while acting as Executor.

Deciding not to Serve

When the Will names an Executor, that person can decline to accept the position with all its tasks and liabilities. If so, the first source you must look to is the Will. Most attorney drafted Wills anticipate that the first named Executor might not serve, and thus name an alternate Executor.

If it does, then that alternate is the person who will serve if the first choice steps aside. If that alternate Executor wants to serve, the process is straightforward. The attorney who is aiding with probate of the Will would draft a sworn waiver of appointment for the first choice to sign (before a notary). It would be filed with the probate clerk along with the Will and Application for Probate, in which the alternate requests appointment as Executor.

Supposing that alternate does not want to serve, he or she must also sign a sworn waiver of appointment. Continue to progress through any other alternates named in the Will, until one of them either agrees to serve or they all waive appointment.

If everyone named in the Will waives appointment, then state law determines the process for appointing someone else. The Probate Code puts tighter restrictions on an applicant when the decedent did not name that person in the Will as a choice for Executor. Assuming that an applicant was not named in the Will, he would have to apply to be "Administrator" rather than "Executor."

Coexecutors

When a Will names more than one Executor at the same time, they are called Coexecutors. It is legal for one of the Coexecutors acting alone to take care of most estate business. Routine matters like collecting funds from a bank account can be handled without unanimous action, without even a majority – unless the Will specifically states that the Coexecutor must act jointly and unanimously.

Even if the Will is silent on that point, any conveyance of real property requires all of the Coexecutors to act jointly and unanimously (a majority is not adequate). Only the probate judge can override that requirement by ordering one of the Coexecutors to sell land acting solo.

Most Wills do not name Coexecutors. Instead, they name a solo Executor and then identify successors to act if the initial Executor dies, resigns or becomes disabled. Having a solo Executor avoids what Judge Grant of the Texas Court of Appeals described as "a hydra-headed administration of the estate in which there is no guarantee that there will not be a duplication of effort, as well as each Executor being able to hire an attorney to be paid out of the estate which would result in double attorneys' fees".[64]

Naming Coexecutors can provide an opening for conflict, because Coexecutors are not bound by law to act unanimously.

For instance, what if funds are limited and one Coexecutor feels it is appropriate to pay off the MasterCard while the other one wants to use the money to pay off the Visa? They might argue over money and how it should be allocated. Both Coexecutors could even hire separate attorneys which would double the cost of administration.

If the Coexecutors are like-minded they can choose to coordinate all of their efforts. Conflict is not a given just because you name Coexecutors. When they get along and work together, Coexecutors share the burden and lighten each other's load. So it depends on the character of the people and their relationship whether naming Coexecutors is a wise or an unwise tactic.

GUIDE TO BEING EXECUTOR

Proving the Will's Authenticity

Consider the appointment of a personal representative from the Judge's perspective. For example:

> Into court walks John Smith, whom the Judge has never met. John has a document that appears to be Betty Smith's Will. The Judge must ask: Is this really Betty's Will, or is it a fake? Is Betty really dead? Is my court the right place for these questions to be asked? Does the Will nominate John as Executor? Your attorney must present the answers to all these questions in a way that allows the Judge to rule in your favor.

The Probate Code tells your attorney what to expect, and provides a method for answering the Judge's questions. First, the authenticity of the Will must be established using one of these methods:

- The witnesses who saw Betty sign the Will can be located and brought to court. They can testify that the Will is really Betty's Will. However, witnesses cannot always be easily located because a Will might be 25 years old.

- If the actual witnesses cannot be located, anyone who knows Betty's handwriting well enough to identify her signature can be brought into court. They can testify that the Will appears to be Betty's. However, sometimes there are no such witnesses.

- If Betty's lawyer had the foresight, her Will might be "self-proved." This is an affidavit attached to the Will and signed by Betty and her witnesses at the time they signed the Will. Under the probate code, a Self-Proving Affidavit alone is adequate evidence for a Judge to admit the Will to probate. This technique is the most reliable and the least expensive.

Other facts must be entered into evidence. Some Probate Judges like you to testify out loud, answering questions posed by your lawyer. Some Probate Judges want everything to be written down before you get to court, so that you can swear to the truth of the written statement in open court.

To activate an Executor's power, the Judge must determine that the applicant is entitled to hold the position. Generally, the person named in the Will is "qualified" to be Executor. Only adults who are legally competent and have never been convicted of a felony may serve as Executor.

Once satisfied, the Judge will sign a written order admitting the Will to probate. That order acknowledges the Will's legal validity and authorizes you to take the next steps.

Will Contests

Legally, anyone has the right to contest a Will so long as the claim is not frivolous. But no one should jump into a Will contest without considering that the battle will be emotionally difficult, financially expensive and time consuming. The person bringing the contest must hire and pay an attorney. Some attorneys accept contingency fees (where you don't pay unless they win), but this is most common in accident cases. In a Will contest, the person bringing the contest should expect to pay the attorney fees.

When a relative dies, a strong emotional reaction is common — sadness at the loss of a loved one, and sometimes anger when inheritance expectations are not met. However, legal proceedings in a Will contest might last longer than the anger. Then the person bringing the contest would be stuck with a complex and expensive lawsuit that remains time consuming and burdensome even though the emotional motive has faded.

Will contests can also cause extensive family conflict. The emotional damage that will be inflicted in the Will contest may never heal. If you are considering starting a contest, factor in your emotional state. If you are defending a Will against a contest, remember that the wishes expressed by the decedent are the real issue. The decedent owned various items and had an undeniable legal right to give them to anyone – and so long as the Will accurately reflects those wishes it should be followed. But if the Will is indeed faulty (for any of the legal reasons set out below) then it may not be worthy of defense.

Burden of Proof

Timing for a Will contest is critical. If a contest is filed before the Probate Judge's initial ruling to admit the Will to probate, then the person who is offering that Will must prove it *is* valid. That proof may not be difficult to obtain, especially if the Will is "self-proven" as discussed earlier.

If a contest is filed after the initial ruling that the Will is valid, then the person filing the contest has the legal obligation to prove the Will *is not* valid. Proving that is a task that is often more difficult that it first seems.

Grounds for a Contest

The law requires that a contestant be able to prove some very specific facts before the court can invalidate a Will. The key issue is evidence, hard evidence. Suspicion, rumor and anger are not enough to stand up in court. Before filing a Will contest, the disgruntled party should look deeply to see if there is any hard proof of any of these things:

- Did the testator (the person whose Will it is) lack testamentary capacity when making the Will? Did the testator understand who was in the family, know what assets exist, and know to whom he/she wanted those assets to pass? Were you there on the day the Will was signed? If not, how do you know the answers to those questions?

- Does the Will meet all of Texas' legal requirements to be admitted to probate? Is it signed by the testator, witnessed and dated? If it is handwritten, is it in the testator's hand or someone else's? Is the Will genuine or a forgery?

- Was the testator "unduly" influenced? Did someone force the testator, through threats and coercion, to sign the Will? Again, were you on the scene at the time the Will was signed, or are you just speculating about these things?

- Is the Will a fake or a forgery? How can you prove that it is not authentic?

I emphasize: you must have solid evidence. Speculation about what happened is not adequate; you must present evidence that satisfies stringent requirements.

When there are two possible Wills – an "older" Will and a "newer" Will that may have replaced the older one – is it worth filing a contest to see if the older Will can win? Depends. Even if the person filing the contest manages to disprove the validity of the newer Will, the older Will is not necessarily restored. While the newer Will may not have been a valid Will, it may have been a valid revocation of the older Will (the standards for creating a new Will versus the standards for revoking an older Will are quite different). If the new Will is invalid but the old Will is revoked, you may end up with intestacy – the absence of any valid Will – requiring application of state law to determine the heirs' identities. The person filing the contest would receive only what the laws of descent and distribution provide. This may be less than expected, perhaps far less than the older Will would have allowed. If you can't achieve your goal, is the Will contest worth the trouble?

Always think long and hard before you start any type of Will contest.

Probating a Lost Will

It is always preferable that the original Will be offered for probate... the actual pieces of paper that the decedent and witnesses signed, not a facsimile or copy. When the original is filed with the court, the court requires that its validity be proved in the ordinary fashion discussed above.

But what if the Will cannot be located? Must we presume that just because the pieces of paper are lost we also lose the intentions of and instructions from the decedent? Well, the answer is "yes" – but it is what the law calls a "rebuttable presumption", one that can be removed if there is proof to the contrary.

The Texas Court of Appeals summed it up by saying, "When a will is in the possession of the testator when last seen, failure to produce the will after the testator's death raises the presumption that the testator destroyed the will with the intention of revoking it, and the burden is cast on the proponent to prove the contrary"[65]. Other courts have ruled that "in the possession of the testator" will be broadly interpreted. For instance, when a Will was last known to be in the possession of the testator's lawyer the court treated it as though it was in the possession of the testator[66]. If it was simply in a place to which the testator should have had access, it is treated as though it was in his/her possession.

But as I said, the presumption that a lost Will has been revoked can be overcome by contrary testimony. For instance, if the Will was last seen after the date of the testator's death then the person who saw it can testify that the fact it is lost is not because the testator destroyed it. Or if the testator was too ill to have destroyed the Will (was, for instance, in a nursing home or was unconscious since the last time anyone saw the Will) the court may agree that it was not revoked.

The probate code says that evidence must also be submitted to prove the contents of the lost Will. In the best case scenario, a photocopy of the Will may be filed with the court as evidence of what was stated in the lost Will. If a copy cannot be found, it is possible for someone who read the Will to testify verbally about what the lost Will stated.

Additionally, the court will want to know the identities of the people who would inherit under the laws of intestacy if the Will had been revoked. Sometimes the Will and the intestacy laws would have yielded the same result, so the court does not have anyone to protect. But if the Will would have left everything to Fred while state law, in the absence of the Will, would have given everything to Wilma, then the court may want to hear Wilma's side of the story before deciding to follow the lost Will or to follow the intestacy laws.

Bond & Oath

Before taking office, an Executor must post a bond unless the Last Will and Testament says that no bond is necessary. The bond is an insurance policy that guarantees honest action by the Executor. If the Will did not waive bond, then the Executor must visit with a bonding agency, obtain and pay for the bond, and return it for the Judge's approval.

After the bond issue is settled, the Executor must take an oath of office swearing to fulfill the duties and responsibilities of the role. Then the clerk issues official credentials, called letters testamentary.

Letters testamentary are signed by a county clerk, bear the county's embossed seal, and identify the Executor. A Letter must be presented to the bank, to the broker and to anyone else who needs assurance that the stranger who has just walked in the door is, indeed, the legal Executor of this particular estate.

Reading of the Will

There is not ordinarily a "reading of the Will." Frankly, in Texas it has never been a popular custom to hold a formal reading of the Will, since our probate procedures do not require it. The large family gathering to hear the Will is seen more often in the movies for its dramatic flair than it is seen in real life.

Notice to Creditors

Shortly after receiving letters testamentary, the Executor must notify the public of the appointment. This notice must be run in a local newspaper. It tells anyone who might care whom to contact regarding any claim against the estate.

Several other notices may be necessary. For instance, if the decedent owes any taxes to Texas (like sales taxes on a sole proprietorship business) then notice must be sent to the Texas Comptroller. If a mortgage exists, the lien holder should be notified. If the Will names any charities as heirs, they must be notified. And general creditors can optionally be mailed a notice that gives then a limited amount of time to present their bill or be barred from future collection efforts.

Notice to Charities

An Executor is legally required to give a formal notice to each charity named in the Will. This must be done within 30 days of the date you are confirmed as Executor by the court. The notice must inform the charity that it has been named as an heir, and must give identifying information (like the decedent's name, the county in which the Will was probated and the case number assigned to the Will by the court). This is a task the Executor should delegate to the estate's attorney.

Along with the notice, the Executor must also mail each charity a copy of the probated Will and the probate application and order. That way, the charity has a great deal of information about the estate.

There is no requirement to specify exactly how much each charity will be receiving. You may not know the exact dollar figures until you have paid the debts and taxes... so if the Will says that the charity should get (for instance) 30% of the estate, there is no way to know the value of that 30% until you are done paying the obligations.

However, when the Executor finishes paying all the obligations, you must calculate the value to be dispensed to each charity (as was called for in the Will). How you disburse the values depends on how the decedent's investments were held. If everything is liquid (cash or CDs) then you can simply gather up the funds and write a check. If the estate contains stocks, bonds or mutual funds then you can work with the broker to distribute them in-kind – that is, you can directly transfer each investment to the charity.

You will want to obtain a receipt from each charity upon making the disbursement, so you will have evidence that each organization has received that which it was due.

Inventory of the Estate

Both Independent and Dependent Administration require filing of a public inventory of the assets of the estate within 90 days of the Executor's taking the oath of office. This does not, under most circumstances, need to include a detailed list of the decedent's personal items. It does include a list of all the financial resources that pass by the terms of the Will. The inventory can be used by anyone with a claim against the estate to decide whether to pursue that claim, and is used by the IRS if any estate tax return is required.

The fact that the inventory is public is a consideration for some people to use a living trust instead of a probated Will. The trust avoids probate and thus avoids the filing of a public inventory after your death. Legislation has been introduced to allow probate inventories to be sealed by the court, but it has never become law. Now that many public records are being posted on the internet, the public inventory could become a source for scammers and identity thieves. To date there are no reports that the information in an estate inventory has been misappropriated, but it is a matter of concern.

Though due no later than 90 days after the issuance of letters testamentary, most courts are lenient in granting extensions. Frequently in larger estates it takes more time to gather the data, and the accountant wants to be sure that the estate inventory closely matches the estate tax return. Since the tax return is not due until 9 months after the date of death, the courts are fairly understanding of a request to extend the 90 days for accounting purposes.

Handling Title to Real Estate

If the deed to the house is in the survivor's name only, then you are already recognized as the sole owner. If you ever decide to sell it, you will have no trouble. However, if the house is in two names (typically husband and wife) the surviving spouse will certainly have difficulty when it comes time to sell.

Why? The buyer expects that everyone who owns an interest in the house will sign his or her interest over upon the sale. If one owner dies (say it was the husband) and his name is on the deed, the buyers will want to know to whom he left his share and who has authority to sign for him. Those questions are answered if he left a Last Will, but the answers are only acceptable to the public when the Will has been probated.

There is four-year statute of limitations on probating a Will and having an Executor appointed. After four years, it is sometimes possible to probate the Will solely to show the change of ownership (using Muniment of Title). Otherwise, the heirs to his share of the house must be determined under the state's intestacy laws, which will likely delay the sale of the house.

Probate of the Will so that the Executor's powers are activated is only the first step. (Unless you can use Muniment of Title in which no Executor is appointed; rather, the order signed by the Judge passes title but does little else.) The Executor is responsible for fulfilling the terms of the Will and should sign an "Executor's Deed" to change title into the name of the heir specified in the Will. The Executor's Deed must be prepared by an attorney, and then recorded with the county clerk. Once done, the heir will be recognized as full owner of the house, with the right to continue to live there and the right to sell it when the time is right.

Distributing Stocks & Bonds

Real estate is not the only valuable asset that an Executor may have to handle. Many estates includes stocks, bonds and other securities that can only be traded or sold through official channels.

If you locate a cache of stock certificates in the decedent's safe deposit box (or, as once happened to me, in a suitcase under the decedent's bed) you have two choices on how to process them and two choices on how to distribute them. By "process" I mean how to handle the paperwork necessary for the companies to change their records of ownership and by "distribute" I mean how to get the value represented by the stocks to the heirs named in the Will.

The processing choices are:

- Handle each stock separately by contacting the transfer agent who has been selected by the company to keep records of who owns their stock. The identity of the transfer agent may be printed on the face of the stock certificate, and is most typically an east coast bank. Phone them for instructions, and they will likely tell you that they need 1) a letter testamentary issued no longer than 60 days ago, 2) a death certificate, 3) the actual stock certificate, 4) a letter of instruction from you, 5) an affidavit as to the domicile of the decedent, and 6) various other papers to annoy and confuse you.

  They will likely also require that your signature be affirmed with a "medallion guarantee" – a method of confirming your identity by having a commercial bank verify your identity. Sometimes finding a commercial bank to apply the medallion guarantee can be frustrating. They won't accept notarization, and they are in control, so you must jump through each hoop they put in front of you.

  Note that you will be repeating all of those steps for each different stock, so the quantity of paperwork and the amount of legwork involved can be quite extensive.

- Open a brokerage account in the name of the estate, and give all the stock certificates to the broker. There is paperwork to open the account, and the broker will ask for a letter testamentary and the death certificate. All of the stocks will be placed into this new account (and the certificates will be replace by a monthly or quarterly statement from the broker listing the various items held in the account). You will not be dealing directly with transfer agents and will not need any medallion guarantees, so this method cuts down the quantity of paperwork and the amount of legwork tremendously.

Now that you have processed the securities so that you have control over them as Executor, you need to follow the terms of the Will. If the decedent has debts that must be paid, the securities are a source of funds (but should probably be used to pay the debts only if there is not enough money in the estate bank accounts). When you know the debts have been eliminated, it is time to distribute the remaining estate as called for in the Will. You have two methods available:

- You can instruct the broker to sell all the securities, placing the net proceeds into a bank account owned by the estate. Then you write checks to each devisee for the proper share of the estate.

- You can instruct the broker to open an account for each devisee named in the Will, and instruct the broker to place into each account the proper share of the securities.

The first method is more work for you, the second method is more work for the broker. The first method eliminates the investments the decedent selected in order to distribute cash, the second method preserves the investments which allows each heir to decide personally whether to sell or keep the investments. The eldest child may nostalgically recall when dad bought those shares in AT&T and told her he planned to hold onto them forever (so she's glad to have her portion of those shares). The youngest child may have no attachment to the stock, or may need funds to pay for a child in college. Each heir's needs are different, and it is often appropriate to allow them to make their own decisions whether to retain or to liquidate the various investments.

Executor's Quandary: Valueless Items

As Executor, you may be dealing with many valuable assets. What do you do when you have to handle an asset that have only minor value, or is even a nuisance? Sometimes undesirable responsibilities are thrust upon us, like an inexpensive, undeveloped parcel of land burdened by property taxes, membership dues and/or maintenance fees.

The Executor is empowered to make an attempt to liquidate a bad investment. However, the Executor does not have unlimited discretion, as the terms of the Will must be followed. If it says that the family's adult children inherit everything, they inherit both the good and the bad investments. If the land cannot be sold so that the proceeds can be split according to the Will, then the Executor may distribute ownership to all the heirs with an Executor's deed. That removes ownership from the estate and makes the heirs into partners who co-own the land with shared responsibility for paying its expenses.

Alternatively, the Executor may be able to give away the property. First, get written permission from each of the heirs. Then contact the local school district, volunteer fire department, a local charity or one of the neighboring landowners. Someone may be happy to take the land off your hands if it serves their own interests to do so.

Executor's Fee

There are two ideas running through Texas law about Executor's fees. First, the legislature has given a very specific set of rules to determine what fees are appropriate. Second, the courts have recognized that the statutory scheme can be disregarded if the Will itself sets different rules for handling the fees.

Under the statutory scheme, the Executor is "entitled to receive a commission of five per cent." That begs the question, "per cent of what?" Calculating the Executor's fee under the statutory scheme can be very involved.

For instance, the statutory scheme forbids any fee "for receiving funds ... which were on hand or were held ... in a financial institution or a brokerage firm." That means that the Executor cannot legally charge anything for just going to the bank or brokerage to get and distribute the estate's money. On the other hand, the Executor can charge 5% for selling real estate, for collecting debts owed to the estate and for paying debts owed by the estate.

The statutory scheme can be easily changed by setting different rules in the Will.

In one Texas case[67], the Will said the Executor should be paid a "reasonable fee." The Executor sold real property belonging to the estate for about $27.5 million, and took a fee of about $2.8 million. One heir sued the Executor, claiming that fee (about 10%) was too high. The court decided that the terms of the Will overrode the statutory scheme; that the 10% fee was allowable because it was within the Will's "reasonable fee" limit.

If the Will says nothing about a fee, the Executor can automatically charge a 5% fee for certain transactions. If the Will says something else about fees, then the terms of the Will must be followed (even if the resulting fee is less, or is more, than the statutory 5% fee).

Is it a good idea to list the Executor as an heir, to be sure he/she gets paid? That depends. If the Executor is someone you would ordinarily include as an heir, then that inheritance is adequate; no additional fee need be allowed unless you really want to give additional funds.

On the other hand, if the Executor is someone you would not ordinarily include as an heir, you might reduce the Executor's future income taxes by deciding to give an inheritance in lieu of a fee. One snag: if that person declines to act as Executor, he/she may get the inheritance without doing any work. The alternate Executor may do all the work without pay.

As a consequence, the best approach is to either 1) say in your Will that there is to be no fee at all, or 2) say in your Will that there is to be a specific percentage of the gross estate as a fee or a specific dollar amount as a fee. Doing so ensures that the Executor or the Alternate (whoever actually serves) will be the one who gets paid, and that calculating the fee will be much easier than it would be under the statutory scheme.

Finding "Missing" Heirs

As Executor, part of your job is to locate the devisees named in the Will so you can distribute to them the items the Will gave them. What if one of the heirs is missing?

If "missing" means this heir is simply hard to get in touch with, or will not reply, or that the family knows vaguely the person is "somewhere in Alaska" but you're just not sure where… then the Executor needs to redouble efforts to make contact. Consider hiring an investigator to track down the heir, or use the internet to do a search. Think about the heirs important connections: children, work at or retirement from a particular company, military service, land owned elsewhere. These are links that may lead you to the lost heir.

Also check to see if there is anyone who is already authorized to represent the heir. Is there an agent who has been appointed in a durable power of attorney? Was there ever any court action to appoint a Guardian for this person before contact was lost? If you can answer "yes" to either question, that representative can work with you.

If "missing" means this heir has truly disappeared (there is suspicion the disappearance is not voluntary) and the property is in danger of being injured, lost or wasted then the Executor proceeds by bringing court action to create a receivership. In this context, "waste" could include losing the opportunity to make a profit from the sale of a piece of land.

When you file an application for the appointment of a receiver, the missing heir's rights must be properly honored. The court clerk must issue a notification that the application was filed and must list the names of all involved parties. The notice must be posted at the courthouse and must also be published in a newspaper in the county where the missing heir last resided and in each county where the missing heir owns property.

Anyone interested in the welfare of the missing heir is given the opportunity to appear in court to contest the application. Additionally, the court must appoint an attorney ad litem to represent the interests of the missing heir (to speak on behalf of the missing person). If the court feels that additional protection is needed, it can appoint a guardian ad litem who also has the job of protecting the best interests of the missing person.

If "missing" means that the heir has been gone for over seven years and there is no indication during that time that person is still alive, the courts can presume that person has died. In that case, the Executor can inquire whether the missing person left a Will naming heirs to that share of the properties, or whether our state laws on intestacy determine who now owns that share.

DEPENDENT PROBATE

So far, all the procedures have applied equally to both Independent probate and Dependent probate. This is where they part. An Independent Executor appears in court after this point only under rare circumstances involving litigation. But a Dependent Executor must, by law, be supervised by the court in nearly every way from this point until the estate's business is concluded. If it is time to pay a debt of the estate, to sell an asset of the estate, or to distribute property to the heirs, the Dependent Executor must first get approval from the Judge. Each time the Dependent Executor goes to court, the Dependent Executor must:

- Hire an attorney (usually the same one who filed the probate originally);

- File with the court a motion requesting approval of the action the Executor wants to take;

- Notify the public, through the Clerk's office, that action is possible and that a public hearing will be held at the time chosen by the court;

- Appear in court at the proper time to present the request to the Judge. At this point, any person who objects to the action may present their opinion to the Court as well;

- Prepare an order for the Judge that approves the desired act (or which disapproves and forbids the act if the Court finds it to be needless);

- If the court approves the desired action, the Dependent Executor may then proceed to sell the asset or to pay the bill. When the action is finished, the Dependent Executor must file a report informing the Court of the action taken and seeking "confirmation." And when the probate is finished, the Dependent Executor must file another inventory and ask the Judge for permission to close the estate.

Those same steps must also be taken by a Dependent "Administrator." The difference between an Executor and an Administrator is that the Executor is selected by the decedent in the Will. An Administrator is selected by the Judge in cases where there is no Will, or if the Will is faulty.

An Administrator is required to post bond and would be subject to supervision of all activities by the court. That supervision can be a big factor in how fast the estate can be handled and how much it will cost. Most actions the Administrator takes would need prior approval by the Judge, which slows things down and increases the attorney's fees.

There is one way, under these circumstances, to avoid court supervision and to eliminate the bond. Under state law it is legal for the distributees to agree to unsupervised administration. The law requires all of the distributees be officially served legal notice of the application for independent administration; it also allows distributees to waive notice or to appear in court. The court must be satisfied that it is hearing from all the heirs, so the proponents must offer clear evidence that everyone is accounted for; no heir can be left out of the process.

Once the facts are established, the heirs may unanimously select a person to serve as independent administrator. Any individual heir who disagrees can prohibit the whole process. But if no heir dissents, the court must appoint the person they have selected (unless the court finds that to do so would not be in the best interest of the estate).

MUNIMENT OF TITLE

Probate of the Last Will and Testament as a Muniment of Title certainly sounds intimidating. But substitute the word "evidence" for "Muniment" and the meaning becomes clear: the Will is evidence of ownership.

Muniment of Title is simpler and less expensive than either Dependent or Independent Administration. However, it is not available in all situations. It can only be used if the estate owes no debts (other than, perhaps, a mortgage) and if there aren't any other reasons for an Executor's appointment.

Sometimes the pattern of heirship set out in the Will makes Muniment of Title impractical. If the Will names several heirs or if the Will contains any type of trust, using the Muniment process does not answer all the questions raised by the Will. Business dealings like rental property, partnership, or being a creditor usually call for appointment of an Executor instead of a simpler Muniment. If the Will leaves everything to just one person, Muniment may be appropriate. For example:

> Harry dies owning a house (with a small mortgage), other land, and a bank account. He does not have any debt other than the mortgage. If his Will leaves everything to his wife, then his estate is a good candidate for probate as a Muniment of Title. On the other hand, if his Will names his children as heirs, or leaves something in trust for one of his grandchildren, then Muniment may be inadequate. Appointment of an Executor would be a better choice.

Similar to the process for appointing an Executor, in Muniment of Title your attorney prepares an application requesting a probate court hearing. About two weeks later, you and your attorney appear in court to testify that the Will is authentic. The Judge reviews the Will, the application and the proof. If the Judge is satisfied that all is in order, the Judge signs an order approving the Will.

That order establishes as legal fact that the Will is authentic, instructs the clerk to record the Will in the county records, and instructs anyone with assets belonging to the estate to turn them over to the heirs named in the Will without further legal complications. This allows the estate to be gathered and distributed to the heirs.

No Executor is appointed in a Muniment of Title proceeding. As such, letters testamentary are not issued. No oath is needed, no bond is posted, no inventory is prepared, and no court approval for future action is necessary. Within 181 days of the order's issuance a report should be made to the court detailing how the Will's instructions have been followed (although many courts will waive the report).

Beyond the Statute of Limitations

When the heirs named in a Will do not bring the Will to court for probate within the four-year statute of limitations, the law says that they have missed their opportunity. It is as though the Will never existed. As a consequence, the people named in the Will are no longer entitled to receive the assets of the estate; instead, the laws of intestacy determine who gets the assets. Failure to probate can have very large financial consequences.

Muniment of Title is the only possible way around the four-year statute of limitations. Before this process can be used, these conditions must be met:

- First, the person offering the Will must not be "in default" which means that they cannot have purposefully waited beyond the four-year limit. It may be fairly easy to find an interested party who is not in default to bring forward the Will.

- Second, the heirs identified by the laws of intestacy must be notified that the Will is being brought to probate, and they must agree that they do not object to its being used. Why? If the Will is accepted by the court, then its wording determines who gets the assets. The intestacy laws no longer decide who is entitled to the assets. Often the Will specifies different heirs than the intestacy laws identify. Before the court applies this exception to the statute of limitations and changes who might be entitled to assets, it wants to clear the process with all interested parties.

The point is this: a Will must be probated to take effect. If you fail to probate the Will you may lose your entitlement to various assets. Although Muniment provides a limited opportunity to use the Will even though you waited beyond the four-year limit, you should take action before this problem arises. If you want to inherit assets under the terms of a Will, start probate within the four-year limit.

Confusion for Stock Transfer?

If the estate has any stocks, the non-Texas transfer agent will insist on letters testamentary. Muniment of Title does not provide such letters, a fact that confuses the out-of-state transfer agent and can result in delays. Under Texas law, the Muniment order is sufficient to transfer stock – but it is not what the transfer agent expects. You might either argue the point, or you might decide that it is better to obtain letters testamentary by probating the Will as an Independent Administration if you will have to deal with out-of-state transfer agents.

SMALL ESTATE AFFIDAVIT

A "Small Estate Affidavit" is an effective process when someone with a modest estate dies without having made a Will. Even so, it can only be used if 1) the estate is valued under $50,000 other than a homestead, and 2) the estate owns no real estate other than a homestead. Since no Will exists, the state laws of descent and distribution determine the identity of the heirs. Also, state law requires that at least 30 days pass since the date of death before the affidavit can be filed in court.

This process is available for transferring homestead ownership but cannot be used to transfer title to any other non-homestead real estate. If other land is involved, then a Dependent Probate may be required.

Your attorney will write the affidavit to include a list of all of the heirs, with their names and addresses. A list of all the assets and debts of the deceased must also be included. All the heirs must join together to sign the affidavit, so this process is practical only if the family is cooperative.

The affidavit must also be signed by at least two people who knew the decedent but who do not receive anything from the estate. All the signatures must be notarized.

After filing the affidavit with the probate clerk, it is assigned a case number. Since this is an abbreviated procedure, no notice of the filing need be given by the heirs or by the court. Your attorney will present the affidavit to the Judge, but no formal hearing is held. No witnesses are needed beyond those who have signed the affidavit, and no testimony is taken in court.

After it receives the Judge's approval, the affidavit is recorded in the probate clerk's records and the heirs get certified copies. If a homestead is included, the approved Affidavit must also be filed in the county's deed records.

The affidavit and approving order identify which assets the heirs are entitled to receive and to authorize banks, transfer agents, and other persons who hold assets of the estate to deliver those assets to the heirs.

AFFIDAVIT OF HEIRSHIP

Affidavit of Heirship is formally called "Affidavit of Facts Concerning the Identity of Heirs." It is the simplest and least expensive probate procedure. It is also the least reliable since a probate Judge never gives approval. The heirs will need an attorney to assist with preparation of the affidavit.

If the estate is mostly personal items or paid-for land, and if the entire family is agreeable so there is little chance of a contest, then an Affidavit of Heirship might succeed. On the other hand, if there are stocks or bank accounts, an Affidavit of Heirship may not be acceptable to either the bank or the broker.

The Affidavit of Heirship is a sworn statement about the life history of the deceased person. If a Will exists, it may be attached to the affidavit. The affidavit is signed by at least one person who knew the decedent's life history, is notarized and is then filed with the county clerk.

The filed affidavit is often, but not universally, accepted as evidence that title to the assets passed to the persons named in the affidavit. If any parties want to contest the information, they can. Once it has been on file for five years, the information in it is presumed to be true in any legal proceeding (but can still be disproved if the information is wrong).

The heirs' preparation of an Affidavit of Heirship is not guaranteed to be the final act in probating an estate. Since it is not court approved, any interested person can impose a more complex procedure requiring court approval. If so, the affidavit is treated as non-binding evidence. This lack of guarantee is the Affidavit of Heirship's weakest point.

Internet Resource:
There is a special Affidavit of Heirship targeted solely at automobiles. You can use it to transfer title to a car after the owner dies, without probate. The form is available free at WWW.PREMACK.COM (click on "legal documents").

Index

List of Tables and Illustrations

About the Author

Paul Premack

Paul Premack has practiced law in Texas since 1982. The Premack Law Office in San Antonio focuses on the legal needs of seniors and their families.

Paul is certified as an Elder Law Attorney by the National Elder Law Foundation, which is accredited by the Texas Board of Legal Specialization and the American Bar Association. He is a founding member of the Council of Advanced Practitioners of the National Academy of Elder Law Attorneys.

Paul is also certified as a Geriatric Scholar by the University of Texas Health Science Center in San Antonio. He earned his BA from the University of Texas at Austin with high honors in 1979, and his Doctor of Jurisprudence from the University of Houston College of Law in 1982.

Since 1989 Paul has written a weekly column for the San Antonio Express-News on legal matters of concern to seniors. The Austin-area Senior Advocate also carries his column in their monthly publication.

Paul holds membership in the State Bar of Texas, in the San Antonio Bar Association, and is a Life Fellow of the San Antonio Bar Foundation. He is also a member of the Texas Chapter of the National Academy of Elder Law Attorneys and served on its Board of Directors for five terms.

Endnotes

[1] Visit www.NAELA.com to search their database of members for a Certified Elder Law Attorney in your area. The author is a Certified Elder Law Attorney.

[2] Chapter XII, Section 481 et. seq., Texas Probate Code

[3] Title 2, Chapter 166, Section 166.001 et. seq., Texas Health & Safety Code

[4] 975 S.W.2d 539, Edward D. Jones & Company, and Delmar "Bo" McKinney, Petitioners, v. Pat Fletcher, Independent Executrix of the Estate of Beatrice Clark Cairns, Deceased, Respondent

[5] 002 S.W.3d 723, Comerica Bank-Texas v. Texas Commerce Bank National Association

[6] 124 S.W.3d 906, Musquiz v. Marroquin

[7] House Bill 1813 passed by the 2001 Legislature and effective September 1, 2001.

[8] 981 S.W.2d 211, James J. Trimble v. Texas Department of Protective & Regulatory Services

[9] 42 USC 1396p

[10] www.hhsc.state.tx.us/si/gat/gat_over.html

[11] Texas Probate Code, §883

[12] 801 S.W.2d 858, Stauffer v. Henderson

[13] The Tax Act of 2001 expanded the exemption from federal estate tax to $1 million in 2001-2002, to $1.5 million in 2003-2005, to $2 million in 2006-2008, to $3.5 million in 2009 and eliminated all estate tax for the year 2010. However, Congress approved a "sunset" provision that would eliminate all those exemptions as of January 1, 2011 and roll back to a $1 exemption for 2011 and on. It will take an act of Congress to change the roll-back. Stay tuned.

[14] Texas Human Resources Code, Chapter 102

[15] Texas Health & Safety Code §242.845et seq.

[16] Texas Occupations Code, Title 3, Chapter 159

[17] Title 22, Part 9 Texas Administrative Code, §165.2

[18] Title 4, Chapter 313, §313 et. seq., Texas Health and Safety Code

[19] Chapter 166, Title 2, Texas Health and Safety Code

[20] 497 U.S. 261, Cruzan v. Director, Missouri Dept. of Health (1990)

[21] Since the Schiavo matter made headlines in 2005, several books have been written from different points of view. Her parents, Mary & Robert Schindler, have authored a book entitled "A Life that Matters: The Legacy of Terri Schiavo" and her former husband Michael Schiavo has authored a book entitled "Terri: The Truth".

[22] 162 S.W.3d 678, Nikolouzos v. St. Luke's Episcopal Hospital (Tex. App. – Houston) 2005

[23] Gonzales, Attorney General, *et al. v.* Oregon *et al.* No. 04-623, 2006

[24] www.cms.hhs.gov/NationalHealthExpendData/downloads/nhe2004.zip

[25] 42 CFR 483.12(d)

[26] Internal Revenue Code, §101(g)

[27] 28 TAC 3.1708

[28] 180 S.W.3d 847, Huse v. Texas (Tex. App. - Eastland), 2005. Rehearing Overruled January 19, 2006.

[29] 28 TAC, Part 1, Chapter 3, Subchapter Y

[30] WWW.MEDICARE.GOV/MPDPF/PUBLIC/INCLUDE/DATASECTION/QUESTIONS/ENROLL DIRECTLY.ASP?DEST=NAV%7CHome%7CQuestions%7CEnDir%7CWelcome&Search Type=Enroll&comingfrom=MPDPFIntro&EnrollDirectly=True&version=default&browser =IE%7C7%7CWinXP&language=English&defaultstatus=0&pagelist=Home& ViewType=Public&PDPYear=2006&MAPDYear=2006&MPDPF%5FMPPF%5FIntegrate=N

[31] New York Times, June 5, 2006 "The Drug Benefit: A Report Card", online at www.nytimes.com/2006/06/05/opinion/05mon1.html?ex=1150257600&en=4efc42995188c697&ei=5065&partner= MYWAY

[32] www.hhs.state.tx.us/medicaid/engApp.shtml

[33] 746 F. Supp. 19, Miller v. Ibarra (D.Colo.1990)

[34] 42 USC 1396p(d)(4)(b) and 40 TAC 15.417(f)(3)

[35] HB 2292, Section 2.17 (78th Regular Session, 2003).

[36] 527 U.S. 581, 138 F.3d 893, Olmstead v. L.C. (1999) affirmed in part, vacated in part, and remanded

[37] Current federal poverty level figures are available at http://aspe.hhs.gov/poverty/figures-fed-reg.shtml

[38] 38 CFR, Part 51.50

[39] A prime example of the Act's bias was displayed in the Fogal matter, in which a new home was severely defective yet the builder avoided liability, forcing the homeowner to protest on the street corner in Houston. Read about it at WWW.MOJONES.COM/NEWS/FEATURE/2005/07/HOME_SOUR_HOME.HTML or read a critique of the agency at WWW.HOBB.ORG/INDEX.PHP?OPTION=COM_CONTENT&TASK=VIEW&ID=344&ITEMID=2

[40] Occupations Code, Chapter 2301 and 16 TAC 107.1-107.11

[41] Human Resources Code, §48.052

[42] Civil Practice and Remedies Code, §74.151

[43] Civil Practice and Remedies Code, §84.001 et. seq.

[44] 42 USC 14501, Public Law 105-19, 105th Congress

[45] HB 202, 79th Regular Session, amending §4.102 of the Texas Family Code

[46] Texas Constitution, Article 16, §15 and Texas Family Code section 4.202

[47] 28 S.W.3d 154, In Matter of Case (Tex. App. - Texarkana) 2000

[48] Texas Probate Code sections 471-471, added by HB 1186, 79th Regular Session

[49] 977 S.W.2d 718, Stubbs v. Ortega

[50] 530 U.S. 57, Troxel v. Granville (2000)

[51] 126 SW3 251, In re Pensom

[52] Texas Family Code, §153..433

[53] In re Keller, 2005 Tex. App (LWC-6924), No. 04-05-00542-CV

[54] 397 F.2d 82, Crummey v. Commissioner (9th Cir. 1968)

[55] 886 S.W.2d 398, Hagaman et al v. Morgan (Tex. App. - Dallas) 1994

[56] HB 204, 79th Regular Session, changing section 162.507(c) of the Texas Family Code and section 40 of the Texas Probate Code.

[57] 993 S.W.2d 298; Estate of Leroy Gorski v. Diane V. Welch (Tex. App. - San Antonio) 1999

[58] 102 S.W.3d 355, In re Estate of Schiwetz (Tex. App. - Corpus Christi) 2003

[59] HB 1190, 79th Regular Session, adding section 112.037 to the Texas Property Code

[60] Texas Health & Safety Code, §711.002

[61] Article 4590i, Vernon's Texas Civil Statutes

[62] 15 S.W.2d 589, Sargeant v. Sargeant (Tex. Commission of Appeals, Section A), 1929

[63] 541 S.W.2d 865, Gonzalez v. Guarjardo de Gonzalez (Tex. App. - Waco) 1976

[64] 33 S.W.3d 282, Lesikar v. Rappeport at page 321.

[65] 735 S.W.2d 924, 927-28, Hibbler v. Knight (Tex. App. -Houston) 1987, writ ref'd n.r.e.

[66] 480 S.W.2d 820, 821, Cable v. Estate of Cable (Tex. App.--Fort Worth) 1972, no writ

[67] 47 S.W.3d 767, Lee v. Lee (Tex. App. - Houston) 2001